D0867017

Local Public Finance in Europe

STUDIES IN FISCAL FEDERALISM AND STATE–LOCAL FINANCE

Series Editor: Wallace E. Oates, *Professor of Economics, University of Maryland and University Fellow, Resources for the Future, USA*

This important series is designed to make a significant contribution to the development of the principles and practices of state–local finance. It includes both theoretical and empirical work. International in scope, it addresses issues of current and future concern in both East and West and in developed and developing countries.

The main purpose of the series is to create a forum for the publication of high quality work and to show how economic analysis can make a contribution to understanding the role of local finance in fiscal federalism in the twenty-first century.

Titles in the series include:

Taxes, Public Goods and Urban Economics
The Selected Essays of Peter Mieszkowski
Peter Mieszkowski

Fiscal Federalism in Russia
Intergovernmental Transfers and the Financing of Education
Kitty Stewart

The Political Economy of Local Government
Leadership, Reform and Market Failure
Brian E. Dollery and Joe L. Wallis

Tax Policy in the Global Economy
Selected Essays of Peggy B. Musgrave
Peggy B. Musgrave

Local Public Finance in Europe
Balancing the Budget and Controlling Debt
Edited by Bernard Dafflon

Political Economy in Federal States
Selected Essays of Stanley L. Winer
Stanley L. Winer

Public Finance in Developing and Transitional Countries
Essays in Honor of Richard Bird
Edited by Jorge Martinez-Vazquez and James Alm

Federal Intergovernmental Grants and the States
Managing Devolution
Shama Gamkhar

Local Public Finance in Europe

Balancing the Budget and Controlling Debt

Edited by

Bernard Dafflon

Professor of Public Finance, University of Fribourg, Switzerland

STUDIES IN FISCAL FEDERALISM AND STATE-LOCAL FINANCE

Edward Elgar
Cheltenham, UK • Northampton, MA, USA

© Bernard Dafflon 2002

All rights reserved. No part of this publication may be reproduced, stored in a
retrieval system or transmitted in any form or by any means, electronic,
mechanical or photocopying, recording, or otherwise without the prior
permission of the publisher.

Published by
Edward Elgar Publishing Limited
Glensanda House
Montpellier Parade
Cheltenham
Glos GL50 1UA
UK

Edward Elgar Publishing, Inc.
136 West Street
Suite 202
Northampton
Massachusetts 01060
USA

HJ9415
.L627
2002

048783099

A catalogue record for this book
is available from the British Library

Library of Congress Cataloguing in Publication Data
Local public finance in Europe : balancing the budget and controlling debt / edited
   by Bernard Dafflon.
      p. cm. — (Studies in fiscal federalism and state-local finance)
   Includes bibliographical references and index.
   1. Local finance—Europe. 2. Local budgets—Europe. I. Dafflon, Bernard.
   II. Series.
   HJ9415 .L627 2002
   3366'.0144—dc21

                                                          2002019151

ISBN 1 84064 878 3

Printed and bound in Great Britain by Biddles Ltd, *www.biddles.co.uk*

Contents

List of figures

List of tables

List of contributors

Lars-Erik Borge, Associate Professor, Department of Economics, Norwegian University of Science and Technology, Trondheim, Norway.

Bernard Dafflon, Professor of Public Finance, Centre for Studies in Public Sector Economics, University of Fribourg, Switzerland.

Gisela Färber, Professor of Public Finance, German Post-Graduate School of Administrative Sciences Speyer, Speyer, Germany.

Angela Fraschini, Professor of Economics, Faculty of Political Sciences, University of Eastern Piemont "Amedeo Avogadro" and Department of Public Economics, University of Pavia, Italy.

Stefan Garbislander, Research Assistant, Institute of Public Finance, University of Innsbruck, Austria.

Guy Gilbert, Professor of Economics, Department of Economics, Department of Social Sciences, Ecole Normale Supérieure ENA-Cachan, France.

Alain Guengant, Director of Research, CNRS-CREREG, Department of Economics, University of Rennes I, France.

Dieter-Jörg Haas, Research Assistant, Institute of Public Finance, University of Innsbruck, Austria.

Niels Jørgen Mau Pedersen, Head of Division, Department of Economics, Ministry of Interior and Assisting Professor, Institute of Economics, University of Copenhagen, Denmark.

Carlos Monasterio-Escudero, Professor of Public Finance, Department of Economics, University of Oviedo, Spain.

Jørn Rattsø, Professor, Department of Economics, Norwegian University of Science and Technology, Trondheim, Norway.

Sergio Rossi, Senior Lecturer, Department of Economics, Università della Svizzera Italiana, Lugano, Switzerland.

Javier Suárez-Pandiello, Professor of Public Finance, Department of Economics, University of Oviedo, Spain.

Erich Thöni, Professor of Public Economics and Public Finance, Department of Public Economics, University of Innsbruck, Austria.

Jacques Vanneste, Professor of Public Finance, Department of Economics, University of Antwerp, Belgium.

Peter A. Watt, Senior Lecturer, Institute of Local Government Studies, University of Birmingham, United Kingdom.

Acknowledgement

This study on local public finance in selected European countries includes Austria, Belgium, Denmark, England, France, Germany, Italy, Norway, Switzerland and Spain. The problems with comparative analysis lie in the diversity of definitions and functions of local authorities between countries or between levels of government within a country, and also with the application of various accounting system and rules. Thus some common stakes were necessary to give a framework to this collection of national case studies. It was not evident from the beginning that the contributors would accept these passage points in order to gain in coherence and comprehensiveness. I would like to thank all of them who have accepted this exigency and played the tune.

We first discussed the issues of balancing the local budget and controlling debt in 1997 at a Seminar in Champéry, where members of the Association of Local Public Economics (ALPES) met at a workshop for post-grade researchers, sponsored by the Conference of the Universities of West Switzerland. We then worked and exchanged ideas for about two years. The decision to collect the research in a volume was taken at the 1999 ALPES Seminar in Rennes, France. Some papers have been presented in other conferences. We would like to thank the numerous participants who made critical comments and suggestions, which certainly improved the end product.

Thanks in particular to Roberto Abatti, from the BENEFRI Centre of Studies in Public Sector Economics for his technical expertise and diligence in preparing the camera-ready copy of the draft papers sent by the contributors. This was not an easy task, but it has been achieved with talent and good spirits. Thanks also to the editorial staff of Edward Elgar Publishing for their helpful assistance and to Wallace E. Oates, for accepting this collection of papers in the Studies in Fiscal Federalism and State-Local Finance Series.

1. The requirement of a balanced budget and borrowing limits in local public finance: setting out the problems

Bernard Dafflon

The idea of this comparative study goes back to the 1997 ALPES[1] Seminar in Champéry (Switzerland) where several scholars presented individual papers on local government budgeting and local debt with similar preoccupations and questions, such as (i) the existence of any legal requirement for a local balanced budget, (ii) a possible control from higher government levels on local budgeting and borrowing and (iii) the implementation of the Maastricht convergence criteria for local public finance. The framework of discussion is given in six sections. The introductory section recalls two issues, Maastricht and recurring public deficits, which give the general background to the chapters. Ten key issues are formulated in section 1.2. Owing to the heterogeneity of the accounting systems of local finance in Europe, some common definitions are necessary and are given in section 1.3. Section 1.4 presents a sequence of six questions with the intent of assessing the degree of budget discipline in the particular country. Questions about how the budgetary rules influence the budgetary position and the fiscal outcome of the communes in one country are presented in section 1.5. Tentative results are discussed in section 1.6.

1.1 INTRODUCTION

The chapter starts with two considerations: one is the local concern with the enforcement of the Stability Pact for the European Monetary Union (EMU), the other is the painful necessity of reversing the recent trend towards growing public deficits.

According to article 109 J (1) of the Maastricht Treaty,[2] the general government's financial position of any Member State must be sustainable, that is (i) the ratio of government deficit to Gross Domestic Product (GDP) must not exceed the reference value of 3 per cent and (ii) the ratio of government debt to GDP must not exceed the benchmark value of 60 per cent. The idea is that there should be budgetary discipline and a procedure to avoid excessive deficits and indebtedness if the Stability Pact is to be successfully enforced and a unique monetary currency created. In the Treaty, "general government" means the public sector in general (central administration, regional and local governments and social security), excluding commercial activities. Yet, the open-ended definitions of the required budgetary discipline to be secured across the whole euro area and the shortcomings of the excessive deficit and indebtedness procedure that will be enforced through the planned Stability and Growth Pact create problems. The European Council in Dublin (December 1996) and in Amsterdam (June 1997) endorsed the same conclusion that a "dissuasive set of rules should have a deterrent effect and put pressure on Member States adopting the Euro to avoid excessive budgetary deficits or to take corrective measures if they occur ... Each Member State will commit itself to aim for medium-term budgetary position close to balance or in surplus".

How is the "medium term" defined? Which "budgetary position" (current or including the capital account) should be close to balance or how much in surplus? To what extent might a deficit be considered as "close to surplus"? When considering the dynamics of general government debt and the sustainability of fiscal positions, the EMI (1996, p. 24) uses a number of locutions such as "actual primary balance", "overall balance excluding interest payments", "required primary balance (typically a surplus) in order to reduce the debt ratio", "sufficiently high primary surplus to regain budgetary room for manoeuvre in the medium term", so it is difficult to organise this into a clear-cut analytical picture. Not surprisingly, the first consideration of the ALPES Seminar was that used at the local level in various national circumstances, the same technical vocabulary has not the same signification (as for example: debt servicing, amortisation, debt instalment, gross savings, the distinction between current and capital accounts, or the requirement of balance in the actual accounts compared to simply a balanced budget).

At the same time, and especially since the beginning of the 1990s, important public deficits have occurred in most European countries at the three levels of government – central, regional and local – as well as in the social security accounts. The average fiscal deficit for the European Union (EU) as a whole widened rapidly from 2.4 per cent of GDP in 1989 to a peak of 6.1 per cent in 1993. At that point in time, most countries faced major challenges in reversing what was clearly an unsustainable trend. National authorities had to take corrective measures in an effort to place their government deficits on a downward path. This has been partly achieved, with an EU-wide budget deficit of 5.0 per cent in 1995, cut down to 2.4 per cent in 1997, unfortunately using also one-off measures and other accounting tricks to qualify for the EMU (Dafflon, 1999). In the same period, the general government gross debt as a percentage of GDP rose from 60 per cent (1990) to 72 per cent (1997) (European Commission, 1998, p. 124). Local governments have been in the forefront in reacting to the trend of growing deficits in their annual accounts and in devising sets of ratios intended to prevent excessive borrowing. Yet, although much has already been said about local budgetary policy-making, and about the policy effects of budget deficits and public debt in fiscal federalism, few empirical studies have been conducted in order to explore how budgetary discipline really functions at the local level. Thus here the attempt is made to organise a comparison on this issue at the local level in ten European countries – Austria, Belgium, Denmark, France, Germany, Italy, Norway, Switzerland, Spain and England – on the basis of an agenda of ten key issues. [3]

1.2 TEN KEY ISSUES

In order to make possible the comparison, questions have been formulated in ten broad key issues. The objective is to compare the issues, both at normative and practical levels, and the solutions in selected European countries. Discussion should include the questions of local budgeting (in particular the rule of a balanced budget) and of borrowing either from the point of view of local government or under regulation (if any) of the regional (central) government. The economic consequences of regulation as well as the institutional concepts and possible sanctions are of interest.

1. In local public finance, one may distinguish between budget responsibility and budget discipline. Budget responsibility is assumed to intervene for each financial decision where self-assessment of benefits and costs intervenes, as for individual investment decision-making. Budget discipline is related to any kind of institutional rules which limit in advance the possibility of deficit spending or borrowing. Is such a distinction of importance in your country? How is it applied and by which level of government?

2. Is the current budget distinct from the capital budget? Is borrowing limited to investment in a pay-as-you-use formula, or is it accessible for financing current deficit? What is the relation (or the compromise) between the rule of a balanced current budget (if it exists) and public investments?

3. How is the capital budget decided? Is there any local discretion in investment decision-making? Does the decision concern the whole capital budget or individual items of the capital budget? Is it necessary to present a programme of investment for each of them? (Such a programme describes the kind of investment, the cost of investment, its duration, depreciation and the future running cost.)

4. Is a separate vote needed or does the referendum exist (i) for the current budget, (ii) for taxes in the current budget, (iii) for particular items of the capital budget or (iv) for the total capital budget?

5. Is a rule of balance imposed on the current (the whole) local public budget? Which level of government sets the rule? What are the reasons for or against such a rule? Is borrowing by local government regulated: if so, by whom and how? Does the rule apply ex ante on the budget and/or ex post on the actual account? Does the rule allow actual deficit to be carried over into the following exercises (and if so, into how many years?) or must a deficit be repaid within the next exercise?

6. Is there any conceptual link between borrowing, debt management and capital expenditures? What is the role of amortisation as a link between investments and debt? Is there a link between amortisation in the books and the financial (annual) repayment of the local public debt?

7. What is the policy of capital amortisation at the local level: the systems of amortisation, the rates of amortisation, the coincidence between amortisation and annual repayment, the duration of debt repayment according to depreciation?

8. The political autonomy of a decentralised government may run against the regulation of budgeting and borrowing: are the rules the same between the local and regional, as between regional and central government levels?

9. How is the local public debt defined? Does a concept of "gross public debt minus capital = net public debt" exist? These concepts are relevant when some kind of limit is set up against borrowing. Do such limits exist in your country, and which ones?

10. How are the Maastricht rules (deficit < 3 per cent of GDP) and (total debt < 60 per cent of GDP) going to be divided between the layers of government?

Starting from the possible answers to these questions, the study explores four main lines:

- definitions;
- the budgetary procedure;
- the structure and organisation of local government finance;

- the incidence of possible rules, budget discipline or responsibility.

1.3 DEFINITIONS

The heterogeneity of local public finance in the EU is reflected in various systems of public accounting at local level, a wide variety of specific concepts and a disparate vocabulary. In consequence, the first objective is to organise an analytical framework that allows comparison not only in term of statistical data and results, but also in term of public finance terminology and bookkeeping definitions. The argument is that if the definitions are not clear, and if the accounting procedures vary widely, then the financial results, and the statistical data based on them, are not comparable. Figure 1.1 is presently used for restoring comparability.

The example of Norway (Chapter 9) will illustrate this issue:

The key financial control is a balanced budget rule implying that current revenues in local governments must finance current spending inclusive of debt servicing. Investments are to a large extent financed by loans, but there is a formal approval procedure for loan financing. The financing of investment is spread over time and the design is assumed to stimulate inter-temporal efficiency.

The questions to be answered are: (i) whether this statement is acceptable for other European countries, (ii) which meaning is given to the key words in each country?

Take the concept of "debt servicing". We found that it can be defined in a number of ways:

- interest payment of the existing debt;
- interest payment + bookkeeping amortisation of the capital assets contained in the opening assessment sheet;
- interest payment + (amortisation in the book = annual regular instalment of the debt, for the current account);
- interest payment + (amortisation in the book = depreciation of capital assets = annual regular instalment of the debt, for the current account), as it is the case in Norway and in many Swiss cantons;
- similar to the two previous points, but (...) is written in the capital account;
- interest payment + contractual repayment of the debt.

In this example, one sees that "interest payment" is always present. But the concept of amortisation taken in addition varies widely: formal amortisation "in the book" only, amortisation in comparison to depreciation, amortisation compared to effective debt repayment, in the current or in the capital account, and amortisation compared to the contractual annual repayment of the debt. For each of the other terms, the scope for interpretation and the variations in the definitions and uses of concepts are quite amazing. This is at the very least a cause for thought and scepticism about the validity of many comparative studies on European local public finance which ignore these aspects.

Setting aside the variations in Norway and in the Swiss cantons, one can refer to the definitions used elsewhere in the EU for the compliance of the national public finance (adding all government layers + social security) with the Maastricht criteria.

The primary balance is the sum of the effective monetary revenues in the current and the capital accounts, minus the sum of effective expenditures, also in both accounts, but without interest payments (accounting item number 32 in Figure 1.1) and amortisation (33). Pure bookkeeping entries without monetary content (38, 39, 48 and 49) are not considered. Explicitly, these six items in Figure 1.1 are excluded from the primary balance.

Investment revenues (61, 62 and 63) are directly balanced against capital expenditure in the year of reference, disregarding the fact that in most cases those revenues are earmarked for specific investment items. This also means that the "net capital outlay" is purely a treasury concept without economic significance.

The "balanced budget/account" requirement is computed from the previous result, but taking into account the interest payments (32). This result, if negative, should not exceed 3 per cent of GDP.

Comparing the Norwegian approach to the broader European definitions immediately signals some controversial issues: the extent of the balanced budget requirement, current or current + capital; amortisation; and investment revenues, if they are earmarked.

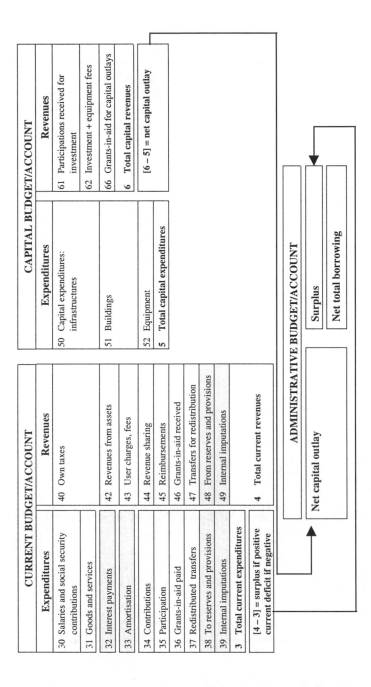

Note: Numbers refer to the categories and items in the harmonised accounting system that is used in the Swiss cantons and communes.

Figure 1.1 Analytical framework for a public budget and account

1.4   PROCEDURE

The procedure which serves as a starting point for the purpose of obtaining valid comparisons in the national definitions is given in Figure 1.2 (Dafflon, 1996, p. 240). Six solutions are possible. Solution 1 corresponds to the absence of any constraint. The other solutions present increasingly tighter constraints, with solution 6 giving the strictest rules. The final position of a particular canton or commune depends on the answers to the following six questions.

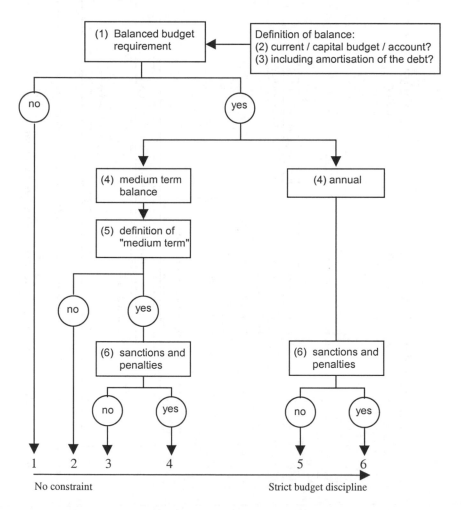

Figure 1.2   Six paths towards a strict budget discipline

1. Is a balanced budget required? Is the requirement extended to the actual account?
2. If the affirmative holds, the rules must define the extent to which the balance is required: total (current + capital) budget or current budget only.

    With the current balanced budget requirement, local governments can legitimately borrow to finance genuine capital investments. Taxpayers during the immediate period of revenue are not charged with the full costs of public projects that promise to yield benefits over a whole sequence of time periods. The intergenerational equity problem can be solved with appropriate rules of amortisation.
3. Is amortisation of the debt included in the outlays of the current budget (which must be balanced)?

    In the affirmative, taxpayers and beneficiaries in periods following the debt issue are faced with contractually committed interest and amortisation charges that are offset by income or utility yielding public assets. The life of the capital public investment, thus the duration of amortisation, should be measured not in terms of physical depreciation but in terms of its economic usefulness following a pay-as-you-use path.
4. If the rule of a balanced budget is constitutionally or legally fixed, is this an immediate or a medium-term requirement, that is, should each successive annual (current) budget be balanced, or is the balance required on average for a sequence of time periods, or is the balance to be recovered for the last annual exercise in a sequence of several predetermined years?

    The rule of annual balance produces a tighter constraint and leaves no inter-temporal budget flexibility to smooth over irregular current outlays and revenues. If the balance is required on average for several current budgets in a row, it introduces more flexibility in budget policies, but it also softens budget discipline and opens the door to political leeway and interest groups' strategies. Hence the importance of the next question.
5. In the case of a medium-term balance requirement, is the medium term properly delimited?

    Limitation must make explicit the beginning of the sequence of time periods and the number of periods. Ideally, these should correspond to terms of office. If, on the contrary, the political time horizon and the balanced budget time horizon do not coincide, asymmetry introduces a premium for the former and debt illusion on deficits in current budgets is likely.

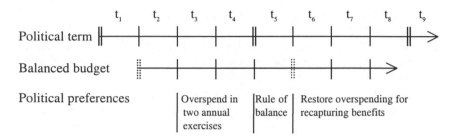

Figure 1.3   The problem of delimiting the proper medium term

Consider that the political term is four years, beginning in t_1 (see figure 1.3). Suppose the periods over which the current budgets must balance on average are also four years long but do not coincide (t_2 to t_5). What will happen? Simple public choice concepts, such as the proclivity of politicians to spend and their reluctance to increase taxes in order to remain in favour with their constituency, explain the prevalence of budget deficits with this asymmetry (of time periods and of behaviour). Politicians will overspend in years t_3 and t_4, incurring budget deficits, leaving their successors to restore the balance. But the medium-term balanced budgets must be obtained by the end of year t_5, which corresponds to the first year of the new political term. Why should newly elected politicians promote a tight budgetary policy to free tax revenue surpluses in order to repay the debt due to past current deficit? And if they obey the rule, why should they not recapture political benefits by overspending even more in years t_6 and t_7, leaving their followers to re-equilibrate, and so on. Who will say how much overspending in years t_6 and t_7 is too much? This attitude will be reinforced if either the length of the "medium-term" or the beginning of the period (the two conditions are not cumulative) are not explicitly defined. Without legally binding definitions, the requirement for balance in a sequence of current budgets is an empty concept.

6.   The last question concerns the sanctions and penalties that could be imposed on local governments when the requirement of a balanced budget or the limits of local indebtedness are not respected.
     The public choice argument is that political sanctions for deficit spending and excessive debt, or political rewards for budgetary discipline, are not likely at the time of election and are not sufficient anyhow because of the time lag between annual budget and periodical elections. Sanctions should apply immediately. The standard penalty is that if a current budget deficit is incurred, local expenditures should be cut and/or taxation would have to be increased. If local authorities do not

follow this rule, the higher government can decide to raise the annual coefficient of taxation in place of the commune. Sometimes, in addition, communal investments and debt financing must be authorised by ad hoc special decree of the higher authorities. If this is so, the latter authority might enforce and control pay-as-you-use finance, that is the coincidence between the residual value of use of the investments and the net amount of indebtedness (or the equivalence between booked amortisation and the effective annual repayment of the debt). If the amount of net debt is higher than the residual value of the investments, the pay-as-you-use rule is not respected. The higher government may defer any new authorisation until the overdue amortisation is paid; meanwhile new investments financed by further borrowing would not be possible.

Paths 1, 2, 3 and 5 in Figure 1.2 might be grouped together. They lead to a situation where no balanced budget is required. The requirement of a medium-term balance in current budgets without explicit definition of the beginning and the length of the period (path 2), or without penalty if adequate measures to eradicate chronic deficit spending are not fixed (path 3), opens the way to any possible budgetary policy. It does not mean that balanced budgets are never implemented, but only that there is no obligation and no constitutional guarantee, so that equilibrium is rather unusual. Unconstrained budgetary discipline is highly vulnerable. Neither does this mean that unconstrained solutions give greater importance to Keynesian demand management policies. Fiscal constitutions without a balanced budget requirement never subject local governments to stabilisation policies which would be decided at higher levels of government. Yet, such a requirement could be a particular case of path 4. Paths 4 and 6 lead to budgetary discipline; the choice between them depends only on whether the current budget/account (path 6) or the current + capital budgets/accounts (path 4) is/are considered.

1.5   STRUCTURE AND ORGANISATION OF LOCAL PUBLIC FINANCE

An additional domain of study is to scrutinise whether specific national structures and organisations of local public finance influence budget results, borrowing and indebtedness in the selected countries. The sequence which we want to explore is the following:

- share of local public expenditures in the total public expenditure, in

percentage of GDP;
- share of local public capital expenditures in the total amount of government investment;
- share of local public investments in total local public expenditures.

From this starting point, we consider local public revenues: how much is financed by own revenues (taxes, fees and tariffs, revenues from patrimonial assets), grants-in-aid (specific, conditional or general) and borrowing. Local tax autonomy is defined as the possibility to increase tax revenues by raising exclusive taxes or supplementary (piggyback) tax rates. What we need to know is how much of the local revenue sources higher government controls; what share of total local revenues is obtained through grants-in-aid and revenue sharing? How much credit and loan do higher government levels control? Other possible, but not exclusive considerations, are:

- debt policy:
  – what sorts of expenditures (current or capital) are thus financed?
  – which debt ratios must be respected?
- credit rules:
  – access to credit institutions
  – what sorts of loan?
  – which interest rate?
- technical control of higher government:
  – authorisation prior to the expenditure and a priori control of fiscal capacity
  – a posteriori control and sanctions.

1.6   INCIDENCE OF BUDGET DISCIPLINE OR RESPONSIBILITY

The last objective of the study is to verify whether stricter rules of control over deficit and borrowing are effective in the sense that the general level of indebtedness is lower where the rules are the more stringent. This could be a more difficult part of the study since the preconditions of deficit financing at local level vary from one nation to another, a situation that complicates international comparisons even with identical rules and definitions. Also several explicative variables are at hand which are difficult to isolate one from another. One set of reasons is probably given by selective access to the capital market, the monopoly power of specific national lenders, the borrowing guarantee given by higher rank government when approval procedure are needed, and extended access to loans at reduced rates (sometimes even negative in real terms).

The growing support for the view that political and institutional settings have a role to play in ensuring fiscal performance has paradoxically been accompanied by an increasing lack of confidence in the results achieved. Apparently, political institutions and budgetary institutions seem to be crucial for fiscal discipline. But, if certain institutions are more favourable to fiscal discipline, it would be possible that these mechanisms have been adopted because voters or politicians in this collectivity are more conservative in their attitude toward debt financing than in other collectivities with more "debt-friendly" settings. Poterba is, to our knowledge, the first author to raise this potential mis-specification of the models, pointing out the problem in a very clear way:

> The critical question for policy evaluation is how to interpret this correlation between budget institutions and fiscal-policy outcomes. It is possible that the correlation simply reflects correlation involving fiscal discipline, fiscal institutions, and an omitted third variable, voter tastes for fiscal restraint. Voters in some jurisdictions may be less inclined to borrow to support current state outlays or to use deficits to shift the burden of paying for current state programs to the future. If these voters are also more likely to support the legislative or constitutional limits on deficit finance, then the observed link between fiscal rules and fiscal policy could be spurious. (Poterba, 1996, p. 399)

If this was the case, public or political preferences could become in the end a main factor explaining the comparative evolution of debt. The argument could be presented in the following simplified way. Let us call "A" the voters' preferences for fiscal restraint, "B" the budgetary or fiscal rules or institutions and "C" the fiscal policy outcome. The possible sequences of argument are: C = function of (B), in this case preferences have no influence; C = f(A), fiscal institutions play no role; and C = f(A,B), both are simultaneously important. The observed correlation could appear as C = f(B) formally, but in fact reflect either C = f(A) or C = f(A,B). Empirical evidence suggests that the political configuration can influence fiscal performance (that is, minority governments, coalition governments and in some cases left-wing governments are related to more deficits, *ceteris paribus*, while direct democracy reinforces debt control). Also, budgetary engineering seems to influence the final fiscal imbalances (negotiations dominated by the prime minister or the minister of finance are related to less indebtedness, and the same occurs if the executive body controls the budgetary process over the legislative branch). As expected, empirical evidence shows that the more a formal rule is stringent against debt financing, the less the level of deficits.

At this stage, the intermediate conclusion is that local practices vary widely from one country to another, and even within the same country in federal states when the intermediate level (Länder, cantons, provinces) sets its own particular rules for local finance. There seems, as a first rough estimate, that although there exist strategic behaviours of local governments when the rules of the game are not precisely defined or with anticipated changes of the rules in the long run, there is no evidence that less control from the centre leads to disastrous effects and excessive indebtedness. No financial crisis or mismanagement on any grand scale have been observed.

NOTES

1. Association of Local Public Economics.
2. The Maastricht Treaty was signed on 7 February 1992 and came into force on 1 January 1993. Convergence conditions for entering the EMU (European Monetary Union) on 1 January 1999 were analysed in the 1997 public accounts. These conditions are given in the Protocol 5 about excessive deficits and indebtedness. See also Conseil de l'Europe (1997, 14).
3. In the same vein, see Conseil de l'Europe (1992).

REFERENCES

Commission Européenne (1998), *EURO 1999, Rapport sur l'état de la convergence*, Partie 2, Strasbourg.
Conseil de l'Europe (1992), *Les possibilités d'emprunt des collectivités locales et régionales*, Communes et Régions d'Europe no 47, Strasbourg.
Conseil de l'Europe (1997), *Les finances locales en Europe*, Communes et Régions d'Europe no 61, Strasbourg.
Dafflon, B. (1996), "The Requirement of a Balanced Local Budget: Theory and Evidence from the Swiss Experience", in Pola, France and Levaggi (eds), *op. cit.*, 228–52.
Dafflon, B. (1999), "Public Accounting Fudges Towards EMU: A first Empirical Survey and some Public Choice Considerations", *Public Choice*, 101/1–2, 59–84.
E.M.I. (1996), *Les progrès de la convergence en 1996*, Eureopean Monetary Institute, Frankfurt, November, French edition.
Pola, G., G. France and R. Levaggi (eds) (1996), *Developments in Local Government Finance*, Edward Elgar, Cheltenham, UK.
Poterba, J. (1996), "Budget Institutions and Fiscal Policy in the US states", *American Economic Review*, vol. 86 (2), 395–400.

2. The theory of subnational balanced budget and debt control

Sergio Rossi and Bernard Dafflon

2.1 INTRODUCTION

In the canon of fiscal federalism, the redistribution and stabilisation functions should be carried out at the central government level (Oates, 1972). By contrast, the assignment of the allocation function is a priori undetermined, since it depends on the weights attached to the costs and benefits educed by centralising or decentralising the provision of public goods (King, 1984). Empirical evidence on the assignment of functions to multi-level governments shows that the three basic functions of fiscal policy are largely carried out by central governments, with varying degrees of decentralisation at one or more subnational levels.[1] This is so because the bulk of public spending concerns policy objectives that cannot be adequately pursued by the non-coordinated actions of subcentral governments (Tanzi, 1995). Revenue collection is in general more efficient and equitable when tax responsibilities are assigned to the federal government, although some taxation powers may have to be decentralised for fiscal accountability reasons (Wildasin, 1997; Tanzi and Zee, 1998).[2]

This chapter focuses on the subcentral government level, with the aim to point out which of these theoretical issues are relevant for the assignment of functions to decentralised governments, in connection with the balanced budget constraint and the control of government borrowing within European countries. Section 2.2 addresses the normative arguments that the theory of fiscal federalism has elaborated for and against the assignment of functions to subnational governments, with respect to the balanced budget requirement. The thread running throughout this approach is that limiting fiscal deficits enables governments to control their debt, without hindering the functions of fiscal policy in Pareto's sense. The next step in Section 2.3 is then to investigate from a positive point of view what arguments have been put forward, in practice, in order to call for balanced budget rules and debt control at the subnational government level.

2.2 THE NORMATIVE ANALYSIS

Let us apply Musgrave's (1959) threefold functional distinction of fiscal policy objectives at the local government level to investigate whether the basic functions of public finance can be decentralised – and, in the affirmative, to what extent.

2.2.1 Income Redistribution

According to fiscal federalism and public choice literature, the redistribution policy cannot be optimally put into practice at the local government level, on either equity or efficiency grounds, because of the required long-time horizon of such a policy, which contrasts with the short-term mobility of voters–taxpayers between local jurisdictions (Tiebout, 1956; Oates, 1972; Walsh, 1993). In this theoretical framework two lines of enquiry can be singled out for discussion, the first considering intra-generational matters of concern and the second dealing with inter-generational issues.

Intra-generational transfers
At any government level, the policy of income redistribution has the characteristics of a pure public good (Thurow, 1971), provided that within that jurisdiction there exists a widespread consensus on imposing on the wealthy and high-income earners for the benefit of the poor and poverty-stricken residents. Two problems need to be tackled for the case in point. They concern local budgeting and the openness of local economies.

The budgetary problem If a local government intends to pursue a redistributive policy, by taxing more heavily its wealthy residents in order to subsidise the penniless citizens, the amount of its financial support to the latter group should not be made dependent on the government's annual budgetary stance. In other words, within the jurisdiction there ought to be either no redistribution policy at all or one which is effectively implemented over the long run, in order to ensure the stability that the less wealthy residents may reasonably expect from such a policy. Further, since the recipients of these intra-period transfers usually belong to the lowest income cohort existing within the jurisdiction, their average and marginal propensities to save are probably close (if not equal) to zero. This amounts to saying that the redistributed income is entirely consumed over the current period, and nothing is left over to finance future consumption. If so, then these intra-generational transfers of income need to take place on a regular basis. In each fiscal year these transfers must be funded by the government's current revenue. Government borrowing would be ruled out for redistribution purposes, owing to the unmanageable, and possibly unsustainable, debt burden that a "roll-over" strategy would be putting on the government's fiscal position as time goes by. This argument is further reinforced by the financial-smoothing effect ensuing from such a redistributive (debt increasing) policy. In fact, over the business cycle the dynamics of the government's grants to indigent residents is such that, generally speaking, the worse the macroeconomic performance, the higher the sums needed for carrying out the redistribution function. Clearly, a redistributive policy has a strong counter-cyclical component. Now, during a recession – and a fortiori in the case of an economic crisis – the income accruing to taxpayers may be curtailed, at least in nominal terms, high-income earners generally being the economic agents worst hit by such adverse conditions (because of the significant decrease in profits and other non-wage shares of national income, or GDP). During an economic downturn, this situation would worsen the already difficult financial outcome of the government's account, therefore putting the dynamic sustainability of the redistribution policy at stake.

One might counter by arguing that government borrowing could actually provide a way out of this impasse. If the redistribution policy is financed (at least in part) by selling government bonds, so the argument goes, in distressed areas the need to curtail fiscal transfers to low-income residents – or to cut back the public goods supplied within the jurisdiction – can be averted. By the same token, amortisation of the public debt (issued to finance the redistribution policy during an economy's slowdown) would take place only in the upturn, when the government's budgetary situation may have recovered and – on account of fiscal surpluses – debt repayment might be less problematic. Yet, this counter-argument does not resist a thorough examination. As a matter of fact, its logic is linked to the idea of using so-called sinking, or rainy-day, funds to offset impending fiscal deficits, an idea which indeed hinges on balancing the budget over the business cycle. The introduction of rainy-day funds from which resources can be drawn during cyclical downturns – so as to avoid government borrowing – calls, in fact, for a certain degree of budgetary discipline, in so far as the current account surpluses recorded during an economic boom are set aside to pay for possible budgetary deficits in bad-weather times. As Balassone and Monacelli (2000, p. 28, n. 20) have recently noticed, "rainy-day funds are used by some American States as a shelter against the effects of the cycle on the deficit in order to comply with balanced budget clauses".[3] On reflection, there is no government borrowing to finance income redistribution in this case, because rainy-day funds are built up beforehand.

There are two further reasons to exclude borrowing for funding redistribution: (1) Empirical evidence clearly shows that the practice of government borrowing to overcome cyclical low peaks is asymmetric from a public choice point of view. Fiscal policy makers are willing to enter into debt when the economy is slowing down, but may be more reluctant to amortise this debt when the economy is recovering.[4] (2) Furthermore, during periods of sustained economic growth local governments are often put under pressure – by a number of voters and vested interest groups – either to decrease the tax burden or to extend the provision of public goods, which in fact amounts to reducing (perhaps to zero) notional fiscal surpluses (Buchanan et al., 1987).[5] Both arguments add to the probability of having an upward trend in government debt over time. They explain in part the need to restrict local government borrowing and the obligation to fund redistribution at the local level out of current revenues.

The open-economy problem   The traditional argument for centralising the redistribution policy is based on the mobility hypothesis (Tiebout, 1956), which applies particularly at the local government level, where there is a relatively high mobility of agents between neighbouring jurisdictions – especially within urban regions. The question one has to ask is whether a local government can implement an aggressive redistribution policy without jeopardising its own existence in the long run (Oates, 1972). Fiscal federalism literature answers in the negative, because the agents' mobility between jurisdictions would theoretically lead to a concentration of low-income earners in the most generous areas, which will eventually impede the financing of the redistributive policy of the latter jurisdictions (Walsh, 1993). In such a jurisdiction, the increasing number of incoming potential beneficiaries keeps increasing the share of the government's revenues allocated to it. Over time, this is bound to bring the local authority to raise taxes, pushing wealthy taxpayers to leave the jurisdiction when they consider that the tax burden has become excessive. If the local government cannot afford to lose its most affluent taxpayers, it has to moderate its redistributive policy, thus reducing the "redistribution differential" between jurisdictions. In the latter situation, there would be no visible difference with respect to a centralised redistribution policy.

There are, however, a number of counter-arguments that may apply in practice. First, owing to several economic and non-economic reasons (particular local customs, established interpersonal relations, geopolitical idiosyncrasies, ethnic and religious factors, language barriers, social security heteronomy, labour market organisation, and so on), interjurisdictional mobility may not be very high, at least in the long run, thus allowing for decentralised redistribution policies to be effective.[6] Second, if central and subcentral governments have heterogeneous preferences for local public goods, it may be optimal, on Pareto-efficiency grounds, to decentralise redistribution policies (Pauly, 1973; Dafflon, 1992). Third, it is often argued that costly information about the potential recipients of these policies can be obtained more effectively by the lower (or lowest) government tier (Rocaboy, 1995). Despite these cases, there is a pretty strong presumption for centralising redistribution policies.

It should nevertheless be recalled at this juncture that zoning and land planning are two policy instruments that may actually serve to select (wealthy) taxpayers or to limit the number of poverty-stricken residents in a particular local jurisdiction. If a local authority organises its territory in such a way as to offer a number of extensive residential, or industrial, areas of land, it becomes attractive for well-off individuals and business activities looking respectively for housing and industrial estates (and/or location advantages).[7] To put the point sharply, through zoning and land planning a local authority can select the kind and financial profile of the residents– taxpayers that it wants in order to implement its specific distributional choices. This form of spatial income redistribution is possible because land is an immovable asset. Note however that, properly speaking, zoning and land planning are not part of the redistribution function. Rather, they are two policy instruments for discriminating low-income residents – firms as well as individuals – from upper-class circles.

Inter-generational transfers

Besides its spatial dimension, the redistribution function of fiscal policy has also a time dimension. In fact, while income redistribution from affluent to indigent residents occurs within the same fiscal year and is basically allotted to consumption purposes by its recipients, there are also several public expenditures relating to investment or capital goods. Now, it is well known that an investment decision made in period one usually yields benefits over several subsequent periods – although the corresponding fiscal generations do not participate in the decision-making process (Alesina and Perotti, 1995). If the period-one investments of a government level were entirely paid for by the current generation of taxpayers – as is the case when these expenditures are entered on a balanced budget – the following generations would benefit from the ensuing public goods without paying a penny for them. This is unfair. In fact, for equity reasons, the cost of those public investments that promise to yield benefits over a number of fiscal years ought to be financed on a pay-as-you-use basis (Buchanan, 1958; Wagner, 1970; Dafflon, 1996). These expenditures may therefore be loan financed (although fiscal surpluses

may also be used in financing them). By loan financing investment projects,
future fiscal generations are indeed made to pay for the benefits they obtain
from these investments, as far as their tax burden covers the corresponding
debt service – inclusive of debt amortisation.[8] As Milesi-Ferretti (1997, p. 8)
clearly puts it, "public debt redistributes the tax burden across time, and can
therefore be a vehicle of intergenerational distribution".

Such an approach is openly disregarded by those economists adhering to
the view that public spending on investment goods is continuous over a
whole sequence of fiscal years, as maintained for instance by Buchanan
(1997). Each fiscal generation would thus benefit from the public
investments made by previous generations for roughly the same amount as
the current period investments. Hence, it would be pointless to loan finance
investment projects (in order to have an inter-generational distribution of
their costs on the basis of a pay-as-you-use finance principle), since in the
end there would be no difference in the actual tax burden of the various,
overlapping generations. However, this line of reasoning applies only to
relatively large subnational jurisdictions. For smaller local authorities, as
those of several European countries, the constant investment hypothesis
seems far less realistic: one large investment in one political period is usual.
In the latter case, it would be wiser to separate the current account from the
capital account in order for the former to comply with a balanced budget
requirement and to limit government borrowing to investment expenditures.

2.2.2 Macroeconomic Policy

Stabilisation and regional growth are twin features in public finance literature
on the macroeconomic objectives of the general government sector. They are
considered in turn in the two following subsections.

Stabilisation
Among economic policy makers, the consensus for centralising the
stabilisation function is general because of free-riding problems that exist
with decentralised counter-cyclical fiscal policy geared to enhancing
macroeconomic performance (Balassone and Franco, 1999). The argument
has traditionally been developed in a prisoner's dilemma framework. In the
most basic terms, any local government represents a small, open economy.
When it comes to counteracting the local effects of business cycles, namely
depression, the subcentral authority's effort may be either vain or Pareto-
inefficient (Derycke and Gilbert, 1988; Bayoumi and Eichengreen, 1995). On
the one hand, those investments undertaken at the local government level to
counteract the effects of a macroeconomic shock and sustain the overall
economic performance tend to benefit also the neighbouring jurisdictions

(that is, those not financing them). It would indeed be extraordinary if all production factors employed in a local investment project proved to be autochthonous. On the other hand, being aware of the existence of such spillovers from local investment expenditures, a local government might actually decide neither to finance a capital project on its own nor to co-operate with another jurisdiction for financing it. No subnational authority would indeed have an incentive to pursue optimal stabilisation policies, since it could free-ride on the fiscal efforts carried out by other jurisdictions having that goal. As the prisoner's dilemma literature indicates, a co-operative Nash-equilibrium would provide a Pareto-efficient solution. Yet, in order to secure the subnational governments' co-operation, the federal government has to intercede with them, either by fully centralising the stabilisation policy on efficiency grounds or by imposing at least a strong co-ordination of subnational stabilisation-oriented fiscal policies.[9]

An analogous conclusion can be drawn when one considers the stabilisation policy from a Keynesian point of view or in a functional finance setting (Lerner, 1943).[10] In this theoretical framework, one is led to ask whether a local authority can implement a stabilisation policy arguing along Keynesian lines, that is, aiming at supporting the economy's effective demand with no consideration at all for the local government's budgetary situation. Two points seem to be relevant to answer this question. First, to the best of our knowledge, neither Keynes nor Lerner ever explicitly considered stabilisation policies at the subnational government level. But, on the other hand, local governments often have an extended control over investment expenditures. In this respect, in order for the public policy to have some bearing on effective demand, it is necessary to co-ordinate the related projects at the different government levels, otherwise genuine co-ordination problems may embarrass the targeted counter-cyclical result. This co-ordination calls for a nation-wide, all-inclusive government tiers approach, which contrasts with decentralised (cacophonous) stabilisation policies. In addition, local governments might also have their own (different) preferences over the evolution of macroeconomic variables, such as inflation and unemployment, which would exacerbate the already mentioned co-ordination problems. As suggested by Cangiano and Mottu (1998, p. 6) "since the magnitude and effects of shocks may vary among regions, intervention by the central government may lower the costs of smoothing out such asymmetric effects".

The size of subnational jurisdictions is also relevant in this respect. Relatively large local governments may determine their investment policy taking into account business cycle forecasts, in order to adjust the magnitude of their capital outlays for counter-cyclical reasons. Or they may be willing to implement an active stabilisation policy and thus to carry out public investments with a counter-cyclical goal, independently of the other local authorities, in order to obtain as a counterpart some particular advantages from the central government, which remains officially in charge of pursuing the macroeconomic policy targets. To state it differently, from a strategic point of view, a relatively large local jurisdiction may be interested in putting the central government under political pressure by sharing the financial burden of the country's stabilisation policy, targeting a number of fiscal advantages as compensation. However, small local jurisdictions cannot do this, particularly when their investment level is unstable over time. Owing to the dynamic discontinuity of their capital expenditures, small subcentral governments may indeed be reluctant to abandon any single investment project for the sake of macroeconomic stabilisation. In this case it is therefore very unlikely that local governments would abide by centrally co-ordinated stabilisation policies. As a result, the central government is left with the obligation to bear more of the financial burden of stabilisation, since it has to compensate for the lack of co-operation in the general government sector in order to meet its macroeconomic policy targets.

Regional growth and fiscal competition
At the local level, the macroeconomic targets of fiscal policy may include elements of regional development, which go beyond the stabilisation function. Fiscal competition can be considered as a regional, or local, fiscal strategy in order to attract to (or to retain within) the jurisdiction the most interesting business activities for a number of macroeconomic reasons – first and foremost to enhance economic development and curb unemployment. In particular, a local authority may be willing to implement a discretionary fiscal policy with respect to firms (and their managers), to boost output growth and labour market clearing within its boundaries. Yet tax competition between local governments does not represent an optimal solution from a political economy perspective (Tulkens, 1985; Wilson, 1999).[11] Over the long run, fiscal competition is harmful since it decreases the revenues of the local governments as a whole. Even if tax competition enables the expansion of the general government sector to be controlled, and perhaps to be limited, (Pommerehne et al., 1996; Feld, 1999), empirical evidence at the European Union level shows that this kind of competition between regions exacerbates structural fiscal deficits and might put the sustainability of government debt at stake (Commission of the European Communities, 1997). This conclusion is strengthened by globalisation, which creates a political and economic setting in which the number of offshore places (the so-called fiscal havens) keeps increasing. Governments are thus stimulated to implement tax systems and fiscal strategies in order to attract those business activities that are highly mobile (Smith, 1996; Tanzi, 1996; Organisation for Economic Co-operation

and Development, 1998). At present, tax competition aims indeed at limiting the firms moving – in terms of fixed as well as financial capital – to offshore places, by decreasing the tax burden on business profits and top managers' earnings. This kind of competition between local authorities (but the argument applies to nation states as well) encompasses a series of drawbacks, namely (i) the risk of reducing the revenues of the local government considerably, (ii) the risk of diverting profitable trade and investment from the jurisdiction, (iii) the risk of transferring part of the tax burden to less mobile factors or activities (that is, labour and consumption), a transfer that is bound to impinge on both employment and fiscal equity between and within the generations of taxpayers, and (iv) the risk of jeopardising the creditworthiness of the local government through erratic strategies that impact negatively on its budget in the long run.

To give a flavour of these problems, let us briefly consider the dynamics of tax competition between two local governments, A and B, of the same country. Assume that the fiscal strategy implemented by A is successful in attracting income-creating firms by granting them a tax bonus. Soon, if the game is symmetrical, B will be offering a similar, but higher, bonus, in order to gain a comparative advantage for business location. This non-cooperative game may go on for quite a long time, with successive rounds that eventually reduce to a minimum the local tax burden in both A and B. Owing to a lack of co-ordination between A and B, any local economic benefit that might result from this fiscal strategy is therefore bound to be nullified in the long run by a dynamic tax competition of the other jurisdiction. In the end, firms are therefore not attracted to a specific location, since the self-reinforcing, downgrading process of tax competition between local governments A and B removes any comparative advantage that these authorities might individually have in the short run.[12] On the whole, tax competition between A and B is such that both lose a considerable part of their fiscal revenues. This situation is further reinforced by the problem of asymmetric information. As a matter of fact, when a firm is looking for fiscal advantages (basically, a reduction of its tax burden), it often starts negotiations with more than one local authority. This allows firms to know, and compare, the various sorts of fiscal advantages offered by competing governments, whereas none of these knows what the competitors are indeed offering. Clearly, the lack of co-operation between (local) governments is such that tax competition is overall detrimental for the general government sector, in terms of both fiscal revenues and economic development (Organisation for Economic Co-operation and Development, 1998).

A first solution to harmful tax competition would consist in establishing a powerful, and independent, observatory for the general government sector, to collect all local authorities' decisions that grant a tax bonus or other fiscal advantages to firms, contributing to establish a nation-wide policy agreement on tax competition, where controls and penalties are clearly indicated.

But a decentralised balanced budget requirement may also be enforced with intent to limit harmful fiscal competition between local governments, "so as to avoid a 'rush to the bottom' of tax systems, which would prevent governments from sustaining desirable tax policies and financing necessary expenditures" (Cangiano and Mottu, 1998, p. 20). The argument runs as follows. A local authority is led to grant a tax bonus or any other fiscal advantage to specific categories of economic agents (firms as well as individuals) in so far as it does not fully, and immediately, support the ensuing negative budgetary effects. In a nutshell, the less the current government's fiscal policy results are affected by such tax strategies, the more the government may be led to play down the negative outcomes of fiscal competition. This occurs indeed when the budgetary process is open ended. In this situation, in fact, fiscal policy makers can more easily yield to firms' pressure or the demands of well-to-do agents, and grant them a specific fiscal advantage or tax bonus, because government borrowing will mitigate the tax bill that has to be presented to the voters–taxpayers – who probably do not fully discount their future tax liabilities resulting from present deficit spending (Moesen, 1993). So, by analogy with earlier discussion, this form of behaviour may give rise to a multiple-round, non-co-operative game with other competing governments, in which case the policy outcome would be twofold. On the expenditure side of its balance sheet, the local authority may record an increasing outlay for the provision of public goods destined to attract business activities within the jurisdiction. On the revenue side, the same authority may notice a rapid decrease in tax collection and/or user charges for the same reason. Taken together, these outcomes would eventually prevent local governments from financing a series of programmes aimed at the general public's welfare. In a system of competing subnational governments it is no exaggeration to say that each local authority is thus faced with a situation similar to the prisoner's dilemma noted earlier.

Again, a solution to this dilemma may be found along two lines. The first, and simplest, way would be for the central government to ban any form of fiscal competition at the local level. However, another route can be worked out, one which actually allows for an interjurisdictional, democratically decided fiscal competition. This solution hinges on a balanced budget requirement to be specified by law or by the constitution. The point is that with a hard budget constraint that excludes government borrowing, fiscal advantages can be granted only as long as they do not threaten budget equilibrium. On the assumption of unchanged policies, with a balanced budget rule a local government has either to limit the amount allotted to policy programmes or to increase the tax burden of the general public, if it intends to pursue a downward tax strategy and/or a strategy of fiscal generosity in favour of selected groups of voters–taxpayers. A closed-ended budgetary process would bring about a democratically voted trade-off between these alternatives. Otherwise, any fiscal bonus granted to a particular firm or individual would have to be compensated by an increased tax burden on other firms or individuals: since this amounts to introducing de facto a system of implicit grants that threaten fiscal justice, it would be rejected by the legislative majority of the local government.

2.2.3 Resource Allocation

So far, the weight of argument against the assignment of redistribution and macroeconomic policies to decentralised governments seems to be prevalent in respect of the points scored by the opposite view. It follows that the control of deficit and debt of the local tiers or, at least, hard rules of balanced budget and debt capping, can be implemented at the central level. We turn now to resource allocation, which can be investigated along two distinct lines of thought, economics or political economy.

The economics of allocative efficiency
As neatly summarised by Cangiano and Mottu (1998, p. 6), "in pursuing *allocative efficiency*, three criteria are usually considered for centralising or decentralising the provision of public goods: their spatial incidence; the existence of uniform or differentiated preferences across subcentral governments; and the presence of economies of scale". The first criterion concerns the spillovers problem (see above). Subnational authorities may ignore any external benefit attached to providing local public goods and may thus be led to underprovide them, unless the concerned local governments agree to negotiate a co-operative allocation scheme that internalises these spillovers (Deloche, 1987). The second criterion is linked to the Tiebout hypothesis discussed above that agents are mobile and can thus "vote with their feet" to choose the jurisdiction offering the combination of local public goods and tax system closer to their preferences (Tiebout, 1956; Rose-Ackerman, 1983; Rubinfeld, 1987). The third criterion assigns the allocation function to the government tier that can provide a particular level of public goods at the lowest unit cost (Tullock, 1969). All the criteria converge on the idea that there ought to be a close correspondence between those who determine the level of provision of public goods, those who pay for this production to take place, and those who actually benefit from it (Oates, 1972; Dafflon, 1992). In fact, when there is an explicit, and simultaneous, link between the benefits of public goods and the taxes or user charges levied to finance them, fiscal accountability is enhanced and

allocative efficiency can be attained more easily (Olson, 1969; Dafflon, 1998). This leads us to explore the political economy of local government finance from a public choice point of view.

The political economy of efficient allocation
As public choice literature points out, a balanced budget constraint provides the necessary institutional framework in order to obtain efficient resource allocation in fiscal federations. The argument has various facets.[13]

First, "the discipline of a balanced budget may produce a more careful weighing of benefits and costs, thus preventing the public sector from growing beyond its optimal size" (Rosen, 1992, p. 458). The optimal size is defined here by the fiscal burden that voters–taxpayers agree to bear in order to finance the desired provision of public goods; it is more easily arrived at when the budgetary process ties together the costs and benefits of such a provision (Gilbert and Guengant, 1991). This is what actually happens with a balanced budget requirement, since each expenditure programme must be linked to the funds that have to be raised in order to finance it. Needless to say, the balanced budget rule does not provide a direct link between a particular expenditure programme and the funds needed to carry it out. Nevertheless, it sets the fiscal boundaries of the public sector by fixing the actual budgetary constraint and the tax burden accepted by the economy. In this respect, tax collection presents several advantages for an efficient resource allocation when it is compared with government borrowing: (i) it makes clear the transfer of financial resources from the private to the public sector that is required in order to implement the selected fiscal policy programmes, thus avoiding the phenomenon of fiscal illusion that may affect the practice of loan financing them (Buchanan, 1964; Buchanan and Wagner, 1978; Tollison and Wagner, 1987); (ii) it enhances fiscal accountability, because it links explicitly the benefits of public expenditure with the costs that taxpayers have to bear collectively if they want to realise a particular policy programme (Lee, 1987; Bennett, 1990; Buchanan, 1997); (iii) it is independent of the agents' mobility between jurisdictions, thus making it impossible for them – when associated with pay-as-you-use finance – to shift part of the fiscal burden of a voted policy programme onto outsiders (Wagner, 1970 and 1987); (iv) it reduces the political and bureaucratic leeway in rent-seeking forms of behaviour – which is bound to limit the allocation choices of future governments and generations of taxpayers in so far as they increase future debt service – since it entails the need for vested interest groups and bureaucrats to defend their expenditure preferences, thus obliging them to compare costs and benefits explicitly (Rabushka, 1983; Shadbegian, 1998).

Second, when a number of local and/or regional governments simultaneously borrow to finance their budget deficits, private investment may be crowded out, a phenomenon that impacts negatively on the overall economic performance: government borrowing represents in this case a non-efficient allocation of resources, since it limits economic growth by crowding out a number of productive investments within the private sector (Cebula et al., 1994; Dalamagas, 1995). This effect has been explained by various reasons that hold good for the general government sector as a whole (Rabushka, 1983; Lachman, 1994; Greffe, 1997): (i) government borrowing draws on the pool of financial resources existing within the economic system, thus reducing the sums available for private investment projects; (ii) this competition exerts an upward pressure on the structure of interest rates, further limiting private investment possibilities;[14] (iii) increasing budget deficits affect negatively the agents' expectations of inflation, which add to the upward trend in interest rates; and (iv) a further reason can be found at the local government level because of the geographical segmentation of capital markets that may exist in practice (Dafflon, 1996, p. 239). Of course, in today's global economy, crowding-out effects may not be observed to the same extent as the theory purports to be the case (particularly at the local level, where capital mobility is higher than at the national and international levels).

On the whole, a balanced budget requirement seems to represent, on allocative efficiency grounds, the best institutional answer to the problems of limiting (1) the size of the general government sector and (2) the crowding-out effects, from both a political economy perspective and a public choice standpoint. It makes ends meet without eating up capital that may be more productive when privately invested. Tested in respect of the other two functions of fiscal policy, as was done above, the normative analysis supporting budgetary equilibrium yields similar results. Yet one may ask whether these very arguments are to be found in practice in defence of those balanced budget rules that have been adopted in fiscal federations. It is to this issue that we now turn, in order to point out where the continuity between normative and positive analysis breaks down.

2.3   THE POSITIVE ANALYSIS

The preceding section has focused on the theoretical arguments that corroborate a balanced budget requirement and, by limiting government deficits, allow for debt control at the local level. The logic of the arguments would lead to a situation where "the rules of the game" are given "top-down". We investigate now what arguments have been put to the fore in practice to explain why a local government ought to abide by a balanced budget rule aiming at controlling public debt. To state it clearly, the purpose of this section is to detect whether the current rules enforcing budgetary discipline are based on a normative analysis or whether, underneath, there exist other lines of argument, which would call for self-discipline.

2.3.1 Multifaceted Budgetary Discipline

Readers will have noticed a slippage between budget balance and budgetary discipline in the previous paragraph. In fact, as the debate in the 1980s and 1990s has shown, the analysis of sound public finance carried out in practice has centred on the idea of budgetary sustainability (which may encompass different forms, as we shall see), rather than sticking to a rigid balanced budget requirement that would apply either to a particular tier or to the general government sector as a whole. Both in theory and in practice budgetary sustainability has a close connection to the balanced budget constraint, and indeed the advocates of the former aim to shape the latter for operational purposes. In this respect, three methodological paradigms have come to light and spawned the academic literature on both sides of the Atlantic.

The golden rule
Generally speaking, the normative arguments supporting a balanced budget rule imply that the overall budget, or account, of a government tier must be in equilibrium; that is, in each fiscal year current tax collection, user charges and received transfer payments have to balance with public spending for both consumption and investment purposes. As already pointed out, those expenditures undertaken for investment projects ought to be financed on a pay-as-you-use basis, because they yield benefits over a number of fiscal years. On equity as well as efficiency grounds, it has therefore been suggested to separate the current from the capital account. This is indeed what the "revisited" golden rule prescribes: a balanced current account combined with a capital account in which government borrowing for investment expenditures is tolerated, or even promoted for inter-generational equity reasons (Eisner, 1984 and 1992; Dafflon, 1998). This distinction has been pushed ahead by arguing that a balanced current account must include debt service, which is defined as interest payment, and debt amortisation according to a pay-as-you-use rule (Dafflon, 1996). This budgetary process has many advantages, which cannot be clearly perceived if one merely considers the normative arguments discussed above. First, it calls for a clear definition of investment expenditures (in order to inhibit various forms of strategic behaviour, inclusive of creative accounting).[15] As a corollary, it

compels governments to present investment plans that consider the ensuing costs and benefits over the whole life span of these projects, thus avoiding the phenomenon of fiscal illusion that may otherwise be elicited by government borrowing. Second, it requires a clear definition of the debt amortisation schedule over the same time span, to avoid spoiling the budgetary choices of future fiscal generations. Third, it does not raise crowding-out problems, unless one is willing to postulate that public investments are less productive than private ones. Fourth, when it is associated with rainy-day funds, it allows for some flexibility in the case of an economic downturn, as far as the balanced budget requirement applies over the business cycle only (but this is bound to introduce political leeway, as we shall see again later from a different perspective). On this last point another line of reasoning has recently given rise to abundant literature, focusing on an intertemporal balanced budget constraint in order to evaluate the budgetary sustainability of fiscal policies over the long run (Balassone and Franco, 2000a; Chalk and Hemming, 2000).

Sustainability or the intertemporal budget constraint
During the last two decades or so, opponents of the application of the (amortisation-augmented) golden rule to local government finance have argued against the limited scope of such a rule on account of two distinct, but interrelated, problems (Balassone and Franco, 2000b). First, focusing on a single fiscal year is not deemed sufficient to evaluate whether a fiscal policy that is currently balanced will be so in the future. Second, by ignoring a number of macroeconomic data (such as output growth, interest and inflation rates), the golden rule would also make it impossible for a government to interact with the actual economic performance and thus allow for some budgetary flexibility in cyclical downturns. This strand of thought has therefore led to the policy proposal for balancing the budget over the business cycle, the relevant target being the so-called primary balance.[16] In short, as the literature on the Maastricht fiscal criteria has recently shown, the analysis of budgetary sustainability aims to establish a numerical benchmark in order to detect when a particular fiscal deficit is excessive with respect to the overall economic situation (Blanchard et al., 1990). This research strategy ties together, via a more or less refined intertemporal budgetary constraint, deficits and debts with given assumptions about inflation, real growth and interest rates (Dietsch and Garnier, 1989). The aim is to bring about a reference value for the targeted variables, like the deficit-to-GDP and the debt-to-GDP ratios enshrined in the Maastricht (or Amsterdam) Treaty, where the stability of these parameters is considered as signalling fiscal policy sustainability.

This approach suffers from a number of methodological shortcomings, which have been pointed out in the literature. By focusing on the primary balance – which amalgamates current as well as capital outlays – the fiscal sustainability approach fails to consider the link that exists in practice between deficit spending and its object, be it consumption or investment goods (Hertzog, 1991). It evacuates pay-as-you-use finance and undermines the very idea of budgetary discipline. Further, how can "sustainability" be assessed on the basis of a "primary surplus" that excludes interest payment? Since it relies purely on bookkeeping relationships that are silent about business cycles and demand-management issues, the analysis lying behind this approach lacks a proper theoretical framework (Mottu, 1997). Moreover, as the debate on the Maastricht fiscal criteria has pointed out, the consistency of the selected benchmarks is problematic, and indeed no grounding in the theory of public finance has been provided to support them (Buiter et al., 1993; Dafflon and Rossi, 1996; Pasinetti, 1998). Another argument is that these criteria refer to GDP figures, which do not fit subnational government tiers. In fact, GDP is a measure of total economic activity, *not* of total government revenue (Spahn, 2000, p. 23). As suggested by the International Monetary Fund, at the local government level one should consider a debt-to-revenue ratio as the numerical benchmark, or ceiling, for assessing the sustainability of local government finance.

In addition, owing to the difficulties in defining, measuring, and forecasting business cycles and macroeconomic performance for the purposes of assessing fiscal sustainability, the actual outcome of such an approach could be pretty spurious if one considers it ex post (Roubini, 1995). This last critique has led some economists with a Keynesian pedigree to put forward a slightly different version of the sustainability approach to fiscal deficits, one where the focus of the analysis is on structural rather than actual fiscal (im)balances.

The structural balance approach
According to a fair number of recent studies, when one ponders a government's fiscal policy outcome, one must distinguish between structural and contingent factors affecting it (Muller and Price, 1984; Giorno et al., 1995). The aim of this distinction is to measure the extent to which a business cycle influences the fiscal policy results, so as to determine whether the actual (primary) balance is structurally sound or not. In the negative, the government would have to act in order to curb the deficit, since in this case the fiscal imbalance can be attributed to structural problems rather than to a mere slowdown of the economic performance. This approach to budgetary discipline is grounded in a concept of fiscal sustainability that is different from the one adhered to by those relying on the excessive deficit procedure

laid down in the Maastricht Treaty. Here the focus is on the structural budget only, around which a number of automatic stabilisers may be operating. This approach, as its advocates claim, has the merit of being independent of the accuracy of the business cycle's forecasts for detecting excessive (that is, unsustainable) deficits and prompting government intervention. Hence, it would also avert those strategic forms of behaviour that may lie behind forecasting methods to cook the government's books. So far, so good.

However, there is no need to go much further here to notice that the same issue can also represent a pitfall in the structural balance approach. In this framework, the problem is to find and apply an objective criterion for defining what a structural balance is. The idea of defining it as the balance that a government would obtain if the economy were at full-employment level does not seem to be free of political leeway. As a matter of fact, in order to put into practice the structural balance approach, one has to define (1) the potential GDP that would result if all production factors were to be employed, and (2) how the resulting (notional) output gap – that is, the percentage difference between output and its reference value[17] – would affect the government's account in terms of fiscal revenues and outlays. Both steps offer room for manoeuvre, since there is no accepted methodology to deal with them.[18] As a result, the figures arrived at in the assessment of fiscal sustainability are problematic, particularly because the possibility that an overzealous measure of potential GDP may underestimate the structural deficit cannot be ruled out. The mismeasured output gap, in fact, may lead fiscal policy makers to overrate the imbalance that they ascribe to economic fluctuations, thus tolerating, willy-nilly, a structural deficit that would have to be reduced. An additional, technical pitfall of this approach is that potential GDP figures are even more difficult to determine at the regional level, not to say are impossible to calculate at the local level. To be sure, granting that an output gap can be measured for the national economy as a whole, national figures cannot be disaggregated at the regional or local level unless one is willing to suppose that macroeconomic shocks and business cycle effects are evenly spread throughout the country. Empirical evidence shows that this is hardly the case.

These worrying conclusions are strengthened by a further consideration relating to the extent to which fiscal deficits can be compensated for during the business cycle. As noted earlier, two lines of reasoning seem to be relevant in this paradigm. Let us call them up here, since this will also serve us as an apposite gambit for the next section. First, it is hardly necessary to stress that an economy's upswing may be softer, or shorter, than the corresponding slowdown, making it theoretically impossible for a one-to-one matching between fiscal deficits and surpluses to occur. Second, owing to various forms of political pressure, during a recovery phase elected government officials may find it difficult to resist the call for increasing public expenditures, thus putting at stake the possibility of smoothing fiscal deficits over the cycle.

In other words, at the local government level it may be as difficult as at the central government level to implement a counter-cyclical fiscal policy because of the nature of the locally provided public goods. Some of them (for instance environmental services, water resources and urban public transportation) relate to other policy goals, which cannot be simply traded off against macroeconomic stabilisation. Others are similar to private consumption goods (for instance nursery and primary schools): during an economic upswing, beneficiaries–taxpayers may want to increase consumption – including quality only (for example fewer children per class) – of these (local) public goods, therefore putting the local government under pressure if it targets a fiscal surplus. Indeed, peer pressure is the main reason behind the introduction of fiscal rules at the local government level, where the lack of institutional controls on public debt may promote bureaucratic leeway and ad hoc bargaining between close-knit politicians and voters– taxpayers.

2.3.2 Approaches to Government Debt Control

As in any "rules versus discretion" debate in public policy, the argument centres on the pros and cons of tying the government's hands by introducing binding rules for fiscal policy makers (Tabellini and Alesina, 1990; Alesina and Perotti, 1996).

> Rigid fiscal rules eliminate (if they are really binding) the possibility of responding to political incentives by running deficits; however, they also depauper the policy-maker of an important tool to stabilise output and/or to smooth tax distortions over time (i.e. run optimal fiscal deficits during an economic recession or when government spending is temporarily high). Conversely, fiscal discretion has the cost of leading to excessive budget deficits if there is a political bias in fiscal policy; however, it allows policy-maker the flexibility of running fiscal deficits in periods (such as an economic downturn or a war) when it is optimal to do so. (Roubini, 1995, p. 6)

Owing to the poor results obtained by decentralising macroeconomic policies at the local level, this debate has led to the adoption of control mechanisms that ought to limit deficits and debts over time independently of political pressure. Clearly, the costs–benefits trade-off between rules and discretion in fiscal policy is such that the advantages of the former overwhelm those of the latter, particularly with regard to the moral hazard problem that may exist in the absence of a legally enforced fiscal discipline (Inman, 1996; von Hagen and Eichengreen, 1996; Buchanan, 1997).

Now, in existing fiscal federations a number of approaches to limit the growth of local government debt have been put forward, within a spectrum ranging from sole reliance on market discipline to direct administrative control of the central government over subnational governments' borrowing. These different approaches reflect different constitutional and institutional frameworks, and also depend on the country's financial and economic situation. Generally speaking, they can be grouped into four main categories (Ter-Minassian and Craig, 1997).

Reliance on financial market discipline

According to the so-called market discipline hypothesis, the regulatory role of modern financial markets would suffice to exert effective discipline on local government borrowing (Breton, 1977; Bayoumi et al., 1995). Adoption of constitutional, or legal, rules would thus be redundant, for tighter credit market conditions – in particular, higher interest rates – would already impose effective sanctions and penalties on those jurisdictions living beyond their means. In practice, however, several stringent conditions need to be satisfied for this to occur (Lane, 1993). First, financial markets should be free and open, so much so that the government must not be put in a privileged position with respect to private borrowers. Second, adequate information on the government's outstanding debt and repayment capacity should be available to potential lenders, who must also be aware of the government's off-balance-sheet operations. Third, lenders should be sure that no chance of bailout exists in case of local government default.[19] Fourth, the borrower should adequately react to market signals before reaching the point of exclusion from the credit market, say, by holding back on excessive spending in response to higher borrowing costs.

Now, these four conditions are unlikely to be observed in the majority of fiscal federations, where free-riding and moral hazard problems may lead to prohibitive credit market conditions and/or the necessity for bailout interventions (Balassone and Franco, 1999). In fact, in developing countries the available information on local government finance often lacks coverage, accuracy and timeliness. When local investment is not continuous over time, but based on one important project for a political term, as is often the case in small jurisdictions, politicians tend to disregard interest rate signals. Additionally, in advanced economies the short-sightedness of government officials that is elicited by relatively short terms of office makes local fiscal policy rather unresponsive to market signals, for the ensuing sanction will bear its effects only over the next political term (through an increased debt burden for future governments). This explains why sole reliance on financial market discipline to limit local government borrowing is not effective in a number of industrialised countries as well as in developing or transition economies (Ter-Minassian and Craig, 1997).

Another market-based alternative to government debt control has recently been brought to the fore (Casella, 1999). Accordingly, a market for tradable borrowing permits could be set up at local government level, where a predetermined debt limit would be institutionally fixed by higher government level in much the same way as this occurs with pollution permits in environmental economics. Once the sum total of borrowing permits and their initial distribution between local authorities have been decided, market forces will enable their efficient allocation with respect to the particular borrowing requirements of different jurisdictions in any given fiscal year. A local government would thus have to obtain the amount of borrowing permits required by its budget deficit, in order to borrow the corresponding financial resources from the capital market. This market-oriented debt strategy suffers, however, from a number of methodological shortcomings. First, it depends on the existence of sufficient competition in the market for borrowing permits, which may not be observed in practice when there are a limited number of competing local governments. Second, even if such a competitive market existed, it would not be enough to stimulate budgetary discipline, in so far as this approach is silent on the very objects that are loan-financed (either consumption or investment outlays). Third, this market would be effective only in so far as local governments do invest on a regular basis, as opposed to a one-off capital expenditure within a single political term. Fourth, on the assumption that the first two problems can be overcome, there remains the conundrum of the initial permit distribution. In fact, owing to the different outcomes elicited by the adoption of different distribution criteria (such as local output, population, revenue collection, grandfathering, and so on), this problem is extremely difficult, unless the centre and the local authorities negotiate over the initial amount of borrowing permits to which any single local government is entitled. This process relies on co-operation, an issue we explore next.

Co-operative bilateral or multilateral control
On account of the various difficulties and "recognition lags" occasioned by market-based debt control, the closest approach hinges on a co-operative scheme in which limits on subnational government borrowing are arrived at through a negotiation process involving the central and local government levels.

> Under this approach, subnational governments are actively involved in formulating macroeconomic objectives and the key fiscal parameters underpinning these objectives. Through this process, agreement is reached on the overall deficit targets for the general government, as well as on the guidelines for growth of main items

of revenue and expenditure. Specific limits are then agreed upon for the financing requirements of individual subnational jurisdictions. (Ter-Minassian and Craig, 1997, p. 164)

In addition, co-operation is needed for the distribution of the shares of the Maastricht fiscal criteria between and within government tiers.

This co-operative approach has certainly the merit to promote dialogue and exchange of information between different government levels. According to its proponents, it should also enable local policy makers to grasp the macroeconomic effects of their budgetary choices, thus raising fiscal responsibility at the lower government level. However, it does not avoid the risk of free-riding forms of behaviour by some local administrators, especially when the number of jurisdictions involved is high and the negotiations may be long and intricate. In addition, if the leadership of the central government in fiscal management is weak, these negotiations may not be effective in limiting local debts. This is why a compulsory scheme seems to work much more effectively than a co-operative process.

The very nature of the negotiating pool may also be considered indirectly as a bailout guarantee in general. The mismanagement of a local government budget after a negotiation round would be sanctioned by imposing a "no debt" ceiling on it in the next round. Whether this sanction mechanism will be effective in practice has yet to be demonstrated. In fact, sanctions are foreign to co-operation and where they exist, they are seldom applied – and if they are, they are re-negotiated in the next round.

Rule-based control
A number of federal countries rely on fiscal rules, specified by the law or constitution, to control local government borrowing. Among these rules, one can find a balanced budget requirement, deficit and debt ceilings (like the Maastricht fiscal criteria), and the golden rule of public finance discussed earlier on. Many countries have adopted a combination of these rules. The advantages of a rule-based control of local debt are manifold. First, its application is fair and immediate, since it does not depend on a contingent, politically biased assessment of local government finance. Second, it avoids time-consuming negotiations between the central and the subcentral government levels, in which asymmetric information and bargaining powers and/or short-term political strategies may prevail over sound macroeconomic considerations. However, as already noted, pure reliance on fiscal rules is deemed rigid in the face of economic fluctuations and may also give rise to various forms of creative accounting in order to circumvent the rules.[20] These practices suggest adopting (1) a well-defined accounting framework for governments, to limit, if not prohibit, off-balance-sheet operations, (2) clear and comprehensive definitions of government deficits and debts, and (3) a

modern government financial management information system, so as to provide timely and reliable data on local public finance (Dafflon, 1996; Ter-Minassian and Craig, 1997).

A crucial issue, only recently debated (Pujol, 2000; Novaresi, 2001), is whether the rules should be set "top-down" or decided on their own by local governments or their leaders. So far, both processes have been based on the same arguments. But are there differences between these two processes? What are the additional reasons, if any, for a local leader of a particular jurisdiction at any given point in time, to decide constitutional binding rules on future budgetary processes and investment funding? What is the effectiveness of "top-down" versus spontaneous regulations? At present, the answers are uncertain and further studies welcome.

Administrative control by the higher government level

The direct control exerted by central government over subnational government borrowing is a sovereign act that may occur in various forms, such as (i) the setting of annual ceilings on the overall debt of particular local jurisdictions, (ii) the review and authorisation of single borrowing operations, (iii) the monitoring of the subnational government's financial operations, and (iv) the centralisation of all government borrowing. As noted by Balassone and Franco (1999), this solution goes against the spirit of fiscal federations, although several considerations argue in its favour as far as local governments' external borrowing is concerned.

> First, external debt policy is intimately linked with other macroeconomic policies (monetary and exchange rate policies and foreign reserve management) that are naturally the responsibility of central-level authorities (in particular, the central bank). Second, a well-coordinated approach to foreign markets for sovereign borrowing is likely to result in better terms and conditions than a fragmented one. Third, a deterioration of foreign ratings for one or more of the subnational borrowers may well have contagion effects on the ratings for other borrowers, both public and private. Finally, foreign lenders frequently require an explicit central government guarantee for subnational borrowing. At a minimum, they tend to count on an implicit guarantee. Thus, the central government is likely, de facto, to bear ultimate responsibility for the subnational governments' foreign debt. (Ter-Minassian and Craig, 1997, pp. 168–169)

These arguments are not so compelling in the case of domestic borrowing of local governments. In fact, owing to the existence of heterogeneous preferences for the provision of local public goods, detailed administrative control by the centre may be suboptimal in Pareto's sense (see above). Additionally, formal approval by the federal government of individual borrowing operations of the local authority entails a moral commitment for the former to provide financial support to the latter in the case of government default. This situation adds to the moral hazard problems raised above and may thus be Pareto-inefficient.

Furthermore, experience shows that regulation by the centre of local government borrowing is not always matched by sound fiscal policies or general macroeconomic targets, but may result in national political strategies giving leeway to politicians at the central government level.

2.4 CONCLUSION

This chapter has considered the normative as well as the positive arguments that have been brought to the fore in favour of the introduction of balanced budget requirements at the subnational government level. On the one hand, the theoretical analysis of the assignment of the three basic functions of fiscal policy to multi-level governments has shown that, both on equity and efficiency grounds, decentralised budget constraints are instrumental in promoting budgetary discipline and fiscal accountability of local authorities. On the other hand, the practice of imposing legally binding fiscal rules is largely explained by the need to restrict administrative leeway and rent-seeking forms of behaviour that have been observed when budgetary processes are open-ended. In short, whereas the theory of balanced budgets focuses on efficient resource allocation and fiscal justice arguments, the practice of budgetary equilibrium relies on a more sophisticated line of reasoning, in which public choice arguments take centre stage.

Now, a further issue that would have to be investigated at the local level concerns the effective contribution of rule-based constraints to balancing the budget or the current account. As a matter of fact, there seems to be little agreement on the extent to which the control of public debt impacts on the observed fiscal performance of the general government sector as a whole (von Hagen, 1991; Elder, 1992; Poterba, 1994; Alesina and Bayoumi, 1996; Shadbegian, 1998; von Hagen et al., 2001). In particular, taking into account the depth and breadth of the analysis of local government finance surveyed in this chapter, several lines of research may be worth exploring, in order to answer a number of questions; for example:

- Do balanced budget rules work effectively at the local government level?
- Is there a positive correlation between stringent rules and fiscal policy results?
- Do fiscal rules have an effect on the extent and volatility of business cycles?

- Do fiscal rules affect interest rates on the credit market for public borrowers?
- Do fiscal rules limit the size of local governments?

Clearly, further work needs to be done in order to assess the operational status of balanced budget constraint at the local government level. The research presented here is just a critical review of the analysis carried out so far. But to our knowledge this is one of the few systematic attempts to bring together normative and positive lines of thought for the control of subnational government borrowing in an increasingly decentralised world.

NOTES

1. "In the five largest OECD federations – Australia, Canada, Germany, Switzerland, and the United States – central governments spend, on average, more than half of total expenditure and collect about 60 percent of total revenue" (Cangiano and Mottu, 1998, p. 7).
2. It is also possible to couch the same argument the other way around: since local governments play an active role in the allocation function of fiscal policy, as we shall see later on, there is a reason to assign particular taxation powers (for instance land taxes and part of income taxes) to the local government level. By contrast, other taxation powers, like VAT and excise duties, should be assigned exclusively to the central government level on equity and efficiency grounds.
3. See also Sobel and Holcombe (1996), Levinson and Knight (1999), and McGranahan (1999).
4. It is sometimes argued that debt amortisation occurs "automatically" during a boom since the nominal burden of the debt diminishes in relative terms compared to the upward swing of macroeconomic magnitudes brought about by real growth, so that it would be pointless to care about debt amortisation when the financial resources are on hand (Thalmann, 1992). Needless to say, if economic growth occurs in nominal terms only because of high inflation, this line of reasoning is flawed. One cannot argue on one side that sound macroeconomic policies aim at an inflation rate as low as possible, and on the other side leave it to inflation to amortise the nominal public debt.
5. Note also that owing to the variability and uncertainty of economic performance, the recovery and boom phase may be shorter than the recession. This would mean that over the business cycle fiscal surpluses could not compensate fiscal deficits entirely, a situation leading to an increasing government debt in the long run.
6. This argument seems nevertheless not to be very robust at the local government level, because for several people it is often possible to commute easily between two neighbouring jurisdictions, the one where the redistribution policy is the most interesting in fiscal terms and the other where these agents used to live and still spend much, or most, of their (working and/or free) time.
7. This argument can be associated with tax competition, an issue we will explore later.
8. On this point see Dafflon (1998, ch. 5). To be true, this line of reasoning pertains to the allocative efficiency argument, an issue we will take up later on.
9. In this latter case, control by the central government of subnational budgets as well as debt capping seem to be the two most frequently used policy instruments to secure co-ordination.
10. See Buchanan and Wagner (1977), and Vaughn and Wagner (1992).

11. "Tax competition is identified by granting preferential tax regimes on easily transportable commodities, inducing cross-border shopping; tax incentives and tax holidays; transfer pricing practices by multinational companies; and proliferation of tax havens" (Cangiano and Mottu, 1998, p. 20).

12. As pointed out by regional economics, however, the location of firms depends on a number of other factors besides fiscal advantages. Among these other factors one may include the proximity of markets, the availability of skilled workers, and easy (that is, low-cost) access to communication networks.

13. For an extensive, in-depth investigation of this subject matter see Pujol (2000), who also provides full bibliographic references.

14. "When the government borrows to finance its budget deficit, it has an unfair advantage in its competition with private borrowers. Since government borrowing is backed up by [...] the power to tax, the government gets first call on the available supply of credit. Moreover, the government will pay whatever rate of interest is required to get the funds it needs to sustain government spending. Private borrowers are not so flexible" (Rabushka, 1982, p. 70).

15. See Dafflon and Rossi (1999) for an investigation of several accounting "fiddles" that have been carried out by some EU countries to meet the Maastricht criteria on public finance in order to qualify for EMU membership as from 1 January 1999. Note also that a criticism raised in the literature against the distinction of a current and a capital account focuses on the dividing line between consumption and investment expenditures (Tanzi, 1993). This (sometimes arbitrary) distinction is considered as leading to endless debate "as special interest groups [would rush] to demonstrate that their favourite programs yield future benefits and should thus be counted as investment and largely excluded from the current budget deficits and the constraints on current spending" (Cavanaugh, 1996, pp. 31–32). This is a pertinent argument indeed, especially in so far as it might lead policy makers to prefer "[investment] expenditures on physical assets rather than greater spending for intangibles such as health or education" (Colm and Wagner, 1963, p. 125). However, this critique does not concern the balanced budget rule per se.

16. According to the 1995 European System of Accounts, ESA95, the primary balance results from the difference between the government's revenues (of both the current and the capital account) and its total expenditures, without interest payment and debt amortisation. See Eurostat (1996).

17. This reference value is defined variously, in different studies, as the trend or capacity or potential or natural-rate or market-clearing value of output.

18. See Giorno et al. (1995), Lambelet (1998), and Nilles and Lambelet (1998) for elaboration on this point.

19. "Additional borrowing will not be discouraged by the capital market if lenders know that local governments cannot repudiate their debt and cannot undergo bankruptcy proceedings; the [higher government level] will eventually repay the debt and hence there is no reason either to restrict credit or to apply a risk premium" (Dafflon, 1996, p. 239). In some cases, the bailout takes a particular form: the regional government assumes the debt, but obliges the local government to amalgamate with a neighbouring commune. As a matter of fact, although a local government's bankruptcy is technically possible, it is politically unacceptable and is thus rarely observed in practice (see Spahn, 2000).

20. "Such practices include, for instance: the reclassification of expenditures from current to capital, to escape current budget balance requirements; the creation of entities whose operations – albeit of a governmental nature – are kept off-budget, and whose debts are not counted against the debt ceilings; the use of state or local government-owned enterprises to borrow for purposes that should be funded through the relevant government budget; the use of debt instruments – such as sale and leaseback arrangements or the so-called private revenue bonds in the United States – that are not included in the debt limits; the resort to arrears to suppliers, which are typically difficult to monitor for inclusion in the public debt ceilings" (Ter-Minassian and Craig, 1997, p. 166).

REFERENCES

Alesina, A. and T. Bayoumi (1996), "The costs and benefits of fiscal rules: Evidence from U.S. States", in *National Bureau of Economic Research Working Papers*, 5614.

Alesina, A. and R. Perotti (1995), "The political economy of fiscal deficits", *IMF Staff Papers*, 42, 1–31.

Alesina, A. and R. Perotti (1996), "Fiscal discipline and the budget process", *American Economic Review*, 86, 401–407.

Balassone, F. and D. Franco (1999), "Il federalismo fiscale e il Patto di stabilità", in Banca d'Italia (ed.), *I controlli delle gestioni pubbliche*, Roma: Banca d'Italia, 225–257.

Balassone, F. and D. Franco (2000a), "Assessing fiscal sustainability: a review of methods with a view to EMU", in Banca d'Italia (ed.), *Fiscal Sustainability*, Roma: Banca d'Italia, 21–60.

Balassone, F. and D. Franco (2000b), "Public investment, the Stability Pact and the 'golden rule'", *Fiscal Studies*, 21, 207–229.

Balassone, F. and D. Monacelli (2000), "EMU fiscal rules: Is there a gap?", *Bank of Italy Discussion Paper*, 375.

Bayoumi, T. and B. Eichengreen (1995), "Restraining yourself: The implications of fiscal rules for economic stabilization", *IMF Staff Papers*, 42, 32–47.

Bayoumi, T., M. Goldstein and G. Woglom (1995), "Do credit markets discipline sovereign borrowers? Evidence from U.S. States", *Journal of Money, Credit and Banking*, 27, 1046–1059.

Bennett, R.J. (1990), *Decentralization, Local Governments, and Markets*, Oxford: Clarendon Press.

Blanchard, O.J., J.-C. Chouraqui, R.P. Hagemann and N. Sartor (1990), "The sustainability of fiscal policy: new answers to an old question", *OECD Economic Studies*, 15, 7–36.

Breton, A. (1977), "A theory of local government finance and the debt regulation of local government", *Public Finance*, 32, 16–28.

Buchanan, J.M. (1958), *Public Principles of Public Debt*, Homewood, Illinois; Richard Irwin.

Buchanan, J.M. (1964), "Public debt, cost theory, and the fiscal illusion", in J. Ferguson (ed.), *Public Debt and Future Generations*, Chapel Hill: University of North Carolina Press, 150–163.

Buchanan, J.M., C.K. Rowley and R.D. Tollison (1987), *Deficits: The Political Economy of Budget Deficits*, Oxford and New York: Basil Blackwell.

Buchanan, J.M. and R.E. Wagner (1977), *Democracy in Deficit: The Political Legacy of Lord Keynes*, New York: Academic Press.

Buchanan, J.M. and R.E. Wagner (1978), *Fiscal Responsibility in Constitutional Democracy*, Boston: Kluwer Academic Publishers.

Buchanan, J.M. (1997), "The balanced budget amendment: clarifying the arguments", *Public Choice*, 90, 117–138.

Buiter, W.H., G. Corsetti and N. Roubini (1993), "Excessive deficits: sense and nonsense in the Treaty of Maastricht", *Economic Policy*, 8, 57–100.

Cangiano, M. and E. Mottu (1998), "Will fiscal policy be effective under EMU?", *IMF Working Paper*, 98/176.

Casella, A. (1999), "Tradable deficit permits: Efficient implementation of the Stability Pact in the European Monetary Union", *Economic Policy*, 14, 321–362.

Cavanaugh, F.X. (1996), *The Truth about the National Debt: Five Myths and One Reality*, Boston: Harvard Business School Press.

Cebula, R.J., J. Killingsworth and W.J. Belton (1994), "Federal government budget deficits and the crowding out of private investment in the United States", *Public Finance*, 49, 168–178.

Chalk, N. and R. Hemming (2000), "Assessing fiscal sustainability in theory and practice", in Banca d'Italia (ed.), *Fiscal Sustainability*, Roma: Banca d'Italia, 61–93.

Colm, G. and R.E. Wagner (1963), "Some observations on the budget concept", *Review of Economic Statistics*, 45, 122–126.

Commission of the European Communities (1997), *A Package to Tackle Harmful Tax Competition in the European Union*, Luxembourg: Office for Official Publications of the European Communities, COM(97) 564 final.

Council of Europe (1996), "Local authorities' budgetary deficits and excessive indebtedness", *Local and Regional Authorities in Europe*, 58.

Dafflon, B. (1992), "The assignment of functions to decentralized government: From theory to practice", *Environment and Planning C: Government and Policy*, 10, 283–298.

Dafflon, B. (1996), "The requirement of a balanced local budget: Theory and evidence from the Swiss experience", in G. Pola, G. France and R. Levaggi (eds), *Developments in Local Government Finance: Theory and Policy*, Cheltenham and Brookfield: Edward Elgar, 228–250.

Dafflon, B. (1998), *La gestion des finances publiques locales*, Paris: Economica, second edition.

Dafflon, B. and S. Rossi (1996), "La logique des critères budgétaires du Traité sur l'Union Européenne: Premiers éléments d'analyse critique", University of Fribourg, *Working Papers* (Faculty of Economic and Social Sciences), 272.

Dafflon, B. and S. Rossi (1999), "Public accounting fudges towards EMU: a first empirical survey and some public choice considerations", *Public Choice*, 101, 59–84.

Dalamagas, B. (1995), "Growth, public investment and deficit financing", *Australian Economic Papers*, 65, 244–262.

Deloche, R. (1987), "La querelle de la centralité ou le paradoxe du passager légalement clandestin", in P. Burgat and C. Jeanrenaud (eds), *Services publics locaux: demande, offre et financement*, Paris: Economica, 81–89.

Derycke, P.-H. and G. Gilbert (1988), *Économie publique locale*, Paris: Economica.

Dietsch, M. and O. Garnier (1989), "La contrainte budgétaire intertemporelle des administrations publiques: Conséquences pour l'évaluation des déficits publics", *Économie et prévision*, 90, 69–85.

Eisner, R. (1984), "Which budget deficit? Some issues of measurement and their implications", *American Economic Review*, 74, 138–143.

Eisner, R. (1992), "Deficits: which, how much, and so what?", *American Economic Review*, 82, 295–298.

Elder, H.W. (1992), "Exploring the tax revolt: An analysis of the effects of State tax and expenditure limitations laws", *Public Finance Quarterly*, 20, 47–63.

Eurostat (1996), *European System of Accounts, ESA 1995*, Luxembourg: Office for Official Publications of the European Communities.

Feld, L. (1999), *Steuerwettbewerb und seine Auswirkungen auf Allokation und Distribution: Eine empirische Analyse für die Schweiz*, University of St. Gall, unpublished Ph D dissertation.

Gilbert, G. and A. Guengant (1991), *La fiscalité locale en question*, Paris: Montchrestien.

Giorno, C., P. Richardson, D. Roseveare and P. van den Noord (1995), "Production potentielle, écarts de production et soldes budgétaires structurels", *Revue économique de l'OCDE*, 24, 179–224.

Greffe, X. (1997), *Économie des politiques publiques*, Paris: Dalloz, second edition.

Hertzog, R. (1991), "Dette publique, déficits budgétaires et financement des investissements", in R. Hertzog (ed.), *La dette publique en France*, Paris: Economica, 567–587.

Inman, R.P. (1996), "Do balanced budget rules work? U.S. experience and possible lessons for the EMU", *National Bureau of Economic Research Working Papers*, 5838.

King, D. (1984), *Fiscal Tiers: The Economics of Multi-level Government*, London: Allen & Unwin.

Lachman, D. (1994), "Budget deficits and the public debt in Sweden: The case for fiscal consolidation", *IMF Staff Papers*, 41, 502–516.

Lambelet, J.-C. (1998), "Assainissement des finances publiques suisses: taille et cause du problème, avec discussion de quelques mesures correctives", University of Lausanne, *Cahiers de recherches économiques*, 98–108.

Lane, T.D. (1993), "Market discipline", in *IMF Staff Papers*, 40, 53–88.

Lee, D. (1987), "Deficits, political myopia and the asymmetric dynamics of taxing and spending", in J.M. Buchanan, C.K. Rowley and R.D. Tollison (eds), *op. cit.*, 289–309.

Lerner, A. (1943), "Functional finance and the federal debt", *Social Research*, 10, 38–51.

Levinson, A. and B. Knight (1999), "Rainy day funds and State government savings", *National Tax Journal*, 52, 459–472.

McGranahan, L. (1999), "State budgets and the business cycle: Implications for the federal balanced budget amendment debate", Federal Reserve Bank of Chicago, mimeo.

Milesi-Ferretti, G.M. (1997), "Fiscal rules and the budget process", *Giornale degli economisti e annali di economia*, 56, 5–40.

Moesen, W.A. (1993), "Community public finance in the perspective of the EMU: Assignment rules, the states of the budget constraint and young fiscal federalism in Belgium", in Commission of the European Communities (ed.), *The Economics of Community Public Finance*, (Reports and Studies, 5), Luxembourg: Office for Official Publications of the European Communities, 167–190.

Mottu, E. (1997), "De la (non-)soutenabilité des politiques budgétaires en Suisse", *Revue suisse d'économie politique et de statistique*, 133, 395–420.

Muller, P. and R.W.R. Price (1984), "Déficits budgétaires structurels et orientations de la politique budgétaire", *Organisation for Economic Co-operation and Development Working Paper*, 15.

Musgrave, R.A. (1959), *The Theory of Public Finance*, New York: McGraw-Hill.

Musgrave, R.A. and P.B. Musgrave (1984), *Public Finance in Theory and Practice*, New York: McGraw-Hill, fourth edition.

Nilles, D. and J.-C. Lambelet (1998), "La situation financière du canton de Vaud: Une vue d'ensemble", University of Lausanne, mimeo.

Novaresi, N. (2001), *Discipline budgétaire: Étude de l'influence du référendum financier et des règles d'équilibre budgétaire sur les finances publiques des vingt-six cantons suisses*, University of Fribourg (Department of Political Economy), doctoral dissertation, 2001.

Oates, W.E. (1972), *Fiscal Federalism*, New York: Harcourt Brace Jovanovich.

Olson, M. (1969), "The principle of fiscal equivalence: the division of responsibilities among different levels of government", *American Economic Review*, 59, 479–487.

Organisation for Economic Co-operation and Development (1998), *Harmful Tax Competition: A Worldwide Problem*, Paris: OECD.

Pasinetti, L.L. (1998), "The myth (or folly) of the 3% deficit/GDP Maastricht parameter'", *Cambridge Journal of Economics*, 22, 103–116.

Pauly, M.V. (1973), "Income distribution as a local public good", *Journal of Public Economics*, 2, 35–58.

Pommerehne, W.N., G. Kirchgässner and L. Feld (1996), "Tax harmonization and tax competition at State-local levels: lessons from Switzerland", in G. Pola, G. France and R. Levaggi (eds), *Developments in Local Government Finance: Theory and Policy*, Cheltenham and Brookfield: Edward Elgar, 292–330.

Poterba, J.M. (1994), "State responses to fiscal crises: the effects of budgetary institutions and politics", *Journal of Political Economy*, 102, 799–821.

Pujol, F. (2000), *L'incidence des préférences sur la discipline budgétaire*, University of Geneva, unpublished Ph D dissertation.

Rabushka, A. (1982), "A compelling case for a constitutional amendment to balance the budget and limit taxes", in J.T. Noonan, A. Rabushka, R.D. Tollison and R.E. Wagner (eds), *Balanced Budgets, Fiscal Responsibility, and the Constitution*, Washington, DC: Cato Institute, 57–86.

Rabushka, A. (1983), *The Economic Consequences of Government Deficit*, Boston: Kluwer–Nijhoff Publishing.

Rocaboy, Y. (1995), "Centralisation ou décentralisation des politiques publiques d'assistance: le jeu de la redistribution", *Politiques et management public*, 13, 93–113.

Rose-Ackerman, S. (1983), Beyond Tiebout: Modeling the political economy of local government, in G.R. Zodrow (ed.) *Local Provision of Public Services: The Tiebout Model after Twenty-Five Years*, New York: Academic Press, 55–83.

Rosen, H.S. (1992), *Public Finance*, Boston: Irwin, third edition (first published 1985).

Roubini, N. (1995), "The economics of fiscal bondage: The balanced budget amendment and other binding fiscal rules", New York Stern School of Business, mimeo.

Rubinfeld, D.L. (1987) "The economics of the local public sector", in A.J. Auerbach and M. Feldstein (eds), *Handbook of Public Economics*, Amsterdam: North-Holland, 2, 571–645.

Shadbegian, R.J. (1998), "Do tax and expenditure limitations affect local government budgets? Evidence from panel data", *Public Finance Review*, 26, 118–136.

Smith, S. (1996), "European integration and local government finance", in G. Pola, G. France and R. Levaggi (eds), *Developments in Local Government Finance: Theory and Policy*, Cheltenham and Brookfield: Edward Elgar, 273–291.

Sobel, R.S. and R.G. Holcombe (1996), "The impact of State rainy day funds in easing State fiscal crises during the 1990–1991 recession", *Public Budgeting & Finance*, 16, 28–48.

Spahn, P.B. (2000), "Decentralization, local government capacity, hard budget constraints, and creditworthiness: macroeconomic aspects", World Bank, mimeo.

Tabellini, G. and A. Alesina (1990), "Voting on the budget deficit", *American Economic Review*, 80, 37–49.

Tanzi, V. (1993), "Fiscal deficit measurement: basic issues", in M.I. Blejer and A. Cheasty (eds), *How to Measure the Fiscal Deficit*, Washington, DC: International Monetary Fund, 13–20.

Tanzi, V. (1995), "Fiscal federalism and decentralization: A review of some efficiency and macroeconomic aspects", in M. Bruno and B. Pleskovic (eds), *Annual World Bank Conference on Development Economics*, Washington, DC: World Bank, 295–316.

Tanzi, V. (1996), "Globalization, tax competition and the future of tax systems", *IMF Working Paper*, 96/141.

Tanzi, V. and Zee H.H. (1998), "Consequences of the Economic and Monetary Union for the co-ordination of tax systems in the European Union", *IMF Working Paper*, 98/115.

Ter-Minassian, T. and J. Craig (1997), "Control of subnational government borrowing", in T. Ter-Minassian (ed.), *Fiscal Federalism in Theory and Practice*, Washington, DC: International Monetary Fund, 156–172.

Thalmann, P. (1992), "Des finances saines", in L. Weber (ed.), *Les finances publiques d'un État fédératif: La Suisse*, Paris: Economica, 265–312.

Thurow, L.C. (1971), "The income distribution as a pure public good", *Quarterly Journal of Economics*, 85, 327–336.

Tiebout, C.M. (1956), "A pure theory of local expenditures", *Journal of Political Economy*, 64, 416–424.

Tollison, R.D. and R.E. Wagner (1987), "Balanced budgets and beyond", in J.M. Buchanan, C.K. Rowley and R.D. Tollison (eds), *op. cit.*, 374–390.

Tulkens, H. (1985), "Analyse économique de la concurrence entre deux juridictions fiscalement souveraines", Belgian Institute of Public Finance, mimeo.

Tullock, G. (1969), "Federalism: Problems of scale", *Public Choice*, 6, 19–29.

Vaughn, K.I. and R.E. Wagner (1992), "Public debt controversies: An essay in reconciliation", *Kyklos*, 45, 37–49.

von Hagen, J. (1991), "A note on the empirical effectiveness of formal fiscal restraints", *Journal of Public Economics*, 44, 199–210.

von Hagen, J. and B. Eichengreen (1996), Federalism, fiscal restraints, and European Monetary Union, *American Economic Review*, 86, 134–138.

von Hagen, J., A. Hughes Hallett and R. Strauch (2001), "Budgetary consolidation in EMU", *European Commission Economic Papers*, 148.

Wagner, R.E. (1970), "Optimality in local debt limitation", *National Tax Journal*, 23, 297–305. See also his (1971), "Reply", *National Tax Journal*, 24, 109–111.

Wagner, R.E. (1987), "Liability rules, fiscal institutions and the debt", in J.M. Buchanan, C.K. Rowley and R.D. Tollison (eds), *op. cit.*, 199–217.

Walsh, C. (1993), Fiscal federalism: an overview of issues and a discussion of their relevance to the European Community", in Commission of the European Communities (ed.), *The Economics of Community Public Finance*, (Reports and Studies, 5), Luxembourg: Office for Official Publications of the European Communities, 25–62.

Wildasin, D.E. (eds) (1997), *Fiscal Aspects of Evolving Federations*, Cambridge: Cambridge University Press.

Wilson, J.D. (1999), "Theories of tax competition", *National Tax Journal*, 52, 269–304.

3.   Local budgeting and local borrowing in Austria

Erich Thöni, Stefan Garbislander and Dieter-Jörg Haas

3.1   INTRODUCTION: THE STRUCTURE OF LOCAL GOVERNMENTS

Constitutionally, Austria is a federal country with three levels, the federal level or Bund, nine states or Länder and 2,359 (1999) local governments (communities) or Gemeinden. Austria also has so-called "charter cities"[1] (Statutarstädte), which execute all functions of the local government as well as those of the district (Bezirk). The latter are administrative bodies below the Länder level; they are the first level of federal and state administration.

With the exception of these "charter cities" and Vienna, all local governments are considered equal in carrying out their responsibilities (Einheitsgemeinde)[2], although they vary significantly in their size, type, economic and administrative capacity, level of development, and revenue (see also section 3.4). Vienna (1.6 million inhabitants in 1999) has a special dual constitutional status as one of the nine Länder, and at the same time as one of the 2,359 Gemeinden. Table 3.1 points to the heterogeneous structure of local governments according to inhabitants.

After territorial reforms ("Gemeindezusammenlegung", "Gebietsreform") in some Länder of Austria, which reduced the number of local governments considerably (from over 4,000 right after World War II to 2,300 in 1980), the total number is increasing again, which points to ongoing (local government) "re-engineering", also called "divorcing". Table 3.2 shows the changes in numbers of local governments over time.

Table 3.1   Distribution of local government size (inhabitants) in Austria

Size of local governments in local inhabitants		Number of local governments in 1999
(1.)	< 500	181
(2.)	501–1 500	992
(3.)	1 501–3 000	755
	Subtotal (1.) – (3.)	1 928 = c. 82 %
(4.)	3 001–5 000	232
(5.)	5 001–10 000	130
	Subtotal (1.) – (5.)	2 290 = c. 97 %
	10 001–20 000	45
	20 001–30 000	12
	30 001–100 000	7
	100 001–500 000	4
	>500 000	1
	Total	2 359

Source: Statistisches Jahrbuch der Republik Österreich.

Table 3.2   Local governments in the Länder of Austria

Year	Burgen-land	Carinthia	Lower Austria	Upper Austria	Salzburg	Styria	Tyrol	Vor-arlberg	Total	Total incl. Vienna
1949	317	244	1 584	444	117	977	285	96	4 064	4 065
1955	320	241	1 652	444	119	875	286	96	4 033	4 034
1960	319	229	1 652	445	119	857	287	96	4 004	4 005
1965	319	204	1 650	445	119	808	287	96	3 928	3 929
1970	319	204	1 160	445	120	551	287	96	3 182	3 183
1975	138	121	558	445	119	546	278	96	2 301	2 302
1980	138	121	558	445	119	544	278	96	2 299	2 300
1985	138	121	562	445	119	544	278	96	2 303	2 304
1990	145	121	568	445	119	544	278	96	2 316	2 317
1995	168	131	571	445	119	543	279	96	2 352	2 353
1996	170	131	571	445	119	543	279	96	2 354	2 355
1997	170	132	572	445	119	543	279	96	2 356	2 357
1998	171	132	573	445	119	543	279	96	2 358	2 359
1999	171	132	573	445	119	543	279	96	2 358	2 359

Source: Statistisches Jahrbuch der Republik Österreich; relevant years.

3.2 THE LOCAL FUNCTIONS AND THE AUSTRIAN CONSTITUTION

3.2.1 The Distribution of Competencies and Local Functions

As in other federal countries (USA, Germany, Switzerland), the Constitutional Law (Bundesverfassungsgesetz of 1920 and 1929, B-VG) specifies the "sovereign" federal legislative functions; the Länder are responsible for whatever is not clearly defined there (Residual clause, Art. 15 Par. 1 B-VG)[3] (Pernthaler, 1984, pp. 62–65). Despite the formal dominance of the Bund, one should not underestimate the strength of the Länder, especially on the executive side. Looking at their status more carefully, one recognises that the Austrian Länder exercise considerable discretion in their relations with the Bund and especially with the Gemeinden. Most federal administration is implemented by the state and local governments.

The constitution guarantees self-government at the local level within a specific area of competencies (Art. 115-120 B-VG), and this authority can be defended before the Constitutional Court. These competencies are specified by a general clause ("those matters that belong to the exclusive or predominant interest of the local community and can be performed by it within its own boundaries and within its own administrative capacity" (Art. 118 para. 2 B-VG) and is limited to specific spheres: *local elections and civil service, local police, local traffic and roads, local markets, emergency and general rescue services, fire protection, building regulations, local land use, cemeteries, elementary schools and school building, as well as hospitals* (Art. 118 para. 3 B-VG).

According to Austrian constitutional experts, "self-government" has to be interpreted dynamically and therefore this delimitation can never be a closed one. In practice, the constitutional interpretation and the evolution of responsibilities between the Bund, Länder, and Gemeinden has restricted local responsibilities to the following areas of activities: *local water and (partly) energy supply, local transport, local sewage, local garbage collection and disposal, hospitals, local sports facilities, local housing, basic social welfare, local subsidies.*

48   *Local public finance in Europe*

Local Functions

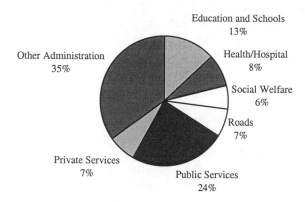

*Figure 3.1   "Functional" share (above 5 per cent of total expenditures –
local level 1998, excl. Vienna)*

This "constitutional invisibility" is further enhanced by the so-called
"Privatwirschaftsverwaltung" (Art. 17 B-VG), according to which Bund,
Länder, and Gemeinden are allowed to intervene into any area of
constitutional competence reserved for the other levels (non-governmental
administration). They do so by means of civil-law arrangements, through
companies and public expenditure, and, especially, through subsidies. Thus it
includes all functions, such as *hospitals, local housing, local roads and
works, local public transport, local water and (partly) energy supply, local
cultural and educational activities, basic social welfare, land zoning, local
subsidies and promotion.*

As already mentioned, local governments also fulfil administrative
functions mandated or delegated by the federal or the state level. In executing
such functions, they are supervised by the districts as the first level of state
administration (see below). These activities must be financed on the local
level but with little or no local discretion (cost-shifting to the local level).
Therefore, the significant autonomy in expenditure decisions in the above-
mentioned range is overshadowed by the functions delegated by Bund and
Länder. As a result, the expenditure levels of each government unit and
government level do not necessarily reflect a real measure of fiscal autonomy
(see below, and see Figure 3.1 and Table 3.2).

Table 3.3   Local responsibilities: constitutional and in practice

Area of local self-government guaranteed by the constitution (formal constitution)	Local governmental responsibilities in practice (real constitution)	Local non-governmental administration (Privatwirtschaftsverwaltung)
• local elections and civil service	• local water and (partly) energy supply	• local water and (partly) energy supply
• local police	• local transport	• local transport
• local traffic and roads	• local sewage	• local roads and works
• local markets	• local garbage collection and disposal	• local housing
• emergency and general rescue services	• local sports facilities	• local cultural and educational activities
• fire protection	• local housing	• basic social welfare
• building regulations	• basic social welfare	• land zoning
• local land use	• local subsidies	• local subsidies and promotion
• cemeteries	• hospitals	• hospitals
• elementary schools and school building		
• hospitals		

With regard to Art 120 B-VG, which permits inter–local co-ordination and co-operation, effective local and state bodies have been formed for carrying out particular service functions. Some Gemeinden have founded "administrative unions" (Verwaltungsgemeinschaften) which act as agents in carrying out delegated functions such tax collection, fire protection, water and electricity supply, but the overall legal and political control still rests with the original local government. "Communal associations" (Gemeinde-verbände) are unions without explicit control functions of the participating Gemeinden. They have been established for *basic social welfare (e.g. care for the disabled), hospital administration, schools, public transport, sewage, promotion of tourism, water and energy supply*. These associations are usually run by the above-mentioned "non-governmental companies" (Privatwirtschaftsverwaltung) (Bennet, 1985, p. 15).

3.2.2 Local Government and Local Supervision

Local resolutions and plans are passed, implemented and controlled by the elected local parliament (based on proportional representation and presided over by a mayor). In contrast to the federal and state level (the "legislative levels"), local parliaments are "quasi-administrative bodies" with "quasi-legislative competencies". Local parliaments have the right to enact decrees (Verordnungen) based on federal and state laws. Besides, in, for example,

Carinthia, the Tyrol, the Burgenland, and Upper Austria, – but not in all states – the mayors are elected directly by the people.

Local government supervision is carried out by the federal and state level. The assignment of supervision competencies to Bund and Länder depends on the local functions concerned. The objective of local government supervision includes:

- *supervision of legitimacy* to ensure the legitimacy of local political behaviour;
- *supervision of efficiency* to ensure the economy, efficiency and effectiveness of the allocation of local financial ressources (which also includes implicitly intergenerational distribution of the debt and tax burden).

Measures of local government supervision are vetoes on local administrative decisions, obtaining information about local activities, dissolving the local parliament, and an authorisation requirement for some special local measures (e.g. local borrowing). According to Art. 127a B-VG, budgets of local communities with a population of more than 20,000 are additionally controlled by the Austrian National Audit Office (Österreichischer Rechnungshof). Considering these activities, supervision by higher tiers of government means a significant weakening of local autonomy in Austria.

3.3   LOCAL FISCAL STRUCTURE AND LOCAL BUDGETING

3.3.1 The Austrian Fiscal Constitution

Austria is a special case in that constitutional financial provisions are not laid down in the constitution. Rather this is done in a separate "Financial Constitutional Law" ("Finanzverfassungsgesetz" (F-VG), first 1922, now 1948). This Financial Constitutional Law assigns taxes to the respective level only within an abstract framework of nine types of joint (shared) or exclusive (separate, own) tax types.

These abstract types are implemented through so-called "Financial Settlement Laws" ("Finanzausgleichsgesetze" – (FAGs)), formally legislated by the Bund. Decisions regarding the FAGs are an example of the Austrian Social Partnership and cooperation and the result of a complex bargaining process between the three levels (Bund, Länder, Gemeinden). These negotiations result in a compromise agreement on joint tax sharing, its ratios and criteria for division, and some vertical grants to and from a level, which brings about important horizontal balancing effects. These agreements used to be valid for six years (up to 1985), but are now valid for three to four years (currently for the period between 2000 and 2004).

As all these financial laws are formally federal laws, the ultimate competence remains with the Bund, and therefore decisions are heavily influenced by its interests, coalitions and logrolling. The consequence is an asymmetrical constitutional structure. Statements like the "Law of Popitz", planning possibilities, the need for federal interventions on reasons of economic stabilisation and redistribution, regional and sectoral federal policies, as well as the above-mentioned historical legacy have all supported this development. Taxing in Austria is a complex mixture of exclusive (separate, "own") and joint (shared) sources.

3.3.2 Local Revenues and Local Budgeting

Under consideration of the F-VG and the present FAG, the local finance system includes mainly three types of revenues:

- local shares of the joint taxation system;
- exclusive taxation of local governments;
- intergovernmental grants or transfers.

Table 3.4   Structure of ordinary local revenues 1998, excl. Vienna

Local revenue	in Million ATS	%
Exclusive local taxes	31 862	30.17
Shared/joint taxes	46 477	44.02
Intergovernmental grants	9 867	9.35
Other revenues	17 385	16.46
Total (ordinary) local revenue	105 591	100.00

Source: Gebarungsübersichten 1998; own calculations.

As Table 3.4 indicates, the main part of local revenues is generated within the joint taxation system. Tax sharing is carried out in a complicated manner. In a first step (Oberverteilung), the total revenue of a single tax is divided among the federal, state and local levels according to the ratios negotiated for the different taxes. In a second step (Unterverteilung), the total state and local community shares are divided among the nine Länder, and the total share of local communities per state is then divided among its communities according

to a weighted population index. Before resources are actually distributed to
the Gemeinden, different types of levies (Umlagen) are withheld by the state
(Thöni, 1996, p. 40).[4]

To finally match the fiscal needs and fiscal capacities – both specifically
defined – of the different tiers as well as the governments of the respective
tiers, a wide range of intergovernmental grants – general, specific and
matched in their form – are used. For many local communities, grants from
the Länder (e.g. education grants, social welfare grants, hospital grants, water
and sewage grants, special needs grants) are more important than grants from
the Bund. However, they are one of the most difficult areas of Austrian
finance and defy generalisation, since each Land has different legislation and
has adopted different political priorities in the allocation of funds. The
principles of cost sharing, cost shifting and grey areas of financial settlement
are the general background from which the grants derive, but in detail, there
is considerable variability in allocation criteria (Bennet, 1985, p. 61).

Unlike the situation of the Länder (exclusive state taxes account for only
roughly 0.6 per cent of the total tax revenue), the tax yield from exclusively
local taxes still forms an important part of the communities' fiscal revenues,
although the share decreased until 1994, increased between 1995 and 1999,
and is at present (2000) again sharply decreasing. Therefore, the figures of
1998 (see Table 3.5) have to be taken carefully. First estimates for 2000 point
to a "new" share of less than 30 per cent.

Table 3.5   Exclusive local taxes 1998, excl. Vienna

Tax	in Million ATS	%
Community tax	15 963	50.10
Real estate tax	4 896	15.37
Excise on drinks and ice-cream	4 618	14.50
Other local taxes and charges	6 383	20.03
Total excl. local revenue	31 860	100.00

Source: Gebarungsübersichten 1998; own calculations.

Today the most important taxes are the community tax
(Kommunalsteuer),[5] the real estate tax (Grundsteuer), and until 1999 the
excise taxes on drinks and ice-cream (Getränke und Eissteuer). The excise
taxes on drinks and ice-cream were levied until spring 2000, when after a
European Court decision[6] the excise tax on drinks was replaced by higher
value added tax rates on food, drinks and ice-cream and with it an up-
levelling of the local share of this joint tax. Concurrently, for reasons of a
strict budget consolidation policy[7] the federal level instructed the local

governments to accept a reduced "new", lower revenue than the former, which they finally agreed to.[8]

Generally speaking, local tax determination is formally reduced to the fixing of tax rates (Hebesatzrecht) and to the decision whether or not to introduce a certain tax already determined and delegated to the Gemeinde (Beschlußrecht) (Thöni, 1996, p. 39).

3.3.3 The Structure of Local Budgeting

In contrast to the Austrian federal budget, whose structure is determined by the so-called "ministry principle", local and state budgets are based on fiscal criteria and therefore divided into ordinary and extraordinary budgets.

Following the VRV (Voranschlags- und Rechnungsabschluß-verordnung) and the budgetary principles, ordinary and extraordinary local budgets have to be classified functionally, and extraordinary expenditures have to be unusual in nature and size. Ordinary expenditures cannot be financed with loans. Therefore, the sustainability of the local financial situation depends on financing public investments with ordinary revenues.

In comparison, the "standard approach" to loan decisions in public finance is to distinguish the current budget (public consumption) from the capital budget (public investment), with the rule that ordinary expenditures cannot be financed by loans. It follows, therefore, that the more public investments can be "self-financed", the better. This approach therefore indicates the local self-financing ability, but in addition allows more guidance of economic policies at the local level.

To overcome the disadvantages of ordinary and extraordinary budgeting, Austria introduced a "half-way" through position. (Only) local communities with more than 10,000 inhabitants have to implement a so-called "budget cross-section" (Voranschlags-querschnitt). The budget cross-section, which is structured according to cost categories, must make an explicit distinction between current and capital budget in order to distinguish between public consumption and public investment expenditures. The distinction makes it possible to indicate the ability of local self-financing, but there is no unified account of public investment activities. Corresponding to the type of financing (self-financing or borrowing), public investments are assigned to the ordinary or extraordinary budget.

3.4   LOCAL FISCAL STRUCTURE AND INSTRUMENTS OF LOCAL BORROWING

An "optimal local finance structure" which means an efficient distribution of the total local revenues on taxes, transfers and borrowing is dependent on (Zeitel, 1970, pp. 1–20):

- the size and structure (e.g. tourist or mountain local community) of local governments;
- the relationship between obligatory and non-obligatory local tasks;
- and the "degree of local centralisation" (Grad der Zentralörtlichkeit).

The differences in size (see Table 3.1), the structural heterogeneity of local governments and therefore the need for different finance structures is politically not really anticipated by the federal level in Austria. The main reason for this is the juridical and normative principle of "Einheitsgemeinde" (uniformity of local governments) which influences the local task fulfilment (and therefore the local finance structure) (Thöni, 1983, pp. 435–437). This principle assumes that all local governments are equal in their function, organisation and structure. The cause for this simplistic and undifferentiated view is the constitutional interpretation of equal local governments (see also section 3.1). But without the anticipation of the economic and social heterogeneity of local communities by the higher government tiers and the Austrian politics in general, it is not possible to adapt their finance and borrowing structure efficiently.

3.4.1 Concepts of Borrowing and the Development of Local Community Debt

In Austria, there are four distinct types of public debt:

- *administrative debts* are financial commitments closely connected with the execution of the local budget concerned (e.g. commitments resulting from local payment extensions);
- *short-term lending* implies temporary injections of new liquidity without real effects on the local budget;
- *contingent liabilities* result from assuming local liabilities and warranties (e.g. in the context of assistance provided for local investment);
- *financial debts* are mostly medium- and long-term loans and bonds to finance public investments.

In this chapter, the authors will concentrate on analysing the fiscal and economic causes and effects of local financial debts.

Table 3.6 compares the local financial debts of 1985 and 1995 according to the size of the local communities. It is obvious that the debts of smaller local communities (especially local communities with fewer than 1,000 inhabitants) have increased at an above-average rate. Reasons for this might be large-scale investments to improve the local infrastructure (water and energy supply, sewage disposal, local transport) interrelated with an inflexible pattern of local revenues (see also section 3.5).

Table 3.6   Local financial debt and local debt service (in million ATS), excl. Vienna

Size of local community	1985 Local financial debt	1995 Local financial debt	Percentage change
0 – 500	208 314	829 180	298.04
501 – 1 000	1 862 858	4 606 771	147.30
1 001 – 2 500	14 824 354	27 886 316	88.11
2 501 – 5 000	10 838 656	20 641 767	90.45
5 001 – 10 000	9 218 660	15 489 804	68.03
10 001 – 20 000	7 475 273	10 524 066	40.79
20 001 – 50 000	5 962 950	8 302 372	39.23
50 001 – 500 000	12 327 470	17 845 876	44.77
Total local debt	62 718 535	106 126 152	69.21

	1985	1995	Percentage change
Total local debt service *	7 431 200	11 085 599	49.18

Note: * Debt service includes interest payments and amortisation payments.

Sources: *Gebarungsübersichten 1985, 1995.*

Table 3.7 indicates a decisive aspect in the development of local borrowing over the past two decades: local debts financed mainly by "general budget funds" (general revenues of the ordinary budget) decreased between 1979 and 1998 and showed below-average increases after 1985. On the other hand, local debts covered by user charges and "specific payments" (revenues linked to the capital good concerned) increased substantially from 31.3 per cent of local debts in 1979 to 64.4 per cent in 1998. This means that there has been a fundamental change in the structure of local debts and its fiscal effects (especially the incidence of the debt burden). The reason for this is that debts financed by user charges and "specific payments" are usually shifted directly to people inside and outside the community.

*Table 3.7   Development of financial local debt under consideration of the
debt structure, excl. Vienna*

		1979	1983	1985	1990	1995	1998	% change 1979–1998
Type 1 of local debt*	in Million ATS	25 504	25 589	24 441	24 240	34 691	35 512	
	in % of the local debt	51.60	42.90	38.97	33.72	32.69	29.33	39.24
Type 2 of local debt**	in Million ATS	15 466	24 143	30 088	40 432	63 081	77 942	
	in % of the local debt	31.30	40.40	49.25	56.25	59.45	64.37	503.95

Notes:
* Type 1 of local debt: debt mainly financed by covering funds (more than 50 per cent).
** Type 2 of local debt: debt mainly financed by user charges and "specific payments" (more than 50 per cent).

Sources: Bauer and Sainde, 1988, p. 21; *Gebarungsübersichten* relevant years; own calculations.

A number of different fiscal instruments to finance public investments by extraordinary budgeting are available to Austrian local governments, but most of the local borrowing in Austria is institutional; that is, local bonds and loans are usually designed to be granted by domestic banks and insurance companies (Smekal, 1987, pp.71–147). As Table 3.8 points out, the foreign debts of local communities are of only minor importance. Local bonds in the form of real marketable issues which are available to all buyers have lost their importance mainly as a result of two economic factors: first, the dominance of the domestic credit market over the capital market and, second, the lower financial requirements of the different local governments compared with the federal level.

Table 3.8   Schedule of local governments' creditors, excl. Vienna

Financial Local Debt	1998	
	in Million ATS	% of total
Financial debt held by domestic banks and insurance companies	84 414	69.71
Financial debt held by other government tiers or funds	33 316	27.51
Financial debt held by foreign banks and insurance companies	3 281	2.72
Stat. Diff.	77	0.06
Total local financial debt	121 089	100

Source: Gebarungsübersichten 1998; own calculations.

3.4.2 The Local Maastricht Deficit

In the course of the financial settlement negotiations of 1996, it was agreed that in 1997 the federal level could use 90 per cent of the public Maastricht deficit (2.7 per cent of GDP), while the Länder and Gemeinden together could use 10 per cent (or 0.3 per cent of GDP). The dominance of the federal level regarding the deficit criterion once again shows the high degree of fiscal and political centralisation. To reach this criterion, the federal level had to reduce its deficit by roughly ATS 50 billion in two years.[9] With respect to the "permissible" Maastricht deficit, the Länder and Gemeinden together had a deficit scope of ATS 7.5 billion in 1997, but there was neither a fixed rule and a political consensus regarding the division of the 0.3 per cent criterion between the Länder and Gemeinden, nor an agreement within the levels about effective deficit distribution.

As indicated in Table 3.9, all government levels had complied with their fiscal restrictions in 1997. In the following year, the overall deficit rose slightly, with the federal level exceeding the agreed deficit and the Länder having a budgetary surplus. In the years to follow, the Austrian Maastricht deficit continuously diminished, which can be accounted for by reduced deficits at the federal level and constant surpluses in the lower government tiers.

Table 3.9   The "Maastricht-deficit" and its division between government levels (as percentage of GDP)

	1997	1998	1999	2000	2001	2002	2003	2004
General government financial balance of which:	-1.7	-2.3	-2.1	-1.4	-0.75	0.0	0.0	0.0
Federal government sector	-2.7	-2.9	-2.4	-1.8	-1.5	-0.75	-0.75	-0.75
Länder and local authorities	0.8	0.5	0.4	0.5	0.75	0.75	0.75	0.75
Social insurance institutions	0.2	0.1	-0.1	-0.1	0.0	0.0	0.0	0.0

Note: The years 2001-2004 are based on estimates and the financial settlement agreement signed on 16 October 2000.

Source: *Statistik Austria*, Federal Ministry of Finance.

On 16 October 2000 the Federal government, the provinces and the local authorities agreed a new financial settlement up to 2004 and a pact on the joint achievement of a "zero-deficit" in 2002. The provisions following directly concern the general government deficit.

One the one hand the Länder undertake, starting in 2001 (this obligation shall apply to the whole settlement period), to contribute an average budget surplus of not less than 0.75% of GDP and at any rate of ATS 23 billion to the general government consolidation path. Temporary shortfalls of –0.15% of GDP are allowed, if over the whole settlement period the average value of 0.75% of GDP is attained. On the other hand the local governments are obliged, during the same period of time, to contribute an average budget surplus of 0% of GDP to the general government consolidation path. Temporary shortfalls of –0.10% of GDP are allowed, if over the whole settlement period an average value of 0% of GDP can be attained.[10]

A financial analysis of the Maastricht deficit development of the government tiers – shown in Table 3.10 – indicates a very heterogeneous fiscal development over the years.

Table 3.10 The Maastricht deficit of state, local governments and social insurance institutions (in billion ATS)

Level	1994	1995	1996	1997
Federal government	–109.7	–111.8	–101.4	–67.0
Länder and local authorities	–3.1	–5.0	7.7	13.6
Social insurance institutions	1.3	–0.9	2.3	3.7

Sources: ÖSTAT relevant years, Federal Ministry of Finance.

In connection with Tables 3.9 and 3.10, it is important to add that the budgetary surplus of the Länder (especially in 1997) arises from the definitions used. In contrast to the usual budgetary surplus/deficit, the Maastricht deficit does not include financial transactions (e.g. loans, repayments, buying and selling of shares), which have a great influence on the state level (especially loans for housing).

The derivation of the "local Maastricht deficit" (see Table 3.11) requires a material and temporal adjustment of the VRV data. The material adjustment concerns the deduction of the following financial transactions: transfer to and liquidation from reserves, buying and selling of securities and stakes, and costs and revenues in connection with loans and bonds. With regard to the temporary adjustment, revenues and expenditures from prior years and the current fiscal year earnings and disposals are deducted.

However, the fiscal success of the local and state level in 1997 was also due to budgetary spin-offs, an increase in federal transfer payments, and cyclical recovery. Therefore, many of these fiscal effects and measures were non-recurring.

The consolidation of all public budgets was reached without needing far-reaching reform of Austrian fiscal federalism. Nevertheless, the political experiences of those years demonstrated the necessity of an institutional framework to co-ordinate fiscal budget policy between all levels. The Austrian answer was the so-called "Consultation mechanism" and the

"Stability pact" (see below and for a detailed analysis, Thöni and Garbislander, 1999, pp. 442–448).

Table 3.11 The derivation of the local "Maastricht revenues and expenditures" (minus sign indicates a Maastricht deficit; plus indicates a Maastricht surplus)

Local revenues	Local expenditures
1 Ordinary revenues	11 Ordinary expenditures
2 + Extraordinary revenues	12 + Extraordinary expenditures
3 – Targeted debit of the current fiscal year	13 – Targeted surplus of the current fiscal year
4 – Payments regarding prior fiscal year earnings	14 – Payments regarding prior fiscal year deficits
5 – New financial deficit	15 – Current fiscal deficit repayments
6 – Liquidation of revenues	16 – Granted loans
7 – Revenues from loan repayments	17 – Transfers to reserves
8 – Sale of securities	18 – Acquisition of securities
9 – Sale of participations	19 – Acquisition of participations
10 Maastricht revenues	20 Maastricht expenditures

Source: Hüttner, 1996, p.13.

3.5 BUDGET DISCIPLINE AND BUDGET RESPONSIBILITY OF AUSTRIAN LOCAL GOVERNMENTS

In fiscal theory, there are two different approaches to analysing the advantages and disadvantages of local debts. The first, the "budget discipline approach", is based on a policy of interventionism and dominates the Austrian discussion of local debt limits via the local supervisory authority. The second approach, "budget responsibility", is based on an economic cost/benefit analysis and is very useful for explaining the economic causes of local debts in Austria. But, as will be argued in the next section, concrete limits of local debts can hardly be deduced from this approach.

3.5.1 Budget Discipline: Limitation of Local Debts Through Federal and State Regulations

Legal and administrative debt limitations are mainly the result of financial covering clauses based on the above-mentioned "treasury orientation" of local budgets. The most important of these financial clauses states that ordinary expenditures have to be covered by ordinary revenues (exclusive of local taxes, shared taxes and intergovernmental grants).

Most local bylaws include the following five conditions of deficit financing: local borrowing is permitted if:

1. revenues from local borrowing are used only for financing extraordinary and absolutely necessary expenditures;
2. no other type of financing is available;
3. the repayment of loans and bonds does not endanger the fiscal sustainability of the local community;
4. other legal local functions and commitments are not affected;
5. the financial transactions are budgeted as extraordinary ones (extraordinary local budget) (Bauer, 1980, p. 43).

It is obvious that condition 5, which is a tautology, will not limit local borrowing: extraordinary expenditures have to be listed in extraordinary budgets because they will be financed by extraordinary revenues. Condition 1 includes a restriction: "to finance extraordinary and absolutely necessary expenditures". Extraordinary expenditures are "unusual in nature and size" - but a clear, respectively precise, financial definition is missing. There is still a wide range of interpretation of what "unusual" actually means. Therefore, every local government decides more or less independently whether expenditures are ordinary or extraordinary. The same argument applies to condition 2. Conditions 3 and 4 imply that debt service payments should not dominate ordinary expenditures. The sustainability of the local budget should be preserved. But the term "fiscal sustainability" is more or less unspecified and implies the political postulates "covering public investments as far as possible with ordinary revenues" and "preserving budgetary flexibility". A special uniform definition of those postulates does not exist and therefore they are, once again, free for interpretation by both local governments and supervisory authorities.

According to Paragraph 14 of the financial constitution (F-VG), the state law has to regulate all types and procedures of local borrowing in Austria.[11] While local statutes include a relatively wide scope for deficit financing, the authorisation procedure for local borrowing carried out by the supervisory institution implies indirect administrative restrictions. This authorisation process can be divided into two procedures: obtaining authorisation for borrowing and permission for or rejection of local borrowing itself.

The conditions under which local governments have to obtain the authorisation for borrowing vary among the different Länder. Differences in the interpretation of Art. 119a B-VG are a main reason for this. Art. 119a B-VG states that only local (fiscal or political) measures with *serious supralocal effects* have to be controlled by the supervisory authority. The divergent interpretations derive from the term "supralocal effects". A legal definition of supralocal effects and an explicit description of externalities to financial measures are not available.

The differences between the local statutes of the Tyrol, Upper Austria, Salzburg, and the Burgenland are exemplary of this problem:[12]

- The Tyrolean local statute, for instance, states *that each loan application with an amount above 10 percent of the ordinary expenditures of the prior fiscal year* has to be approved by the district authority[13] (see paragraph 115 sec. 1 Tiroler Gemeindeordnung, 1993);
- In Upper Austria, local borrowing depends on the approval of the supervisory institution, if *the level of local indebtedness exceeds (or will exceed as a result of the loan application in question) one third of the ordinary revenues of the current fiscal year* (see paragraph 84 sec. 3 Obcrösterreichische Gemeindeordnung, 1990);
- In Salzburg, local borrowing requires official approval by the state government, *if local indebtedness exceeds (or will exceed as a result of the loan application in question) the ordinary revenues of the previous fiscal year*[14] (see paragraph 85 sec. 1 Salzburger Gemeindeordnung, 1994);
- According to the local statute of the Burgenland, *all local borrowing depends on state government approval*. Exceptions to this regulations are short-term lending and special loans granted by the state or federal government (see par. 80 section 2 Burgenländische Gemeindeordnung, 1965).

These procedures and the criteria are quite unusual in the international discussion concerning local deficits, because there is no comparison between debt service payments and current revenues and/or expenditures. In this discussion it is a comparison between stock criteria (the single loan amount in the case of the Tyrol and the total local debt in the case of Upper Austria and Salzburg) and flow criteria (ordinary expenditures of the prior fiscal year in the case of the Tyrol and ordinary revenues of the current fiscal year in the case of Upper Austria and Salzburg). But the aim of these procedures is not to discuss the sustainability of local budgetary decisions, the criteria determine only under which conditions local governments have to obtain authorisation for borrowing. In this context it seems also obvious that the "European discussion" of local borrowing will force some changes of "the Austrian way" in the near future.

The problem of unclear and inconsistent legal definitions also applies to the regulations governing approval and refusal of local borrowing. Most local statutes comprise the following reasons for refusing deficit financing:

- a disproportionately high fiscal burden or fiscal risk for the local community;

- a serious risk for local liquidity (this is the case if debt service and absolute local obligations are not covered by ordinary revenues);
- a serious risk for other regular local functions.

It is obvious that the terms "disproportionately high" and "serious risk" give the supervisory authority wide scope for interpretation.

As an example of one possible interpretation, the Tyrolean screening process for local finance (in comparison with other Austrian Länder, designated as "progressive and strict") will be described. As discussed before, this procedure will only be implemented if the local community has to obtain authorisation for borrowing, which means that the loan amount in question exceeds 10 per cent of the ordinary expenditures of the prior fiscal year.

Local governments in the Tyrol are required to divide ordinary budget into recurring (periodic) and non-recurring revenues and expenditures. If annual debt payments exceed 80 per cent of the continuing (periodic) budget surplus, the supervisory authority recognises local over-indebtedness. Authorisation is in principle refused. If debt service payments are between 51 and 80 per cent, a high local debt ratio is indicated. Authorisation will be restricted. The reason for this is that the continuing surplus has to finance not only debt payments, but also (at least partly) some non-recurring expenditures. If the annual repayments exceed 80 per cent of the continuing surplus, the fiscal scope for the local community will be too narrow. This is illustrated in Table 3.12.

Table 3.12   The Tyrolean scheme of local debt appraisal

Ratio: debt service payments/current budgetary surplus	Fiscal appraisal
> 80%	local overindebtedness
51% – 80%	high local debt ratio
< 51%	fiscal stability

Considering the "local self-government postulate" and the economic conditions of effective fiscal federalism, the authorisation process described is not really an efficient instrument for limiting local debts. As mentioned above, the various legal regulations give the supervisory authority excessive scope for interpretation. In principle, local self-government and restrictive local supervision by higher government tiers seems incompatible (Bauer, 1980, p. 50).

3.5.2 The New Consultation Mechanism and the Stability Pact between Federal, State and Local Governments

Paragraph 2 of the F-VG 1948 comprises the so-called "cost-bearing rule" (Konnexitätsgrundsatz), which states that each level of government has to finance its own political functions. In political practice, the "cost-sharing principle" and the "ultimate competence" (Kompetenz-Kompetenz) of the Bund made it possible for the central (but also for the states) level to shift costs and tasks to the lower tiers of government without adjusting financial structures.

Therefore, the two levels of government, Länder and especially Gemeinden, have long requested that the Bund contacts the partners concerned before amending tax laws and/or expenditure competencies. The Bund itself felt that for reasons of distribution and stabilisation policy, the co-operation of the other levels would be important.

As mentioned above, a further problem was the intra-level division of the allowed Maastricht-deficit volume. The deficit criterion has the quality of being a "national public good": compliance with the criterion is a requirement of fiscal sustainability and participation in the EMU. The absence of fixed multi- and intra-level budget rules and the possibility of effective political and/or financial sanctioning would encourage free-ride behaviour by the different tiers of government. If only one government unit (one local or even one state government) extends its deficit financing, it will benefit from both the positive effects of the national fiscal stability and its own expanded financial scope. It is obvious that in this case, individual economic and rational behaviour leads to collective irrationality ("prisoner's dilemma"), and therefore an "Austrian stability pact" with concrete conditions of deficit financing followed (see Table 3.13).

Table 3.13 The instability of an Austrian stability pact without (political) effective sanctioning measures

		One government unit:	
		obeys the fiscal rules of the stability pact	does not obey the fiscal rules of the stability pact
All other government units:	obey the fiscal rules of the stability pact	*Maastricht criterion fulfilled; fiscal stability of all government tiers*	*Maastricht criterion fulfilled; extended fiscal scope of the specific government unit*
	do not obey the fiscal rules of the stability pact	*Maastricht criterion not fulfilled; national fiscal instability*	*Maastricht criterion not fulfilled; fiscal instability of all government units*

The "Consultation mechanism" and the "Stability pact" were implemented on 1 January, 1999 after difficult negotiations. Superficially analysed, all levels "gained" from this.

States and especially local governments are now equipped with the constitutional possibility of confronting a one-sided amendment of tasks and their financing by the federal level (for local governments also by the states level), the Bund succeeded in co-ordinating the budget policies of the states and the local governments through the explicit fixing of deficit quotas. The consultation mechanism was therefore invented to settle disputes on cost-bearing and/or cost-shifting with the enactment of new laws and decrees. The final aim was and still is to intensify cost-consciousness on all levels.

According to the consultation mechanism, Länder and local governments vis-à-vis the federal level and the federal level and the local level vis-à-vis the Länder have a veto "on laws which cause costs" on the respective levels. Negotiations in a well-defined governmental, but not parliamentarian, committee would follow. Should there be no settlement, the level which passed or enacted the law or decree will automatically be responsible for financing it.

One subject for negotiation pertains to additional necessary expenditures due to a law or decree above a certain insignificant amount (Bund ATS 15 million per law and not more than ATS 105 million per year; Länder ATS 1–3 million according to Länder size). Legal transfer payments are excluded according to EU regulations (Thöni, 1997, p. 14).

The essential point of the stability pact is the division of deficit quotas in the public sector. The central division remained the above mentioned sharing in the ratio of 90:10 per cent between the federal and the joint treated states and local level. But if the Maastricht 3 per cent level was to change and, for example, be reduced, the quote for the states and local levels would in principle remain 0.3 per cent.

Of this 0.3 per cent of GDP the Länder (excluding Vienna) hold 0.11 per cent, Vienna holds 0.09 per cent and 0.1 per cent are for the 2,358 local governments. Tables 3.14 and 3.15 show in detail what was agreed (leaving out Vienna).

The fixing of the states' shares and the local governments' shares was based on the one hand on the corresponding population and on the other, on "at present special [fiscal] necessities". There was no fixing of detailed shares for each local government. It was believed that this would lead to more and more inflexibility of local budgets, blocking the important local investments.[15] But, should local governments of one state exceed the respective quota, all local communities together would share the responsibility. Also, all states and local governments are allowed to hand quotas over to other states and local governments at the respective level.

Table 3.14 The division of the 0.11 per cent deficit quota between the Länder (excl. Vienna)

Länder	Share (%)
Burgenland	8.361486
Kärnten	10.507517
Niederösterreich	24.457642
Oberösterreich	17.067903
Salzburg	6.174039
Steiermark	21.106987
Tirol	8.081744
Vorarlberg	4.242682

Sources: Hüttner, 1999; BGBL. I Nr 35/1999.

Table 3.15 The division of the 0.10 per cent deficit quota of the local governments by Länder

Länder	Share (%)
Burgenland	4.055238
Kärnten	9.044265
Niederösterreich	22.887226
Oberösterreich	21.525546
Salzburg	7.963123
Steiermark	19.078515
Tirol	10.080573
Vorarlberg	5.365514

Sources: Hüttner, 1999; BGBL. I Nr 35/1999.

3.5.3 Budget Responsibility: Economic and Theoretical Arguments for Local Borrowing

As Musgrave states, borrowing at the local and the state level differs from borrowing at federal level (where stabilisation and distribution policies are central) for two main reasons. First, the reason for borrowing occurs at the lower tiers of government, primarily when substantial public investments with intergeneration effects are to be financed. This concerns the demand side of the finance problem. On the supply side, local and state governments have no or at most a very limited influence on the market conditions under which they have to borrow (Musgrave and Musgrave, 1989, p. 561).

Concerning the Austrian situation, one can state three reasons for the propensity to incur local debts:

- the inflexibility of the local system of revenues;
- the (political) aim of the intergeneration distribution of the tax and debt burden;
- the fluctuating capital investment needs of the local level.

The inflexibility and "resource squeezing" of the Austrian local budgets (only about 14 per cent are manoeuvrable) are caused by the high degree of rigidity of current expenditures (e.g. personnel costs, pension fund costs, debt servicing, charges to other government tiers) and changing local functions (e.g. health care functions) with only a partly corresponding reform of the financial structure in 1997.

Table 3.16 indicates the relation between the fiscal development of some rigid expenditure areas and local (exclusive and shared) tax yields. It is obvious from this that the relative increase in inflexible expenditure accounts is not the only reason for unstable local budgets. Cyclical and structural revenue shortfalls have restricted the local fiscal scope over time. It is expected that especially the amendment of the excise taxes on drinks and ice-cream will reduce this further.

Table 3.16 The increasing rigidity of local budgets (expenditures in million ATS), excl. Vienna

	1991	1993	1995	1997
(1.) Personnel administration	24 150	26 859	30 612	30 852
(2.) Pension expenditures	4 077	4 673	5 106	5 143
(3.) Transfer payments to other government tiers	12 087	15 039	17 985	18 536
(4.) Debt servicing	8 409	9 843	11 085	13 423
(5.) Total (1.)–(4.)	48 723	56 414	64 788	67 954
(6.) Exclusive and shared local taxes (without fees)	58 784	67 045	68 668	78 339
(7.) Share (5.) in % of (6.)	82.88	84.14	94.35	86.74

Source: *Gebarungsübersichten,* relevant years; own calculations.

The so-called surplus of the current budget (see Table 3.17) is another measurement of local budgetary flexibility. The current budget involves all transactions which do not directly affect the capital budget of the local community.[16] This indicator determines how much of the current financial means can be used to cover non-recurring and extraordinary payments. Table

3.17 also indicates the inflexibility of the financial manoeuvrability of local governments during the past years, which confirms the figures of Table 3.16.

Table 3.17   The surplus of the "current budget" as an indicator for local budgetary flexibility (inmillion ATS), excl. Vienna

	1993	1995	1997
(1.) Current revenues	108 001	117 455	127 249
(2.) Current expenditures	92 561	103 808	110 238
(3.) Surplus of the "current budget"*	15 440	13 647	17 011
(4.) Share (3.) in % of (1.)	14.30	11.62	13.37

Notes: * Incl. debt service payments.

Source: *Gebarungsübersichten*, relevant years; own calculations.

As a consequence of the increasing restriction of local fiscal scope on the one hand and the prevailing financial requirements (especially for local investments) on the other, local governments had and still have to reconsider their financial and organisational structures. New instruments of local financing and local task fulfilment, such as leasing transactions and the so-called "private operator model" (privatwirtschaftliches Betreibermodell), are increasingly used by local governments. The private operator model, for instance, means that local functions (e.g. sewage disposal) are executed by private enterprises but continue to be regulated by local governments as well as financed through local user charges (Bauer et al., 1996, p. 113). The local government therefore still has jurisdiction over these functions. The use of these instruments and the possibility of local non-governmental administration (as discussed in section 3.2) could increase hidden public debt on the local level (Dafflon, 1997, p. 106).

Intergenerational externalities of investments into infrastructure financed mainly (in Austria, about 60 per cent) by local governments are another argument for borrowing on the local level. Theoretically, in contrast to federal debt, local borrowing is often classified as external debt. The externality of the debt is discussed as an important consideration for an intergenerational distribution of the debt burden. Although a strong asymmetric relationship between federal and local (state) borrowing is controversial in fiscal theory and practice, a transfer of the debt burden to future generations seems to be more probable in the case of local borrowing. A future increase in debt service payments will disturb the investment function of local budgets, and future generations will therefore inherit a smaller capital stock.

The postulate of equalising local income and living standards, which is still an important political priority in Austria, requires a continuous and sufficient degree of investments in public service organisations and public infrastructure. On the local level, public investments are not used as an instrument of stabilisation policy (with its multiplier effects on income and capital stock). Although it would be necessary to integrate local investment activities in a kind of "multilevel mechanism of stabilisation policy", Austrian policy emphasises equalising distribution effects of public investments. This constellation results in a pro-cyclical local investment policy, followed by cyclical fluctuations of local revenues. To reduce the non-congruence of local fiscal policy, the local business tax was replaced by the community tax, as mentioned above. Besides the funding of financial reserves, borrowing is, for this reason, the only opportunity for local governments to cover the difference between disposable revenues and investment expenditures. In this context, it is important to add that the structure of local investments varies significantly between local communities of different size. While smaller local communities (up to 5,000 inhabitants) focus their investment activities on water supply, sewage disposal, and primary schools, Gemeinden with more than 10,000 inhabitants invest mainly in areas such as public traffic, public housing, and social services.

3.6   CONCLUSION: BUDGET DISCIPLINE VERSUS BUDGET RESPONSIBILITY?

One effective opportunity to ensure fiscal sustainability and responsibility on the local level would be the implementation of medium-term financial planning. At present, local (and state) budgeting in Austria is still rather short term and input orientated and therefore involves some problematic economic effects:

- insufficient consideration of financial consequences of current budgetary measures;
- lack of budgetary priorities (especially investment priorities) and the extrapolation of expenditures from the previous year;
- ineffective performance review of financial measures.

To overcome these inefficiencies, the following political and financial measures should be discussed by the lower tiers of government in Austria:

- the extension of the financial planning period (to between two and five years);

- output-oriented instead of input-oriented financing;
- the use of cost/benefit analyses and cost/effectiveness analyses.

Local governments should prepare urgent and long-term target projections (output orientation) for both investment projects and current expenditures (e.g. personnel costs and local operating expenditures). Financing within the planning period should be connected with the efficiency of target performance. At present, the selection of investment projects is determined by the local administration and supervised by the local authority. To improve the consideration of medium- and long-term financial effects, local governments need to use cost/benefit and cost/effectiveness analyses more often. The outcome of these analyses could help the local authority to decide whether or not to approve the local financial planning. Therefore, the financial role of the local authority institution would also be redefined: instead of the supervision of short-term local fiscal structures (as a result of the short-term orientation of local budgets), medium- and long-term fiscal sustainability would be emphasised. As a consequence, the implementation of medium-term financial planning on the local level could improve the fiscal flexibility and autonomy of local communities.

The budget responsibility approach and medium-term financial planning on the local level provide economic reasons for local borrowing; but as mentioned before, specific economic restrictions for local debts are hard to deduce.

The common economic potential of local governments is important, and their future participation in public economic and stabilisation policy is desirable not only on a theoretical level. In Austria, as in most other European countries, the multilevel co-operation of economic and fiscal policy is strongly co-ordinated and influenced by the federal level (Thöni, 1986, p. 55). The basic philosophy behind the Austrian fiscal federalism arrangement can be summarised as "diversity within strong unity". Therefore, the motives for and the restrictions on borrowing at the local level are not only economic ones.

In contrast to the federal level, local governments have fewer opportunities to influence the maturity of loans and interest rates. Effective local debt management requires inter- and intra-level co-ordination of refunding and repayment operations. This kind of co-ordination mechanism and the required fiscal instruments are still not available on the local level. Therefore, the local debt limit is determined by the liquidity principle. Local solvency is ensured if all expenditures are covered by revenues. It is important to define the liquidity principle dynamically, which implies that the local debt limit is dependent on various economic and institutional factors. Decisive economic and institutional factors are:

- the stage of regional/local economic development; the structure of the regional/local economy;
- the cyclical sensitivity of the local economy;
- the structure of local budgets and local debts;
- cost- and task-shifting activities of higher government tiers;
- inter- and intra-level fiscal adjustments (Bauer, 1980, pp. 35–36).

A uniform local debt rule for all local communities (as the "budget discipline approach" suggests) or even a quantitative determination of the permissible local debt would therefore seem to be neither efficient nor effective. But as discussed above, without fiscal rules, local and other government units will have no incentive for achieving fiscal stability. The Austrian consultation mechanism and the stability pact could be a solution for this economic and political dilemma, if fiscal rules are flexible and if the multilevel agreement brings about real co-operation instead of simply co-ordination still dominated by the federal level.

NOTES

1. Wien, Eisenstadt, Rust, Klagenfurt, Villach, Wiener Neustadt, St. Pölten, Krems an der Donau, Waidhofen an der Ybbs, Linz, Steyr, Wels, Salzburg-Stadt, Graz, Innsbruck.
2. The reason for treating local governments equally is twofold: intergovernmental equity ("Einheitlichkeit der Lebensverhältnisse") and a pressure to reach minimum levels of administrative size.
3. (a) *Exclusive federal competence in both legislation and administration* (Article 10, Article 14 para. 1, Article 14a para. 2 *B-VG*). More than 100 important functions belong to this type, including all courts (there are no state courts), civil and criminal law, police, armed forces, banks, industry, national roads and rail transport, mining, forests, water supply, hydroelectric power, health, social security, unemployment, education services except for elementary and some agricultural education (school building and maintenance are state responsibilities), and national economic planning.

    (b) *Federal legislation but state administration* (Article 11, Article 14 para. 2 *B-VG*). Only six matters belong to this type: citizenship, traffic regulation on roads and non-frontier waterways, social welfare housing, urban redevelopment, control of environmental affairs, and administrative procedures in relation to state competencies.

    (c) *Federal legislation to establish general principles, with states responsible for by law legislation and administration* (Article 12, Article 14 para. 3 *B-VG*). Only a few matters belong to this category: basic social welfare, hospitals, land reform, electricity (except the national grid, national power plants and emergency policies and planning), school building and maintenance (except for high schools and universities), and employee protection.

    d) *Complete state competencies in both legislation and administration* (Article 15 para. 1 *B-VG*). Formally this category includes all matters that are not specified as federal competencies. This gives the states a residual or general competence, but since most important functions have been specified as federal either by the constitution or by interpretation, there are only a few matters left for this type of full state legislative and administrative competence. These include some aspects of environmental protection; building laws, city and rural planning, hunting, fishing, some aspects of agriculture, theatres, some aspects of youth welfare, sports, tourism, and local government (including local police).

4. These are the following. The first is a contribution to the state, which is fixed by federal law at 8.3 per cent. The second is a deduction for community equalisation funds (special needs grants) fixed by federal law at 13.5 per cent. The third is a per capita fiscal equalisation grant.

5. The "community tax" (Kommunalsteuergesetz 1993) was introduced to substitute a former business tax and payroll tax. The tax base is formed by the payroll, the enterpreneurial status was extended. The Kommunalsteuer no longer ties to the "Gewerbebetrieb", it now ties to the "Unternehmen" as fixed in the "Umsatzsteuergesetz 1972" (VAT Law). Changing from business tax and payroll tax to the community tax did cause quite extensive redistribution of revenues between local governments. A financial compensation for relevant hardships in 1994 and 1995 was introduced.

6. The European Court decision pointed to the fact that these excises would clash with the "guide line" on consumption taxation. They would neither include an "earmarking" nor would they truly support "aims of health or tourism policies", which was argued on the Austrian side.

7. Fiscal aim 2000: by 2002 the Austrian government aims at reducing the public deficit to 0% of GDP.

8. First revenue estimates point to the fact that the compromise on the so called "substitute of the excise on drinks", which meant higher shares on the joint VAT, plus a substitution of the former "advertising tax" through a general "publicity better promotion tax" will result in heavy losses of revenue for 2000, but less for 2001 and future years due to an inherent dynamic of the VAT and its distribution.

9. The federal level had to reduce its deficit from ATS 111.833 billion in 1995 (5 per cent of GDP) to ATS 67.019 billion in 1997 (2.7 per cent of GDP).

10. The results agreed are binding; a penalty system reflecting corresponding arrangements at European level will be set up as a safeguard. An information system with similar penalties will also be set up to support the amended stability pact.

11. In principle, the federal government has the opportunity to raise objections to decisions of state and local supervisory institutions.

12. There are also special regulations for some "charter cities".

13. Not all states use the district authority for approval, i.e. it could be also the state government itself.

14. Loans granted by the water resources fund must only be approved by the state government if local budgets are concerned.

15. Local governments, if Vienna is included as local government, do invest more than 60 per cent of all public investment.

16. *Current expenditures*: expenditures for active local government employees, current expenditures for goods and services, interest payments, current transfers to other government units, current transfers to financial institutions, current transfers to households and non-profit organisations, current transfers to foreign countries.

    Current revenues: current revenues for goods and services (refund of costs), income from local property and local non-government enterprises, own and shared taxes, current transfers from other government units, current transfers from financial institutions, current transfers from households and non-profit organisations, current transfers from foreign countries.

REFERENCES

Bauer, H. (1980), *Grenzen der kommunalen Verschuldung – Argumente und Verfahren zur Beurteilung der Schuldengrenze österreichischer Gemeinden*, Institut für Kommunalwissenschaften und Umweltschutz, Wien.

Bauer, H., H. Gruber and B. Hüttner (1996), *Gemeindehaushalte und die Maastricht-Kriterien*, Wien.

Bauer, H. and K. Saindl (1988), *Kommunale Finanzwirtschaft und Haushaltsführung*, Kommunalwissenschaftliches Dokumentationszentrum, Wien.

Bennet, R.J. (1985), *Intergovernmental financial relations in Austria*, ANU, Canberra.

Dafflon, B. (1997) "Les critères budgétaires de Maastricht: quelques éléments de réflexion pour le finances publiques suisses", in Schmid, H., and T. Slembeck (eds), *Finanz- und Wirtschaftspolitik in Theorie und Praxis*, Schriftreihe Finanzwirtschaft und Finanzrecht 86, Bern, Stuttgart, pp. 96–116.

Hüttner, B. (1996), "Der Finanzausgleich 1997 und sein Umfeld", *Österreichische Gemeindezeitung* 8/1996, Wien, pp. 2–16.

Hüttner, B. (1999), "Konsultationsmechanismus – Kosten rechtsetzender Maßnahmen – Stabilitätspakt", in *Österreichische Gemeindezeitung* 1/1999, Wien, pp. 5–12.

Musgrave, R. and P. Musgrave (1989), *Public Finance in Theory and Practice*, Singapore.

Pernthaler, P. (1984), *Österreichische Finanzverfassung: Theorie – Praxis – Reform*, Wien.

Smekal C. (1987), "Verschuldungsbeschränkungen und Verschuldungsverhalten der Gebietskörperschaften – Ein Vergleich zwischen der Bundesrepublik Deutschland und Österreich", in G. Kirsch, *Beiträge zu ökonomischen Problemen des Föderalismus*, Berlin, pp. 71–147.

Thöni, E. (1983), "Das 'Prinzip der Einheitsgemeinde' - rechtlich zulässig - ökonomisch obsolet?", in K. Korinek (eds), *Beiträge zum Wirtschaftsrecht*, Festschrift für Karl Wenger, Wien, pp. 431–446.

Thöni, E. (1986), *Politökonomische Theorie des Föderalismus*, Baden-Baden.

Thöni, E. (1996), "Regional and local government in the European Union: Austria, in EU – The Committee of the Regions / Subcommission on Local and Regional Finances", in *Regional and Local Government in the European Union*, Brussels, pp. 30 – 47.

Thöni, E. (1997/1999), "Fiscal Federalism in Austria: Facts and new developments", in *Diskussionsreihe des Instituts für Finanz-wissenschaft Innsbruck*, Heft Nr. 2/1997, Innsbruck, published in Fossati A. and G. Panella (eds), *Fiscal Federalism in the European Union*, London, New York, 1999, pp. 103–121.

Thöni, E. and S. Garbislander, (1999), *Konsultationsmechanismus und Stabilitätspakt im Bundesstaat*, in Wirtschaftsdienst 7/1999, Hamburg, pp. 442–448.

Zeitel, G. (1970), *Kommunale Finanzstruktur und gemeindliche Selbstverwaltung, in Archiv für Kommunalwissenschaften (AfK)*, Stuttgart 1970/I, pp. 1–20.

Data and Source Documents

Österreichische Finanzverwaltung (1996), *Amtsblatt 1996*, part 51, number 96, Finanzausgleichsgesetz (FAG) 1997, Wien, pp. 369–449.

Österreichisches Statistisches Zentralamt (ÖSTAT), *Gebarungsübersichten, relevant years*, Wien.

Österreichisches Statistisches Zentralamt (ÖSTAT), *Statistisches Handbuch der Republik Österreich*, relevant years, Wien.

Vereinbarung zwischen dem Bund, den Ländern und den Gemeinden über einen Konsultationsmechanismus und einen künftigen Stabilitätspakt der Gebietskörperschaften, BGBL. I Nr. 35/1999, Wien, pp. 249–252.

4. Local public finance in Belgium: structure, budgets and debt

Jacques Vanneste

4.1 INTRODUCTION

The 1980s and the 1990s were quite captivating for public finance in Belgium. First, Belgium became a federal country. This restructuring implied a shift of budgetary autonomy from the central to the intermediate government level. Second, the convergence towards the EMU implied strong austerity programmes for the public sector. Section 4.2 discusses the role of the local public sector in both macro perspectives.

Section 4.3 sketches the institutional and managerial framework of the local public sector in Belgium, not only focusing on the municipalities but also on the different intra- and inter-local government authorities with which the budgets of municipalities are interwoven.

Local public debt and capital expenditure are the topics of section 4.4. First the scope of local public debt is developed. Different concepts of debt are defined and documented for the Belgian local public sector, such as own versus debudgetised debt and gross versus net local public debt respectively. Debt financing is most often linked to local public investments, but also other sources of investment funding are considered. Due to the dual approach of local budgets – current budgets and capital budgets – special attention is given to the interference of debt financing with the budget cycle. Debt financing appears first in the capital budget at the period of investment, then the debt service appears in the current budgets of subsequent years.

4.2 THE LOCAL PUBLIC SECTOR AND FISCAL FEDERALISM IN BELGIUM

The key issue in this section is the budgetary autonomy of local governments in Belgium. Since 1989, Belgium has been a federal country in which budgetary competence is spread over a federal government level, an intermediate government level (three regions and three communities) and a local government level. The following sections give some further information on the budgetary relevance of each government level.

4.2.1 Revenue, Expenditure and Net Financial Balance by Government Level

Table 4.1 illustrates the key characteristics of fiscal federalism in Belgium for the budgetary year 1996. The data on revenue, expenditures, primary balance and net financial balance are reported for the federal government level, the social security system, the communities and regions and finally for the local government level. The latter consists of the provinces, the municipalities and the public centres for social welfare.

The federal government level together with the social security system constitute what is called "Entity I" when monitoring of the public finances is addressed by the "Higher Finance Council".[1] In the same context "Entity II" is made of the communities and regions (i.e. the intermediate government level) together with the local government .

The data for the general government in Table 4.1 are consolidated for intergovernmental transfers. The revenue and expenditure figures at different government levels do not thus simply add up to the figure in the first column. A second remark relates to the budgetary system at different government levels. At the federal government level, for example, current and capital expenditures are presented in one single expenditure budget. Similarly there is one revenue budget including current as well as capital revenue. However this is not the case at the local government level where both a current budget and a capital budget are still en vogue. The current budget registers current revenue and expenditure; the capital budget registers capital revenue and expenditure. Notwithstanding this variation in budget format, the concepts in Table 4.1 have the same content at all levels.

On the revenue side we consider tax revenue, nontax revenue and grants from other government levels. Substracting from this all kinds of expenditures except interest payments we reach the primary balance. The net financial balance takes account of these interest payments. Finally we end up with the net financial balance. Clearly the repayment of debt is not considered.[2]

As can be inferred from Table 4.1 tax revenue represents 39.1% of local government revenue while 52.3% stems from grants from other governments. On the expenditure side, wages and salaries represent 63.6% of current primary expenditures; transfers to individuals some 26.5%. Clearly, local governments have the most labour intensive outlays of all government levels in Belgium. A rather striking fact has to do with capital expenditures. With gross investments in fixed capital assets at the local government worth 64.3 billion BEF in 1996 the local government sector is the most important government vehicle for capital expenditures in Belgium.

Table 4.1   Revenue, expenditure and net financial balance by government level (1996, in billion of Belgian francs)

		Entity I		Entity II	
	General	Federal	Social Security	Communities and Regions	Local
Revenue	*3 908.1*	*1 473.0*	*1 641.4*	*938.3*	*528.4*
Tax revenue	3 772.0	1 407.6	1 352.8	856.1	206.7
Direct taxation	1 488.9	854.8	38.0	437.4	158.4
Individual	1 224.3	621.3	38.0	435.8	128.9
Corporate	264.6	233.5	0.0	1.6	29.5
Indirect taxation	1 034.2	507.2	99.2	389.4	38.4
Social security contributions	1 214.5	40.6	1 214.6	0.0	9.9
Capital revenue	34.3	5.0	0.0	29.3	0.0
Nontax revenue	136.2	58.0	31.9	19.9	45.2
Grants from other governments	-	7.4	257.7	62.2	276.5
Expenditures excluding interest payments	*3 483.7*	*1 078.8*	*1 634.8*	*956.8*	*473.9*
Current expenditures	3 293.3	1 054.6	1'627.0	834.7	406.0
Wages and salaries	753.4	177.2	44.7	324.7	258.1
Expenditures on goods and services	188.4	70.4	19.6	63.5	35.3
Transfers to individuals	2 058.7	232.3	1 564.6	154.4	107.6
Subsidies to enterprises	171.4	100.6	0.0	67.8	3.0
Transfers abroad	121.5	120.9	0.0	0.6	0.0
Transfers to other governments	-	353.3	0.0	223.6	2.0
Capital expenditure	190.4	24.2	0.6	122.1	67.9
Gross investment in fixed capital assets	105.3	3.0	0.6	37.5	64.3
Other	85.1	14.9	0.0	66.7	3.5
Transfers to other governments	-	6.3	0.0	17.9	0.1
Primary balance	*424.5*	*394.2*	*12.8*	*– 18.5*	*54.5*
Interest payments	*703.4*	*640.9*	*6.2*	*32.0*	*42.8*
Net financial balance	*– 278.9*	*– 246.7*	*6.6*	*– 50.4*	*11.7*

Source: Nationale Bank van België, *Statistisch Tijdschrift*, Brussels, 1997-I, blz. 93–97.

4.2.2 Belgium and the EMU: A Multi-layer Responsibility for Convergence and the Stability and Growth Pact

In June 1992, the convergence programme laid down in the Maastricht Treaty was adopted by the Belgian authorities. From that time the convergence criteria became the leading guides for the budgetary policy of the Belgian authorities in order to qualify for admission in the EMU. The Higher Finance Council which includes representatives of the federal, community and regional levels, was entrusted with the task of following the implementation of this strategy.

The responsibility of bringing the overall budget in line with the objectives set out in the Maastricht convergence programme was distributed among the different levels of government. For reasons of effectiveness government levels have been grouped in two specific entities. The monitoring in entity I including the federal government and the social security system was entrusted to the federal government. As already documented in Table 4.1 entity II covers the community and regional governments and the local authorities. As for entity II, the regional governments have been given the responsibility for the budgetary outcome.

The objectives and achievements are measured in terms of net financing capacity; that is the balance of income and expenditure determined using the methods of the ESA national accounts. Consequently, this balance includes debudgetisations but excludes credit granted and shares (participating interests) taken.

Table 4.2 clearly illustrates that the EMU convergence process induced by the Treaty of Maastricht mainly involved the federal government and only to a lesser extent the communities and regions. Except for 1993 the balance of the local public sector always showed a small net financing capacity contributing marginally to the 3% budget deficit threshold.

Table 4.2   Net financing capacity or need by government level (in % of GDP)

	1992	1993	1994	1995	1996	1997*
Revenue	45.4	46.0	47.1	46.8	46.9	47.0
Primary expenditures	41.6	42.4	42.0	41.7	41.6	41.3
Primary balance	3.8	3.6	5.1	5.1	5.3	5.6
Interest payments	10.7	10.7	10.0	9.0	8.5	7.9
Net financing capacity(+) or need(−)	− 6.9	− 7.1	− 4.9	− 3.9	− 3.2	− 2.3
Federal government	− 6.1	− 6.2	− 4.8	− 4.0	− 3.0	− 2.5
Communities and Regions	− 0.9	− 0.6	− 0.7	− 0.7	− 0.5	− 0.2
Local government	0.2	− 0.2	—	0.4	0.2	0.2
Social security	− 0.1	− 0.1	0.7	0.4	—	0.2

Note: * Figures for 1997: estimates.

Source: Nationale Bank van België, *Verslag 1997*, Brussels, 1998, p. 61.

At the end of December 1996, Belgium introduced a new convergence programme covering the period 1997–2000. The objectives are in line with those of the preceding programme, namely to reduce the net financing deficit and the level of indebtedness of the Belgian public authorities. The budgetary standards for both entities underlying this programme are summarised as follows: for Entity I (federal authorities and social security):

- The stabilisation of the primary surplus at 5.3% of GDP;
- A zero real growth rate of primary expenditure at the federal government level;
- A development of tax receipts in line with that of GDP (i.e. a macro-economic tax elasticity coefficient close to 1);
- A balanced budget in the social security sector.

And for Entity II (communities, regions and local authorities):

- A balanced budget for the communities and regions by 1999;
- A balanced budget for the local authorities.

The budgetary path for the public authorities between 1996 and 2000 is sketched in Table 4.3. The projections take account of the above budgetary standards and are implemented within the following cautious macro-economic scenario: a real economic growth of 2% a year throughout the period 1998–2000; a long-term interest rate of 6.3% throughout the period 1998–2000 and a short-term interest rate of 3.7% in 1998 rising to 4.0 % in 1999 and 2000.

As can be inferred from Table 4.3, the net financing deficit would decrease to 1.5% by the year 2000, while the level of indebtedness would decline to 120.4%. A more favourable macro-economic scenario (with real growth rates of 2.6%, 2.7% and 2.5% between 1998 and 2000) would bring down the net financing deficit to 1.1% GDP and the level of public indebtedness to 117.8% of GDP.

Generally speaking the local governments' expected budget track is a small primary surplus and a net financing surplus. The monitoring of the local governments' budget de facto does not operate via the Higher Finance Council. Indeed local governments – and more precisely the municipalities – are faced with a "hard" budget constraint which was already enforced by central government in 1988. At the beginning of the 1980s municipal budgets had reached historic levels due to a combination of reasons. Budget recovery was driven through increasing taxes, national and regional loans accorded to municipalities under strict austerity schemes, and so on. Gradually, municipal accounts improved.

Table 4.3   Budgetary path for the public authorities (in % of GDP): cautious economic scenario

	1996	1997	1998	1999	2000
Entity I					
Primary surplus	5.1	5.3	5.3	5.3	5.3
Interest charges	8.0	7.8	7.4	7.0	6.8
Net financing deficit	2.9	2.5	2.1	1.7	1.5
Entity II					
Primary surplus	0.4	0.5	0.6	0.8	0.8
Interest charges	0.9	0.9	0.8	0.8	0.8
Net financing deficit*	0.5	0.4	0.2	0.0	0.0
Entities I and II					
Primary surplus	5.4	5.8	5.9	6.1	6.1
Interest charges	8.8	8.6	8.2	7.8	7.5
Net financing deficit	3.4	2.9	2.3	1.7	1.4
Level of indebtedness	130.4	127.0	125.2	122.9	120.4

Note: * These are objectives the executives of the regions and the communities have undertaken to meet.

Source: Ministry of Finance: Administration of the Treasury, *Public Debt: Annual report 1996*, Brussels, 1997, p. 104.

The municipal budget's equilibrium is audited at the provincial level, and they have the coercive power to enforce expenditure reductions or tax increases if necessary. There is no formal permission needed for an individual local government to borrow.

4.3   THE LOCAL PUBLIC SECTOR IN BELGIUM: AN INSTITUTIONAL AND MANAGERIAL APPROACH

The most important sub-sectors of the local public sector in Belgium are the ten provincial and 589 municipal governments. Provinces and local governments have the following characteristics in common:

- a jurisdiction within one of the regions, i. e. Flanders, Brussels Capital and Wallonia;
- a general set of allocative and redistributive functions;
- budgetary autonomy, i.e. the competence to decide independently on the level and structure of revenues and expenditures;
- a democratic council elected for a fixed term of six years.

The other sub-sectors of the Belgian local public sector are the public centres for social welfare, the church fabrics and the intermunicipal agencies. They operate either as intra- or as inter-local government authorities and diverge on one or more criteria specified above. The first section hereafter discusses key characteristics of provinces and municipalities; the second section deals with the inter- and intra-local government authorities.

4.3.1 Provinces and Municipalities

Provinces
The territory of Belgium is subdivided into ten provinces, five of which are situated in the Flemish Region and five of which lie in the Walloon Region. Brussels Capital is excluded from the division in provinces.

Provinces are governed by the provincial council, the permanent deputation and the provincial governor. The provincial council is the deliberative body of the province. It decides on all matters of provincial interest. A councillor's term of office is six years. The permanent deputation is the executive provincial committee in charge of the everyday administration of the province. The governor is appointed by the King for an unlimited term. The governor acts in a dual capacity: he acts as a provincial body, while, at the same time, he is a representative of the higher authorities.

Table 4.4   Provincial expenditure: functional classification (budgets 1999)

Public administration	21.1 %
Roads, waterways	5.6 %
Industry	6.1 %
Education	34.6 %
Culture	13.2 %
Social services	4.1 %
Health care	6.2 %
Environment	5.0 %
Others	3.2 %
TOTAL	100.0 %

Source: DEXIA, *De Financiën van de Lokale Overheden in 1999*, Brussels, 2000, p. 46.

The scope of the provincial powers has been described in general terms: the province is allowed to act in all matters which it considers to be of provincial interest on the condition that a higher authority (the federal state, the community or the region) has not yet ruled on the matter concerned. In particular, provinces take action in the organisation of technical and special education and to promote culture and tourism. Furthermore, they elaborate initiatives concerning economic expansion and restructuring. Nevertheless, the budgetary impact of the provinces is relatively small compared with the municipalities. According to the 1999 budgets, provinces spend 56 billion BEF, the municipalities 431 billion BEF (see Table 4.4).

Municipalities
The average number of local residents in Belgium's 589 municipalities is 17,267. The population density in the average municipality is about 332 residents per km².

Municipalities are governed by the local council and the committee of mayor and aldermen. The local council is the deliberative body of the municipality, composed of from seven to 55 members, depending on the number of local constituents. The local councillors are elected for a period of six years. They can be re-elected. The committee is the executive body of the municipality. It is in charge of the everyday administration of the municipality. The aldermen (from two to ten) are elected for a fixed term of six years from the members of the council. The mayor is appointed by the King. Usually, the mayor is a member of the local council.

Local governments are authorised to pursue any policy to promote the interests of their local constituents. To this end the local council can take any initiative that is not prohibited explicitly by central legislation. The circumscription of the powers of the local authorities is thus very general. Table 4.5 and 4.6 give an insight into the actual policies carried out at the municipal level. Both tables are drawn from the current municipal budgets in which expenditures are reported in a twofold way: a functional and an economic classification.

Table 4.5 shows how municipal current expenditures are allocated over eight broadly defined service sectors. The most important expenditure shares are public administration, public safety, education and social services.

Table 4.6 shows how municipalities allocate their expenditures among four economic categories: personnel, operating costs, transfers and debt service. In the average municipality, the costs of personnel amount to more than 50% of the total budget. This is not much of a surprise as the most important services provided at the local level (i.e. public administration, public safety and education) are very labour intensive. Over the observed period, operating costs took a share of approximately 15% of total expenditures and are on an increasing trend. The expenditure share of transfers has been rising at a steady pace since 1993. In 1999, 15% of the budget was allocated to transfers. Finally, the budgetary weight of interest and capital payments that stem from the outstanding local debt can be seen to decrease over time. As a consequence, the budget share of the debt service fell from 22.8% in 1993 to 15.9% in 1999.

Table 4.5   Municipal expenditure shares according to the functional classification (budgets 1999)

Public administration	17.0 %
Public safety	13.6 %
Roads, waterways	11.9 %
Agriculture, industry	2.2 %
Education	17.1 %
Culture	11.5 %
Social services	12.5 %
Environment	9.9 %
Others	4.5 %
TOTAL	100.0 %

Source: DEXIA, *De Financiën van de Lokale Overheden in 1999*, Brussels, 2000, p. 14.

Table 4.6   Municipal expenditure shares according to the economic classification (1993-1999)

	1993	1994	1995	1996	1999
Personnel	50.4	52.0	51.7	51.7	52.5
Operating costs	14.8	15.4	15.2	14.8	16.2
Transfers	12.0	12.5	13.4	13.8	15.4
Debt service	22.8	20.1	19.7	19.7	15.9

Source: DEXIA, *De Financiëen van de Lokale Overheden 1993-1999*, Brussels 1994-2000.

4.3.2 Inter- and Intra-local Government Authorities

Public centres for social welfare
The territorial scope of the public centres for social welfare (PCSW) coincides with that of a municipality but it has a specific statutory mission, that is, to guarantee a minimum of social welfare to all its inhabitants through information, social counselling and material support. In addition a PCSW, especially in large cities, often develops a wide range of activities including public hospitals and rest homes, for example.

The council of a PCSW is not directly elected by the local constituency. Instead it is constituted by the municipal council. The voting process guarantees a similar political composition in both councils. This democratic deficit is justified by the municipality's final budget responsibility.

A PCSW can be considered as a functionally deconcentrated public agency without budget autonomy. Its revenue mainly consists of grants from other levels of government (federal, regional and municipal). It cannot raise own taxes. On the expenditure side we find operating costs for the social network as well as lump sum or even in kind transfers to the indigent. Current deficits have to be covered by the corresponding local government.

Table 4.7 shows relevant data concerning the 1997 budgets of Belgian public centres for social welfare. Expenditures of PCSW are estimated to amount to 3.3% of total government expenditures and 1.4% of GDP. The major share of the budget (47.8%) is spent on personnel outlays. Almost one third (31.5%) of the expenditures are transfers such as the minimum income guarantee, supplementary financial aid to individuals or subsidies to rest homes, hospitals, and so on.

Table 4.7   Public centres for social welfare: 1997 current budget (in billion BEF)

Revenue		Expenditure	
Own resources Activities	29.1	Personnel	56.9
Transfers	86.3	Operating costs	15.6
Municipality (deficit covering)	*34.1*	Transfers	37.5
Federal government (subsistance level)	*10.7*		
Debt	0.5	Debt service	9.0
Total	**115.9**	**Total**	**119.2**

Source: DEXIA, *De Financiën van de Lokale Overheden in 1996*, Brussels, 1997, pp. 53–56.

About one quarter of the current budget is covered by own resources, for example: the renting and leasing of property, the use of the benefit principle for certain services and the interests on savings. The latter are reported as debt revenue. Clearly the major source of revenue is intergovernmental transfers.

Transfers from federal and intermediate governments are mostly matching grants to cover outlays in a variety of fields such as the payment of the statutory minimum income guarantee, the wage cost of subsidised personnel, or the debt service of loans. In some cases the transfer is of the unconditional block grant type using poverty and need criteria for horizontal distribution. The municipal transfer covering the PCSW deficit is an unconditional block grant. In 1997, only one PCSW in Belgium managed to balance its budget without municipal funds. Between 1990 and 1997, the municipal transfer increased by 60%.

The per capita expenditure level of a PCSW increases with the size of the municipality as Table 4.8 clearly shows. The average is 11,183 BEF in Flanders, 11,017 BEF in Wallonia and 17,634 BEF in Brussels. The average municipal deficit covering amounts to 29.4%.

Table 4.8   Public centres for social welfare: expenditures, municipal deficit covering and population size (budget 1997, in BEF per capita)

	Flanders			Wallonia		
	Number	Current expenditure	Municipal deficit covering	Number	Current expenditure	Municipal deficit covering
< 2 500	6	3 971	1 609	97	5 095	1 972
2 500 – 4 999	9	5 409	1 558	65	5 651	2 129
5 000 – 9 999	82	6 890	2 070	83	7 408	2 524
10 000 – 14 999	87	7 565	2 197	42	8 419	2 644
15 000 – 19 999	48	9 034	2 500	17	11 056	2 928
20 000 – 29 999	38	10 248	2 599	25	9 815	2 926
30 000 – 49 999	26	11 588	3 058	4	10 323	3 336
50 000 – 129 999	10	14 543	4 014	7	15 397	3 539
> 130 000	2	21 053	6 862	2	20 483	4 986
TOTAL	**308**	**11 183**	**3 191**	**262**	**11 077**	**3 100**

Source: DEXIA, *De Financiën van de Lokale Overheden in 1996*, Brussels, 1997, p. 91.

Church fabrics
Church fabrics are (budgetary) small local public sector authorities operating at the parochial level. Churchwardens manage the assets and liabilities of a parish. A municipality can have a number of church fabrics within its constituency. Again there is a clear budgetary link with the local budget: budget deficits from church fabrics of recognised religions have to be covered by the municipal budget.

Intermunicipal agencies
Local governments can agree upon the creation of intermunicipal agencies on such specific items as household refuse collection and processing, electricity distribution or regional economic development. The profits or losses of these "local public enterprises" are shared by the participating municipalities according to statutory rules. Neither the council nor the executive board are

elected in a direct way. As each municipality elects representatives within its council, intermunicipal agencies show a democratic deficit.

Table 4.9 draws a picture of intermunicipal activity in Belgium. Throughout the country, 243 intermunicipal agencies are in operation, mostly within one of the three regions but sometimes in a cross-border setting. The total assets for the financial year 1998 were worth 735 billion BEF.

Table 4.9   Intermunicipal agencies: financial statements by sector of activity (1998, in billion BEF)

Sector of activity	Number of observations	Total assets (in billion BEF)
Electricity, gas, cable television	72	550
Water provision and distribution	27	69
Medical social institutions	34	3
Economic development, environmental planning, household refuse, water purification	70	104
Others	40	9
TOTAL	**243**	**735**

Source: DEXIA, *De Financiën van de Lokale Overheden in 1999*, Brussels, 2000, p. 62.

The partners of an intermunicipal agency can either be exclusively public authorities or a joint venture of public authorities mixed with private sector companies. The latter is quite frequent in the energy and cable television sector.

4.4   LOCAL PUBLIC DEBT AND CAPITAL EXPENDITURE

4.4.1 The Scope of Local Public Debt

The budgetary impact of local public debt

From a legal point of view, local public debt consists of all debt types for which a local government is the debtor. The local government is responsible for the debt service; that is, the capital reimbursement and the interest payments. However, in some cases, only part of the debt service has to be paid by the local government itself. This happens when a higher level of government subsidises a part of the yearly debt service through a specific grant. This grant then becomes current revenue of the local government.

By the end of 1999, gross local public debt amounted to 628 billion BEF which represented 5.8% of total public debt. The major part (596 billion

BEF) was completely the responsibility of the local public sector; the minor part (31 billion BEF), was shared between the local public sector and other levels of government.

Gross versus net local public debt
Correcting gross local public debt for local financial assets yields the net local public debt. By the end of 1999 gross local public debt amounted to 628 billion BEF while the net local public debt was worth 479 billion BEF.

Gross local public debt: structure and evolution
Table 4.10 depicts the structure of the gross local public debt between 1995 and 1999, including investment financing loans, short-term financing, and financial retrenchment loans. A striking fact is the quite stable level at which gross local public debt remained over the period covered. Since 1986, local public bonds are no longer in circulation.

Long-term debt has two different sources: local public investment or financial retrenchment schemes. The latter were started at the beginning of the 1980s first by the national government, later also by each regional government. Cities and municipalities with large current budget deficits and a high burden of debt received consolidating loans provided a tight budgetary retrenchment scheme was adopted. At the same time, two important legislative measures were taken: the compulsory budget equilibrium and the deregulation of the supplementary local tax rate on the federal personal income tax. Previously, this supplementary local tax rate was limited to a maximum of 6%. As a result of all these measures the local public finances improved considerably.

Table 4.10 Gross and net local public debt 1995–1999 (end of year, in billion BEF)

	31/12/95	31/12/96	31/12/97	31/12/98	31/12/99
Investment financing loans	443.3	449.3	436.5	448.3	459.3
Financial retrenchment loans	116.1	109.5	99.8	102.4	99.3
Total long-term debt	559.4	558.8	536.3	550.7	558.6
Short-term debt	79.2	76.3	60.3	58.0	69.0
Total debt	638.6	635.1	596.6	608.7	627.6
Financial assets	145.3	133.3	168.9	161.9	148.8
Net public debt	493.3	496.4	427.7	446.8	478.8

Source: DEXIA, *De Financiën van de Lokale Overheden in 1999*, Brussels, 2000, p. 75.

A significant one shot reduction of gross debt was induced by the stock exchange introduction in 1996 of Dexia Belgium shares. Until then Belgian provinces, cities and municipalities were almost the exclusive shareholders of the Gemeentekrediet, a public credit institution devoted to financing the local public sector. The former shareholders were urged by their respective supervising authorities to use the yield of this exceptional dividend (33 billion BEF) to reduce their outstanding debt.

4.4.2 Municipal Investments and the Budget Cycle

Whenever a municipality invests in public infrastructure it has the opportunity to finance it either through borrowing, grants from higher government levels, disinvestments or other own resources. This is traced on the revenue side of the capital budget. Capital reimbursements following an amortisation scheme are part of the debt service and are registered in the current budget. Both are discussed in more detail hereafter.

Investment funding and the capital budget
The funding of investments is registered on the revenue side of the capital budget which has a threefold structure: transfers, investments and debt, each of them corresponding to a specific type of investment financing. Transfers related to capital expenditures come, for example, from an investment fund. In the Flemish community each local government has drawing rights in this investment fund, which is a block grant. Specific matching grants are allocated for investments in local public schools, and so on for the rebuilding of the historic patrimonium. The major part of investment funding, however, is made up of new loans. This debt financing is detailed in the debt section of the capital budget. Another less important source of investment funding is disinvesting some local patrimonium (buildings, land, etc.). This category – somewhat misleadingly – is characterised as "investment".

The major capital expenditures are planned investments by the local government itself. However if municipalities want to support investment by a third party, they can set this up either through a grant or through a loan. The former is registered as a transfer; the latter as a debt expenditure on the capital budget.

The debt service: a current budget entry
The current budget reflects the impact of outstanding debt on local public finance. Each functional expenditure category (see Table 4.5) is divided into personnel expenditures, operating costs, transfers and debt service (see Table 4.6). The latter includes interest payments and capital amortisation on gross local debt.

In some cases (a part of) the capital reimbursement and the interest payments are subsidised by a higher government level, or refunded by a third party. Loans to finance local public works (roads, and so on) may benefit debt service support from a regional or a community authority. Investments on churches are executed by church fabrics, the legal proprietor of this patrimonium. Nevertheless, it is the local government that enacts these so-called "pass through" loans. The church fabrics acting as a third party vis-à-vis the municipality have interest payments and capital reimbursements 100% at their charge.

The link between depreciation of assets and amortisation of debt

There is no formal link between the amortisation period of the loan and depreciation period of the investment good. The "municipal accounting code" states that the depreciation period of the fixed assets (tangible or intangible) must be shorter than the amortisation period of the loan.

The only accepted depreciation method is the linear method. Also in some cases reassesments are allowed. For example administrative buildings must be reassessed annually on the basis of the construction price index.

4.4.3 Municipal Investment Funding

The financing structure of the 1999 Belgian municipal investments is detailed in Table 4.11.

The highest proportion, 56.1%, of the investment funding stems from "own share" loans; that is, loans of which the debt service completely falls at the municipal budget's charge. About 24% of local public infrastructure funding derives from capital transfers from federal or intermediate government.

Referring to section 4.4.1, where the scope of local public debt was discussed, 1.3% of municipal investment is funded through "government share" loans. This is debudgetised debt at a higher government level. Conversely 1% of the investments were in fact prefinancing activities for third parties, for example public centres for social welfare or church fabrics.

Own financing accounts for 16.4% of total investments through either a disinvestment of patrimonium, the use of a surplus on the capital budget, a transfer from the current to the capital budget or a dip into the municipal reserve fund.

Figure 4.1 sketches the investments of the local public sector (municipalities, provinces, PCSW, etc.) between 1990 and 1999. Clearly local public investment shows a "political" cycle. In election years (1988, 1994 and 2000), peak investment levels are recorded as compared with other years.

90   *Local public finance in Europe*

Table 4.11   *The financing structure of municipal investments in Belgium (1999, in %)*

Source of finance	%
Loans "own share"	56.1
Loans "government share"	1.3
Loans at charge of a third party (PCSW, church fabric, etc.)	0.9
Capital transfers from other governments	23.8
Autofinancing	16.4
Other	1.7
Total	**100.0**

Source: DEXIA, *De Financiën van de Lokale Overheden in 1999*, Brussels, 2000, p. 68.

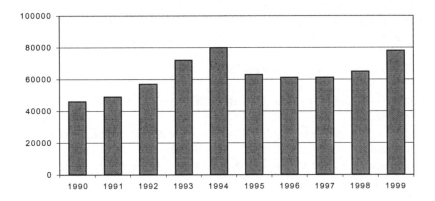

Source: DEXIA, *De Financiën van de Lokale Overheden in 1999*, Brussels, 2000, p. 69.

Figure 4.1   *Local public sector investment 1990-1999 (in billion BEF)*

4.5   SUMMARY AND CONCLUSIONS

The overall picture of the local public sector in Belgium reveals a set of public authorities with a net financial surplus in recent years. Though marginally, the local government contributed to the convergence threshold of 3% budget deficit laid down in the Maastricht Treaty. The objectives for the near future are a balanced budget. The second general conclusion relates to the structure of fiscal federalism in Belgium. Despite the federalisation process, fiscal federalism in Belgium left the local government untouched.

Therefore fiscal autonomy at the local level is quite limited. Local expenditures represent only 6.2% of GDP, which is well below the EU-15 average. Tax autonomy is increasing: tax revenue represented 44% of local government revenue in 1999; in 1980 it was at only 35%.

The municipalities and the public centres for social welfare represent the major local public sector authorities. The former have budgetary responsibility for the latter as current deficits of public centres for social welfare have to be covered by the municipal budget. A public centre for social welfare can be considered as a functionally deconcentrated public agency devoted to a specific statutory mission: to guarantee a minimum of social welfare to all its inhabitants. Its democratic deficit is justified by the municipality's final budget responsibility. The current activities of Belgian municipalities are allocated mainly to public administration, infrastructure, education, culture and social services. According to the economic classification 52.5% of their expenditures are personnel costs.

The gross investment in fixed capital assets of the global local sector is more important than any other government level in Belgium. "Own share" loans are the most common investment funding (56%).The debt service of these loans appears on the current budgets of the subsequent years. Capital transfers account for 24% of the investment funding. Also local public sector investment shows a "political" cycle.

NOTES

1. See section 2.2 for comments on the role of the "Higher Finance Council" in the convergence of Belgian public finances.
2. The repayment of debt is treated differently at the local level compared with other government levels. At the federal government level, for example, this simply does not figure in the expenditure budget. The net financial balance plus the amortisation of debt is the gross financial balance. At the local government level on the other hand, the repayment of debt is part of the current budget. The current budget for public administration for example thus reports on wages, operating costs, transfers and the debt service (interest payments and amortisation) related to this specific function.

REFERENCES

Belgium (1997), Ministry of Finance, *Public Debt: Annual Report 1996*, Brussels.
DEXIA (2000), *De Financiën van de Lokale Overheden in 1999*, Brussel, p. 95.
Jones B. (1995), *Local Government Financial Management*, ICSA Publishing, Hertfordshire.
Moesen W., *Assignment Rules, the Status of the Budget Constraint and Young Fiscal Federalism in Belgium*, (Commission of the European Communities).
Nationale Bank Van Belgie (1997-I), *Statistisch Tijdschrift*, Brussels.
Nationale Bank Van Belgie (1998), *Verslag 1997*, Brussels.

5. Local government and debt financing in Denmark

Niels Jørgen Mau Pedersen

5.1 INTRODUCTION

Denmark has not acceded to the third stage of the EMU, but is none the less committed to respecting the convergence criteria relating to the general government fiscal balance and the public debt.

These convergence criteria for national public finance have really not been a political issue in Denmark. After all, there has been a – more or less tacit – consensus about those criteria being sensible and in line with the policy of both the social-democratic and liberal/conservative parties usually in government in Denmark.

The Achilles' heel of the Danish economy has for generations been the external balance – the balance of payments – due to a low level of public and private savings. That problem is, of course, connected with the fiscal policy and with the public finances. The Maastricht criteria have not changed the agenda here, but have highlighted the demands on the public finances.

In this connection local government finances play an important role. However, it is not possible to articulate the policy objectives in a very simple manner, such as, to "keep the primary local fiscal balance in surplus", "reduce the debt", or the like. Rather the challenge is to organise and regulate the public sector – and here especially the sector of local governments – in a manner that encourages the local governments to contribute in a predictable way to "sound" public finances, which usually means keeping a relatively tight fiscal stance. Besides, it would also be preferable if the local governments could contribute to a reduction of the public debt. Although the total public debt has been markedly reduced in the late 1990s, the gross debt still – at the end of 1999 – ranges at a level of around 52 per cent of GDP.

Those challenges cannot, of course, be dealt with in an institutional vacuum. There are a number of institutional and ideological factors that must be taken into consideration. The list of those conditions, which will be spelled out in more detail below, includes:

- local *accountability* is – actually as a sort of social heritage of the Danish society – seen as an important means of securing public welfare,
- Denmark is a unitary country, but with significant *autonomy* vested in the local authorities,
- the *distribution of tasks* between the layers of the public sector is fairly clear-cut,
- the sector of local governments is *economically very important* both in absolute figures – e.g. number of employees – and in relative terms – i.e. compared with the central government,
- the *revenue system* of the local governments supports the autonomy and accountability of the local governments, and
- the impact on fiscal policy from the sector of local governments is *negotiated*, among other items, once a year between the associations of the local governments and the central government, the latter being in charge of the national fiscal policy.

The programme of the chapter will be as follows. Sections 5.2 and 5.3 will describe the main characteristics and political guidelines of the Danish local governments on the expenditure side and the revenue side. Based on this background, in section 5.4 we will go through the borrowing regulations and their implications. In section 5.5. the special Danish system of macroeconomic control via consultations/negotiations will be discussed. Some statistical measurements of implications of the regulations on borrowing and so on will be presented in section 5.6. In section 5.7 a few policy matters will be discussed before the chapter is concluded in section 5.8.

5.2 THE DANISH MODEL OF LOCAL GOVERNMENTS – TASKS AND RESPONSIBILITIES

5.2.1 The Autonomy of Local Governments

A certain type of fiscal federalism characterises the Nordic countries – and not least Denmark – with local governments in a very prominent role. Many of the tasks managed by the central level and state level ("Länder" or "cantons") in other Western countries are here handled by the local government level (Söderström, 1998, p. 2).

Although Denmark after all must be characterised as a unitary country, the municipalities and counties have a significant degree of autonomy. In some expenditure areas, such as child care, care for elderly people and hospitals, the role of the central level is primarily to arrange suitable economic conditions for the proper handling of tasks at the local level, rather than making discretionary interventions in local government behaviour. Although – in round figures – 90 per cent of the local government expenditures are legally authorised by parliament (the rest of the activities are carried out referring to historical practices or unwritten law), the laws normally allow for a considerable degree of freedom for local action. Some areas, such as schools and in particular income transfers to households, are more regulated, and the room for local discretion rather limited, but both parliament and central government are generally cautious not to intervene directly in decisions on the local level.

In harmony with this, the Danish system attaches importance to budget responsibility at the local level. Local politicians cannot – unless in some extreme situation – pass responsibility for budgetary failures on to central government, but will be accountable for the budget to the local citizen/elector via the local effects of the budget and via the tax rates (see the section below). Consequently, there is no system of budgetary approval from "higher" levels of the public sector, but instead general rules on economic management and central government supervisory councils. Moreover, there exists an obligation for local authorities to have their budgets audited by an external auditing company.

The autonomy of local governments derives from the constitution, which states in section 82: *"Kommunernes ret til under statens tilsyn selvstændigt at styre deres anliggender ordnes ved lov"* or, in English translation: *"The right of the municipalities to manage their own affairs independently under the supervision of the Central Government shall be laid down by statute"*. Those statutes or rules, already mentioned, are laid down in the Local Government Act.

From an ideological and historical viewpoint the structure of the public sector in Denmark has its background in a kind of liberalism. This liberalism has historical roots in the socio-economic system prevailing in the latter half of the 19th century, characterised by an economy with land ownership widely dispersed and a strong tradition of organising agricultural production through local co-operatives (Stanton, 1996, p. 153).

5.2.2 The Distribution of Tasks at Different Levels of Government

The assignment of expenditure responsibilities to three layers of the Danish public sector in a way also demonstrates the autonomy of the local governments. This comes from the fact that the Danish public sector is characterised by a comparatively sharp borderline between tasks carried out by, on the one hand, local governments, i.e. municipalities and counties, and on the other hand central government. Also, there is a sharp distinction, except for certain social tasks, between municipal tasks and county tasks. Finally there is a dividing line with the private sector.[1] This creates a high degree of homogeneity of the units at a certain public sector level and also - by experience - a kind of information monopoly on each level concerning how to handle "their" tasks. This hampers any intervention from other levels, such as intervention from central government in local government tasks, even if national politicians from time to time have the will to correct what they see as budgetary mistakes at the local level.

What is the institutional outline of the Danish public sector then? As already mentioned, the sector is organised in three tiers: central government, the counties and the municipalities. The administrative units on all three levels are managed by parliaments/councils elected directly by the (local) citizens. It should be noted that the counties are not administrative extensions of the central government, but possess the same kind of autonomy as the municipalities. In accordance with this fact, the municipalities and counties are sometimes referred to as *primary* and *secondary* municipalities. There are 14 counties, with an average of roughly 320,000 inhabitants, and 275 municipalities with 19,000 inhabitants on average, including the cities of Copenhagen and Frederiksberg, which are unitary authorities with responsibilities for both local and county authority tasks.

The main functions of the municipalities are local road networks, pre-schools and primary schools, children's health care, home nursing and kindergartens, social services and local cultural activities. The municipalities also organise a major set of capital-intensive services (public utilities) in the areas of energy, water, sewerage systems and waste disposal. Finally, the municipalities are responsible for a number of social security and benefit schemes.

The counties are responsible for – compared with the municipalities – more specialised tasks, typically covering a larger number of citizens. Those tasks include major highways, secondary education, hospitals and primary health care, residential care for people with disabilities and environmental protection.

This leaves police, defence, higher education, unemployment insurance and old age pension schemes as central government (including the sector of social security funds) responsibilities.

The size of the Danish public sector is – as in other Nordic countries - relatively large compared with most OECD countries. Public expenditures make up 61 per cent of GDP and around one-third of the workforce is employed here. The majority of public tasks – handled by around two-thirds of the public sector employees - are organised by local governments, as most so-called individual public consumption is offered by the local government sector. The main figures from 1999 accounts are shown in Table 5.1.

Table 5.1 *Tasks of municipalities and counties, 1999 accounts: Gross operating costs, exclusive of VAT payments*

	Counties	Copenhagen*	Municipalities	Total
Total costs (billions DKK)	83.2	39.6	190.2	313.1
Percentage of total costs:				
0. Urban development	1	3	5	4
1. Public utilities, environment, transport	2	13	7	6
2. Roads	2	1	2	2
3. Education and culture	12	9	19	16
4. Hospitals and health services	57	17	0	17
5. Social welfare**	22	48	57	46
6. Administration	5	8	10	8
Total	100	100	100	100

Notes:
* Including the municipalities of Copenhagen and Frederiksberg.
** Cash benefits, day care institutions for children, services for elderly, etc.

Source: Indenrigsministeriet, 2000b.

5.3   THE FINANCIAL SYSTEM OF THE LOCAL GOVERNMENTS

5.3.1 Main Sources of Revenue – The Principle of Self-financing

The autonomy of local governments on the expenditure side is mirrored on the revenue side. The guideline seems to be a principle of self-financing; that is, local governments, having the powers to decide the level of expenditures, must also confront the citizens directly by imposing taxes necessary for financing the outlays.

The strong emphasis on self-financing of local governments particularly appears through the use of personal income tax, which accounts for more than 90 per cent of all tax revenue.

Central government, the counties and the municipalities all tax personal incomes, but each authority is legally free to set its own tax rate. The income tax system can be characterised as a so-called piggyback system, where the central government and the national parliament have laid down the tax rate schedule, the tax base and the tax deductions, but where each unit of government can freely decide its own tax rate (or tax coefficient). This is probably the single most important factor behind characterising local governments as quite autonomous (see above).[2] This model of local government finance contrasts with the system in the majority of other European countries, where shared taxes are common.[3]

In addition to income tax revenue, local governments receive tax revenue from land taxes.[4]

Besides charges and user fees, general grants are the most important revenue source for local governments (see Table 5.2). General grants are allocated in proportion to the tax base of individual authorities, and thereby do not disturb the relative prices of various activities that the local governments engage in. Finally, local governments receive reimbursements (specific grants) for income transfers to households; that is central government reimburses a certain percentage of such local government expenditures. The policy development in Denmark for the last 20–30 years has been to move away from reimbursements, and replace them with a combination of additional user charges and with an increase in the general grants and local taxation.

Table 5.2   Finance of local government, 1999 accounts

Gross income 1999	billions DKK	%
Reimbursements	27.4	8
Charges, user fees etc.	78.9	23
Net interest	−0.5	0
Taxes	198.4	58
General grants[*]	39.1	11
Total	343.3	100

Notes:
* Including some minor discretionary specific grants.
Total gross income of 343.3 exceeds gross operating costs of 313.1 (see Table 5.1), by billions DKK 30.2, which consists of gross investment expenditures (14.3), VAT payments (11.0) and a net financial surplus for 1999 (4.9).

Source: Indenrigsministeriet, 2000b.

5.3.2 Equalisation – Supporting Self-financing

The principle of self-financing of each local authority must, to be credible to the public, be supported by an effective equalisation system. If not, economic opportunities for individual authorities would be very uneven, making it unrealistic that all authorities could operate with a minimum of intervention from central government. At least, that has been the philosophy of the Danish local government system for a number of years.

The equalisation transfers mainly take place between local authorities, with central government having the role mediator. The equalisation system consists of two mechanisms: one for equalisation of differences in the tax base and one for equalisation of differences in expenditure needs. Both have at their heart the "zero sum" or "Robin Hood" principle of equalisation, namely that equalisation is achieved by taking resources from richer authorities and giving them to poorer authorities. Thus in large part central funds are not needed and the impact on the central government budget is broadly neutral.

The mechanism to achieve equalisation of differences in tax bases is the more straightforward part of the system. The tax bases consist of total taxable personal incomes and a percentage of taxable land values. The tax bases are measured on a per capita basis for each jurisdiction, then compared to the average tax base per capita for the whole country, and finally the differences measured in tax values are equalised with a certain equalisation level. The magnitude of the equalisation level, which is decided by parliament, ranges from 45 per cent to 85 per cent depending on the scheme.

The method of equalising differences in "expenditure needs" is more complex, although it resembles equalising tax bases by comparing figures for the individual jurisdictions with a national average, and then equalising part of the differences (also here with an equalisation level between 45 and 85 per cent). To measure the expenditure needs the Ministry of the Interior collect information from municipalities and counties on demographic and socio-economic factors – so-called objective criteria. The values of those criteria are weighted together for each local government to constitute a measure of the expenditure needs; that is, a measure of the expenditures the local government would have to incur to provide its citizens with services in amounts and standards equal to the national average.[5]

The general grants and equalisation system is formula driven, which underlines the financial responsibility of the local governments, and the sizes of those revenues are communicated to the local authorities in advance of their budgetary decisions for the coming year. Except for some special grants of limited size, which central government can pay out on a discretionary basis, local governments therefore normally have to solve their economic challenges and problems within those given economic conditions, but can use the tax rate as a "buffer". Local governments are allowed to build rainy-day funds – positive cash balances – which can also serve as financial buffers. Using borrowing to smooth economic conditions is, however, restricted (see section 5.4.2 below).

In all circumstances, local governments have by law to *balance the budget*. This is, however, close to a tautology since it just means that total expenditures have to be explicitly financed in the budget; that is, first and foremost by taxes or other revenue sources or – possibly – by a specified reduction of cash balances/rainy-day funds. Local governments are consequently not allowed to settle a budget which includes unspecified items as "savings".

5.4   THE BORROWING REGULATIONS OF THE LOCAL GOVERNMENTS

5.4.1 Background and Main Rule

Since local independence and autonomy is stressed in the Danish model of the public sector, it could be expected that local governments would also have the power to choose between debt financing and current financing of activities. That is not the case, however. Actually, as a main rule, every local authority has to finance its activities, both operating costs, investments and debt service, by way of current revenues and not by loans.[6] Three main factors or explanations for the existence of this main rule can be presented.

First, the rule of current financing can be interpreted partly as a means of underlining the *financial responsibilities to the local citizens* of the local government council for their decisions on investments expenditures.[7] In other words, by demanding that local governments must abstain from using loans, the taxpayers will be confronted more directly, compared with the situation where the financial consequences of, for example, investment decisions could be postponed to the local politicians of the future and the future citizens. The purpose should be to avoid investments that prove to be too costly compared with the benefits derived from them.

The rationale behind this reasoning is that politicians and/or citizens are *myopic* – or short-sighted; that is, there is a risk that the financial consequences of investment decisions for future generations would not be taken sufficiently into account by today's politicians if investments could be financed by borrowing.[8] Those consequences consist primarily of future debt service on the investment. But, moreover, increased operating costs of new or enlarged activities can often be derived from investments, for example the subsidies for running a municipal museum after having erected the house for exhibitions. The arguments here can obviously be questioned, however. Wouldn't it be more in harmony with having a widely decentralised public sector with autonomous local governments, to assure a close connection between what the citizens get and what they pay for from investments, that is, allowing for financing investments by loans being amortised in tandem with physical depreciation? Also, by demanding current financing of investments there is a risk that citizens moving from one jurisdiction to another could be "trapped", because they cannot bring with them the investments made in their former home community, although they already have financed them via taxes. It is only if the local governments' investments are capitalised in land values – which among other things demands a high level of information among the citizens – that the risk of such traps would be trivial.

Second, local autonomy for the major part of public sector expenditures demands some co-ordination of impact on the national economy of local decisions. Especially, the impact of investment decisions on the activity level of the building and construction sector, often being a forerunner of the business cycle, is important to the national economy. Tightening or loosening the restrictions on local governments' borrowing can here be used as a *tool of macroeconomic policy* by central government, which is made specific as a part of the annual agreements between central government and the organisations of local governments (see section 5.5 below).[9] Other instruments of macroeconomic policy involving the local government sector are available and potentially more powerful, such as regulating the size of block grants for local governments. However, regulating borrowing is less complicated – and a lot faster to implement – than reducing block grants since it does not require approval from parliament.

As a kind of side-benefit, central government also gets the opportunity to stimulate certain kind of investments (see examples below) by relieving the borrowing restrictions for those investments. This, however, weakens the use of borrowing regulations in macroeconomic policy.

Third, borrowing restrictions help in *reducing the financial risks*, which will be connected with extended decentralisation. There is a potential risk that, if every local government could freely raise loans to finance investments and maybe even current expenditures, some would run into a financial crisis and would have to pay back excessive loans by increasing taxes. Even though local income tax is a robust and sustainable tax source, the sustainability has its limits. This is partly because taxpayers can move to other, more well-off localities if the tax rate gets so high that they find it unacceptable or unfair. In this situation, central government would probably have to make some, presumably costly, financial interventions to help solve the local financial problems. Borrowing restrictions, however, can prevent or reduce this kind of risk to the local taxpayers and, ultimately the risk – or what could also be called the negative externality of local government decisions – to central government.[10]

5.4.2 The Regulations and the Budget Balance Rule Revisited

As already mentioned the *main rule* for local governments is the following: no access to borrowing for local governments – municipalities as well as counties. This is expressed in an indirect way in the Local Government Act, which authorises the Minister of the Interior to regulate borrowing by local governments.

Borrowing includes both short-term and long-term borrowing, and also financial arrangements with strong similarities to borrowing, such as renting and leasing arrangements (discussed in more detail in section 5.7 below).

However, there are important *exceptions* to this main rule. For counties, long-term borrowing within 25 per cent of the total net outlays for investments for the fiscal year is accepted. That is, however, the only exception to the rule of current financing concerning counties. For municipalities, central government sanctions long term borrowings under two headings: automatic and non-automatic (discretionary) permissions.[11]

The municipalities have so-called *automatic permission* to raise loans for investments in two areas: public utilities and investments which have been given a special political priority.

The municipalities in Denmark own utilities in a number of fields usually run by inter-authority companies: the distribution of electricity, district heating, water/sewerage systems, and so on. The investments of those utilities can be debt-financed by local governments for two reasons. First, those public utilities are wholly user-financed by charges and user fees. This means that for a single year but not in the longer run user fees and charges can deviate from cost, implying that the debt in the long run will be fully redeemed by user payments. In other words, there should be no risk to the taxpayer as such. Second, the investments usually are relatively high compared with current revenues, which means that the user payments would vary dramatically from year to year if investments had to be financed within the current year.

The municipalities also have automatic permission to borrow for investments in certain areas, some of which are given a high political priority; for example, sheltered accommodation for the elderly, energy conservation measures, conservation of buildings, purchasing of land for planning and development purposes. By allowing borrowing for those purposes, central government actually can stimulate those investments.

Furthermore, the Ministry of the Interior grants municipalities *discretionary permissions* to borrow. In practice, the central government announces annually a ceiling on the aggregate value of such discretionary approvals. The aggregate value is explicitly treated as an instrument of macroeconomic policy. This policy is part of the framework of the government's annual budgetary co-operation agreements with local authorities' associations, which is explained more in the next section. Table 5.3 shows the annual variations of the size of the ceiling. Usually, the smallest municipalities are given special attention when applying for a loan sanction, since it generally is more difficult for them in comparison with the bigger authorities to even out investment projects between the years and thereby avoid inappropriate swings in the yearly tax rate. The Ministry of the Interior does not usually examine the economy of the applying municipality in depth, except to establish that it is "needy" and does not have an abnormally high level of debt, that is, not higher than 30 per cent of the total gross outlays. The municipality also has to specify the project the borrowing is intended to finance, since certain investment purposes usually are given priority (e.g. schools in year 2000), but the Ministry does not monitor afterwards how the project is actually carried out.

Table 5.3   *Discretionary permissions for loans, municipalities, annual maxima: annual real growth of GDP*

Year	Pool – annual maxima of loans, bn. DKK	Real GDP growth (%)
1990	150	1.0
1991	400	1.1
1992	750	0.6
1993	2 550	0.0
1994	2 700	5.5
1995	700	2.8
1996	300	2.5
1997	1 300	3.1
1998	700	2.5
1999	500	1.6
2000	1 100	–

Source: Data from the Ministry of the Interior and the Danish Bureau of Statistics.

Besides, it should be mentioned that if the local government has permission to raise a loan there are relatively few restrictions on the kinds of borrowing instruments that the local governments can use. Most important, new loans have to mature within 25 years at the latest (15 years for bullet loans). There exists no requirement for a annual, minimum debt repayment, and there are also no restrictions about the currency in which the loans should be denominated.

As far as short-term debt is concerned, local authorities are free to use this financial instrument in the daily management of cash balances, provided that the annual average (computed for the latest 365 days) of cash balances net of short term loans is positive. This is the so-called *"kassekredit-regel" (overdraft facility rule)*. It allows, as can be seen, the authority to draw on its overdraft facilities in periods with high demands on the liquidity, such as when the authority pays wages to its employees. But this has to be balanced out with periods of surplus payments *to* the authority, for example when tax incomes and general grants are received from central government.

A violation of this *overdraft facility rule* is considered as a rather serious matter and the Ministry of the Interior intervenes, demanding specific provisions to be taken by the local government concerned. Those provisions consist of establishing a plan for economic restoration of the local government economy – with special attention to the cash balances. The restoration must be made within a shorter period (usually three years), by use of saving measures and possibly limited and/or temporary tax increases. If the local government does not meet those obligations it acts illegally.

Finally, the *rule of balancing the budget* of Danish local governments can now be restated: a local authority has, as the main rule, to balance the budget each year. This implies that both current and investment expenditures have to be financed by current revenues, so not by loans, unless the local government has accumulated cash balances (rainy-day funds) from former years to be used now. There are some exceptions, however, for long-term loan financing of local government investments in certain areas (e.g. municipally owned utilities) or when the local government has a special borrowing permission. Also, the local government can use short-term loans as an instrument of financing daily swings of payments, but only as long as the average cash balances exceed the short-term debt.

5.4.3 The Implications of the Borrowing Regulations

On the practical implications of the borrowing regulations, it can be noted that local governments do come into conflict with the overdraft facility rule. Usually – based on the experiences from the last ten years – there are one to four authorities in a "restoration situation" at any given point of time. Until now, every local authority in this situation has managed to rebuild its liquidity reserves within the restoration period, however, in some cases they have needed the help of transfers and provisional loan sanctions from the Ministry of the Interior.

The relatively restrictive regulations of local borrowing should also imply certain outcomes concerning the debt levels of local governments, the fraction of investments financed by loans, and so on. Those statistical matters will be dealt with in section 5.6. The next section will explain the system of annual negotiations between central government and local governments since this system has some implications for the size of the discretionary approvals for raising loans.

5.5 MACROECONOMIC CONTROL VIA NEGOTIATIONS

One of the important reasons for restricting and controlling debt financing of local governments in Denmark is as a means of implementing macroeconomic policy, as has already been described. To be able to understand how this works in practice, it is necessary to look at the Danish system of negotiations/consultations between central government and local governments, since borrowing restrictions are regularly among the items negotiated.

The system of annual negotiations and annual agreements between central government and the organisations of local governments has been a well-established institution in Danish economic policy for nearly 30 years. Such negotiations are also known in other Nordic countries, the Netherlands and the UK, but, it seems, with more limited economic significance than in Denmark.[12] Probably, an important necessary condition behind the Danish system of negotiations is the fairly clear-cut distribution of tasks between the tiers. This division of tasks makes it possible for only two local government organisations to be able to negotiate on behalf of their (in respect of tasks and responsibilities) relatively homogeneous members: the municipalities and the counties.[13] On the other hand, the economic importance of local governments creates the need for co-ordination within the public sector, as already described, and preferably in a way that preserves the autonomy of the single governmental units. Here, agreements aiming at the average behaviour of the local governments but still allowing single units to deviate, have been useful.

The negotiations take place every late spring/early summer between government ministers, notably the ministers of finance, of interior affairs and of economic affairs, and a few elected local government politicians from the organisations. The meetings are prepared by civil servants, who thoroughly calculate the economic scenarios for the coming budgetary year, the fiscal stance, and so on. Normally, the negotiations are concluded by an agreement between the parties. The agreement usually includes a number of items, ranging from declarations of intent about, for example, waiting lists for hospitals, to the average size of the local governments tax rates. Also, the agreements normally include the size of the block grants for the next year and the size of the borrowing opportunities; that is, the ceiling on the aggregate value of the discretionary approvals for raising loans that the central government intends to give. The agreement is not legally binding to either members of the local government organisations or the central government. However, the members of the organisations (i.e. the single municipalities and counties) are expected to be loyal to the agreement since they have authorised their representatives to negotiate on their behalf. Furthermore, the municipalities and counties must face the risk of some sort of financial punishment if they *on average* depart from the agreement. The risk of punishment is usually, however, only modest and will, due to experiences, very seldom be individualised to the single local government, but will instead be implemented on a collective basis (e.g. via reduction of block grants). Central government, for its part, has the job of getting the agreed size of block grant approved by parliament. The size of the borrowing, however, does not have to be approved by parliament, as already mentioned.

As explained, the size of the ceiling of borrowing opportunities is negotiated, but the outcome of the negotiations on this item is not always easy to estimate in advance. The reason for this is that the preferences of the negotiating parties are often unclear or mixed. First, it could be expected that central government would always try to keep the approvals for loans as low as possible to reduce the public debt. However, taking into account that the agreed outlays have to be financed in one way or another, fixing a low ceiling for borrowing could be at the cost of a higher block grant if central government at the same time wants to avoid tax increases. Seen from a central government fiscal point of view, block grants appear more costly than loan approvals, since block grants increase the deficit (or reduce the surplus) of the central government's own budget. On the other hand, the motivation of the local governments' organisations is the opposite, since they will – everything being equal – prefer block grants to loans which restrict the economic room for manoeuvre in the future. Finally, central government has to take into account the fiscal stance of the total public budget for the next year.

As could be seen from Table 5.3 above, the size of the ceiling varies from year to year. The size has some connection with the business cycle. For instance the ceiling was increased in 1993 and 1994, which was part of the so-called "kick-start" of the Danish economy hampered by high levels of unemployment and slow growth of GDP in the early 1990s. When the GDP growth increased markedly in the mid-1990s the ceilings were reduced.

It can be mentioned that the agreement for the year 1999 included a relatively low ceiling. At the same time the conditions for new loans raised by local governments were restricted somewhat. The background for this was, at least partly, central government's priority of reducing the so-called EMU debt, that is, the total public sector debt calculated by EMU definitions for the Maastricht criteria. The objective of central government was to reduce the EMU debt from 65.1 per cent of GDP in 1997 to around 40 per cent in 2005. If the debt of the local government, as an example, was fixed at the absolute level of debt in 1997, it would be reduced from 4.1 per cent of GDP in 1997 to 2.5 per cent in 2005, and thereby contribute to the 2005 objective for the total public sector.

5.6 SOME STATISTICS: LOCAL GOVERNMENT BORROWING AND DEBT LEVELS

The main rule of current financing is mirrored in the low level of debt of local governments. The debt amounted to around 54 billion Dkr (around 7 billion euro) at the end of 1998. This compared with the debt of central government of 650 billion Dkr. As can be seen from Figure 5.1 the long-term debt measured against the tax base is about 10 per cent – or about 4.5 per cent measured against GDP, with central government debt amounting to 56 per cent of GDP. Furthermore, around 1/5 of this can be identified as debt of public utilities owned by the local government. Finally, the debt has been stagnating and falling in relative terms against the tax base for the latest years.

The main rule of no borrowing also explains why a part of local governments' investments is financed, not by loans but by taxes or other current revenues (see Figure 5.3). Actually, the figures for several years (1993–1994 and 1996–1998) exaggerate the importance of debt financing investments to a considerable extent, since an important part of the loans raised in those years – years characterised by a falling interest level – concerns restructuring of debt. Unfortunately, the data do not allow a correction for this.

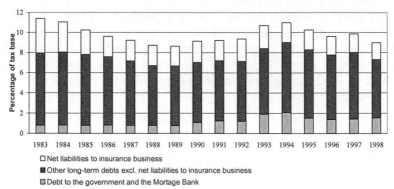

Source: Local governments' accounts.

Figure 5.1   Long-term debt of local governments, percentage of tax base, 1983–1998

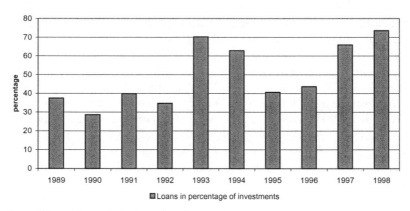

Note: * Borrowing excludes loans from the central government.

Source: Local governments' accounts.

Figure 5.2   Loans raised by governments, percentage of investments, 1989–1998*

Figure 5.2 illustrates, on the other hand, that although current financing is the starting point for local governments when financing investment, this does not in practice means that debt financing is ruled out. As explained above in section 5.4.2, the Ministry of the Interior grants discretionary permissions for raising loans as an instrument of macroeconomic policy, aiming at controlling the local governments' investment level and – ultimately – the level of building activity. In this respect it is of interest if this instrument is actually effective. Figure 5.3 seems to confirm this, since there is a significant correlation between the level of investments of local governments and the extent of raising loans.

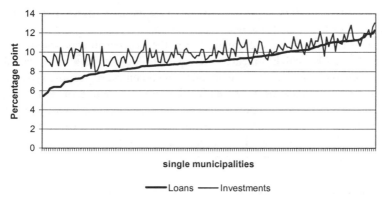

Source: Local governments' accounts.

Figure 5.3   Investments versus loans, individual municipalities, 1995

5.7   POLICY DISCUSSION

The way of regulation borrowing of local governments in Denmark has come under some pressure at the start of the new century. Two problems have arisen, which will be discussed below.

5.7.1 Implications of Lack of Savings

Seen over ten to 20 years the liquidity reserves, including bonds and similar financial assets, of Danish local governments have been falling. Most of the municipalities and counties seem to have tailored the cash reserves to the need for liquidity for transaction purposes and to meet the precautionary motivated need for reserves for extraordinary situations. In this connection, local governments have to take into account that they must at any time of the year, observe the overdraft facility rule (see section 5.4.2 above). However, they have not, as a general rule at least, made financial savings to meet future needs for investments. Although no thorough investigation of this has been made, it seems that the behaviour of local governments has changed here.

This change of behaviour could – maybe – also be seen as a result of central government's attempts at keeping surplus liquidity down as part of the macroeconomic control, such as in the booming economy in the mid-1980s. Whatever the cause, however, it is a fact that financial savings cannot generally be relied on as a mean of financing investments. This implies that if the need for investments rises significantly from one year to another it will require either tax increases or increased block grants from central government or – if those options are not acceptable – more borrowing opportunities for local governments.

The actual background is a dramatic rise in the number of school children from the late 1990s, which, together with the run-down condition of school buildings, demands significant investments. Since central government wants to avoid tax increases and/or increased block grants, loosening of borrowing regulations seems to be the outcome, also because the need for investments is very unevenly distributed among the municipalities. This will mean – and has already meant for 2001 – a significant weakening of the main rule of current financing of local government investment.

5.7.2 Implications of Sale-and-lease-back Arrangements

Another kind of threat to the borrowing restrictions is *sale-and-lease-back* of local governments' buildings – institutions, schools, office-building, and so on – which has become widespread in the last years. Since sale-and-lease-back at first implies a way of converting fixed tangible assets into liquidity reserves it also involves a risk of local governments avoiding the borrowing regulations. The response to that risk from central government initially was to extend the regulations to take into account those situations by putting local governments under the obligation to, for example, deposit the liquidity in a bank account for a minimum of ten years.

However, it has proven that liquidity consequences are not the only controversial financial aspect of sale-and-lease-back or similar arrangements. Thus it has emerged that, in spite of the restrictions on the use of liquidity from those arrangements, some local governments still see a possibility of making a profit from financial sale-and-lease-back. The potential of profits stems from the possibility of depositing the revenues in long-term bonds and making an agreement with the leasing company based on short-term financing, for example a sort of arbitrage between long- and short-term loans. This arbitrage is illustrated by the appearance of the *rent curve*. As can be seen from Figure 5.4 the short term rent is normally somewhat lower than the long-term rent. However, this phenomenon is, of course, connected to the *risk premium* on long-term investments versus short-term investments. Similarly, local governments engaging in these kinds of arrangements expose themselves to a risk, which in the end can be at the risk of the local taxpayers or ultimately central government (in other words, all taxpayers). To handle those consequences as well, central government has recently decided to make a prohibition against local governments' use of sale-and-lease-back, unless central government itself grants an exemption.[14]

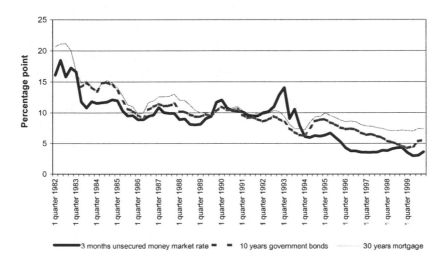

Source: Indenrigsministeriet, 2000b.

Figure 5.4   Danish interest rates, 1st quarter 1982 – 4th quarter 1999

5.8   CONCLUSION

The Danish borrowing regulations for local governments take as their starting-point "no borrowing". This must be seen against the background of several factors. First, the autonomy of Danish local governments has as its counterpart local responsibility for the actual taxpayers – a responsibility, which should not be eroded by postponing the financial burden to future generations of taxpayers. Second, the access to local income taxes as a sustainable income source, combined with a rather sophisticated equalisation system provides local governments with a considerable degree of economic freedom, which – in ordinary circumstances – helps to keep the financial need for borrowing down. Third, this economic freedom, however, also creates a demand for central government to be able to carry out some macroeconomic control by regulating borrowing of the local government sector, also against the background of the Maastricht criteria. These regulations also fulfil the purpose of avoiding the situation where municipalities put themselves into an untenable position by exposing themselves financially.

The borrowing regulations do not, on the other hand, totally rule out debt financing of local governments. Thus some areas of investments are excluded from the restrictions, for example investments in public utilities owned by local governments. Moreover, central government grants discretionary permissions for loans, which in practice softens the tight general restrictions. This element of the system of borrowing regulations also has to be seen in connection with the Danish system of yearly negotiations between central government and the local governments' organisations, where discretionary loans often facilitate agreement.

It is not very surprising that, in figures, Danish local governments have rather low levels of debt, and local investments are only partly financed by borrowing. Or – in other words – local governments usually run an operating surplus and are able to, at least partly, finance their investments.

However, the Danish way of regulating borrowing also has its problems. First, using tight financial conditions as a way of securing macroeconomic control probably does not encourage saving for future investment purposes, and therefore in itself creates a need for loosening borrowing restrictions if investment needs rise above usual levels. Second, local governments searching for other ways of financing investments and engaging in financial arrangements for making profits (e.g. via sale-and-lease-back arrangements) demand that the regulations are constantly under supervision to ensure they are able to handle those situations without creating distortions against "ordinary" borrowing. Finally, it can of course be questioned whether it is in harmony with local governments' autonomy and accountability to intervene in local inter-temporal decision-making by restricting borrowing.

NOTES

1. Contracting out has become more widespread in Danish local governments, which has dimmed the borderline somewhat here. The political responsibility is, however, still ruling. For discussion of contracting out in Danish Municipalities see Christoffersen and Paldam, 1998.
2. Central government has some influence on the average tax level of the local governments via yearly negotiations with local governments' organisations (see section 5.5). Agreements between central government and organisations of local governments are, however, not legally binding, and therefore do not impose any formal restrictions on the single local governments. There is also no formal minimum or maximum level for local

income tax rates, which vary among the municipalities by around 30 per cent and among counties by around 10 per cent.

3. See Lotz and Mochida, 1999.
4. For the land tax there is by law a fixed minimum and maximum tax level, 1.6 and 3.4 respectively. See note 5 above about local income tax levels.
5. See Council of Europe, 1993. For a discussion of objectivity and expenditure needs criteria see Kabelmann and Mau Pedersen, 1999.
6. Mentioning debt service, i.e. interest and amortisation, indicates on the other hand that this main rule is not – and has not been – without its exceptions, which we will return to in section 5.4.2.
7. When the rule of "no-borrowing" was established in the late 1970s and 1980s it was referred to as "rules of self-financing". (see Indenrigsministeriet, 1989). This is, however, another meaning of "self-financing" than the one used above, in section 5.3.1, since there it concerned the character of the revenue source as autonomous from the point of view of local government (c.g. own taxes) and not the intertemporal choice of financing.
8. Studies on Danish municipalities indicate that politicians – but not the electors – show a degree of myopia when it comes to creating political cycles, see Mouritzen, 1991, ch. 16.
9. Actually, this has been the most often mentioned official reason behind the borrowing regulations of local governments in Denmark, see Indenrigsministeriet, 1998.
10. It should be noted here that the Danish equalisation system does not equalise for differences in financial burdens between local authorities.
11. See Stanton, 1996, pp. 167f.
12. See Blom-Hansen, 1998, which compares the system of managing the economy of local governments in the Nordic countries.
13. See Mau Pedersen, 1998.
14. Recommended by a committee including representatives from both the Central Government and local governments' associations (see Indenrigsministeriet, 2000a).

REFERENCES

Blom-Hansen N. (1998) "Studier i statens styring af den kommunale sektors økonomi" (Studies in Central Control of the Economy of Local Governments). Final report from a Ph D project, University of Aarhus.

Christoffersen, H. and M. Paldam (1998), "Market and Municipalities. A study of the behaviour of the Danish Municipalities". Memo 1998-3. Department of Economics: University of Aarhus.

Council of Europe (1993), "Equalisation of resources between local authorities". Recommendation No. R (91) 4. Strasbourg.

Indenrigsministeriet (1989), "Aftaler og henstillinger vedr. den kommunale økonomi i 1980'rne" (Agreements and recommendations about the economy of the local governments in the 1980s). Copenhagen.

Indenrigsministeriet (1998), "Den kommunale låntagning" (Borrowing of local governments). Report from a committee appointed by the Government. Copenhagen.

Indenrigsministeriet (2000a), "Den kommunale låntagning og deponeringsreglerne" (Borrowing of local governments and rules about depositing liquidity from borrowing). Report from a committee appointed by the Government. Copenhagen.

Indenrigsministeriet (2000b), *Det kommunale regnskab – 1999 (Local Governments' Accounts – 1999)*. Copenhagen.

Kabelmann, T. and N.J. Mau Pedersen (1999), "Measuring social expenditure needs and equalization – is it possible to be obejctive?" The case of Denmark. Paper for the IIPF Congress, Moscow.

Lotz, J. and N. Mochida (1999), "Fiscal Federalism in Practice, the Nordic Countries and Japan", *The Journal of Economics*, Vol. 64, No. 4.

Mau Pedersen, N.J. (1998), "Aftalesystemet mellem staten og kommunerne – opgaver og udfordringer" (The system of negotiating between the central government and the local governments – task and challenges), in Indenrigsministeriet – 1848–1998. Copenhagen.

Mouritzen, P.E. (1991), *Den politiske cyklus (The Political Cycle)*. Politica. Odense.

Stanton, R. (1996), *Funding the Fabric: Access to Capital for Local Services*. London Research Centre. London.

Söderström, L. (1998), "Fiscal Federalism: The Nordic Way", in J. Rattsø, *Fiscal Federalism and State-Local Finance – the Scandinavian Perspective*. Edward Elgar, Cheltenham.

6. The public debt of local governments in France

Guy Gilbert and Alain Guengant

6.1 INTRODUCTION

Since the 1982 Decentralisation Bills, the French lower tiers of governments (36,000 *communes* at the local level, 100 *départements* and 22 *régions* at the intermediate level) have a quasi-totally free access to the financial markets. Neither ex ante nor ex post controls of the central state remain: the only exception is that the borrowings must be exclusively earmarked to capital expenditures. The volume, the interest rate, the duration of the borrowings, and the identity of the lender can be freely chosen by local authorities. The banks receive aggregate demands for borrowings from the local entities, all investment projects are taken together instead of separate demands for each project. Thus the borrowings are considered by the local authorities as a global (i.e. non-earmarked) revenue source for the investment projects.

The loans supplied by the banks cover almost entirely the needed capital requirements (circa 70 billion FF, net of debt restructuring operations). Consequently, the local governments rely relatively less on bond finance (circa 5 billion FF for 1997). Bond finance to the local governments appears more expensive and less flexible than loan finance. The greater reliance on intermediate finance results from the high degree of competition in interest rates and other credit conditions prevailing in the market.

In the market for loans, the Crédit Local de France, a private bank, has a leading position (overall 40%); the Crédit Agricole and the Caisses d'Epargne are among the main followers.

The liberty given to the local governments in these matters has a legal counterpart: they have to balance their accounts. This "balance constraint" aims both at ensuring for the lenders that the debt repayments will be made in due time, and at protecting the local authorities against the risk of over-indebtedness. As it is the case for other tiers of government in France, the law protects the local authorities from the risk of bankruptcy. The effective degree of risk is therefore rather low for the lenders to the local public entities. But it is no longer nil. Thus since the beginning of the 1980s, the banks have relied more and more on various techniques of financial diagnosis in order to avoid potential risks. Even if the degree of legal protection is high, asymmetries of information remain in this sector. The fine-tuning of risk management is required in order to detect, behind the official reports, the actual fiscal health and the actual degree of fiscal sustainability of the local authorities.

The local representative of the central state checks every year that local decisions are in accordance with the legal requirements. If not, it transmits the case to the CRC (Chambre Régionale des Comptes) which proceeds to an audit. The auditing procedure bears on both provisional accounts (*budget primitif*) and actual accounts (*compte administratif*).

Section 6.2 of the chapter defines the concept of balance of annual accounts and describes the controls exerted by the central state and the financial courts (CRC). It is thus shown how the balance in accounts requirement directly influences the need for local public saving, in addition to the savings needed for depreciation compensation. Section 6.3 deals with the basic failures of legal protection against over-indebtedness of local authorities. These legal rules do not efficiently guarantee the future solvency of local governments. The auditing procedure is shown to be strongly biased. However, as it is shown in section 6.4, the present state of finances of French local governments is satisfactory on average. The level of indebtedness is globally sustainable and efficiently managed, even if there are some exceptions. Section 6.5 is devoted to the future of local public finances in France in the Maastricht Treaty perspective. Some concluding comments are provided in section 6.6.

6.2   AUDIT AND CONTROL ON THE BALANCE OF ANNUAL LOCAL ACCOUNTS

The concept of an annual balance in the accounts of local governments might appear easy to define. It would be so in the absence of borrowing. The balance between the annual outlays and the annual incomes would thus provide a necessary and sufficient condition for the public budget to be balanced in a static way. In the case where local governments are net borrowers, the static rule of balance in accounts provides only an accounting equilibrium. Even if the expenses for debt repayment and for interest were taken into account, it would not ensure that a financial equilibrium is reached and a posteriori an economic equilibrium. More precisely in the latter case, the budget constraint might take into account the intertemporal flows of money induced by the borrowings. The static rule of balance in accounts must move to a dynamic one. The auditing procedure must be suited to these new requirements.

6.2.1 The "Ex Ante Balance in Accounts" Rule

For the sake of auditing, the concept of actual balance in accounts *équilibre réel du budget* is written down by law (Art. L 1612;4 du CGCT (Code Général des Collectivités Locales)) (Guengant, 1998).
The accounts are "substantially balanced"

> *lorsque la section de fonctionnement et la section d'investissement sont respectivement votées en équilibre, les recettes et les dépenses ayant été évaluées de façon sincère, et lorsque le prélèvement sur les recettes de la section de fonctionnement au profit de la section d'investissement, ajouté aux recettes propres de cette section, à l'exclusion du produit des emprunts, et éventuellement aux dotations des comptes d'amortissements et de provisions, fournit des ressources suffisantes pour couvrir le remboursement en capital des annuités d'emprunt à échoir au cours de l'exercice.*

More precisely, the legal definition of the "balance in current accounts" refers to the structure of the local accounts that are separated into two parts; the "current operations budget" and the budget for "capital operations". The interests paid are imputed to the former budget, but the reimbursement of the capital borrowed is imputed to the latter. The legal definition states that the surplus of current incomes (increased with some – limitatively defined – receipts in capital) is sufficient enough to reimburse the debt in capital over the annual period to come. The gross savings ("épargne brute") defined by the French legislation strictly correspond to Swiss legislation (SEC 95) concepts of cash flow or gross savings. The French concept of "current savings" ("épargne de gestion") is equal to the sum of the gross savings and of the interests: it corresponds to the "primary result" (SEC 95). The "net savings" ("épargne nette") or self-financing capacity, is defined as the difference between the gross savings and the reimbursement in capital of the borrowings; it exactly coincides with the equivalent concept in the Swiss legislation. Using these concepts, the legal rule of "balance in accounts" reduces to the following requirement; gross savings plus some additional incomes from the locally owned capital must be at least equal to the reimbursement in capital of the borrowings. Adding interest to the two sides of the constraint above, this is equivalent to saying that the primary result plus the incomes of the locally owned capital must be at least equal to the annual repayments of the borrowings (interest plus capital).

The only difference from the Swiss rules of public accounting lies with the location of the capital repayments on debt. They are located in the current budget in Switzerland, in the budget for capital operations in France. Thus, ceteris paribus, the balance in current accounts in France is more positive than the Swiss ought to be. The depreciation of capital equipment is limited in France to renewable equipment (motor vehicles for example). The allowance for depreciation of capital equipment added to the financial result of the current year equals the gross savings. These savings are devoted in priority to the annual reimbursement in capital of the borrowings. The depreciation of capital equipment helps to finance the financial depreciation of the debt. The two types of depreciation (the physical one and the financial one) are not cumulative. In other words, the equilibrium requirement is designed to secure debt repayment by local governments. The surplus of current incomes over current expenditures plus the incomes in capital (borrowings excluded) plus occasionally the amount of depreciation allowances, is sufficient enough to cover the pay off of the debt over the current year. If it is not so, the law (art. L 1612.5 CGCT)[1] makes it compulsory to the local assembly to restore in less than one month a substantial equilibrium by an increase in the incomes and/or a cut in the expenses.

More precisely, the content of the legal constraint on a "substantial balance in accounts" is twofold. The first part is a purely accounting rule of balance in accounts. The second consists of two restrictions in the use of borrowings. The first of these derives from the legal rule of balance in the current operations. The use of income from borrowings is not allowed to finance a deficit in the current budget. The second makes it compulsory for the local authority to save yearly as much as necessary to fully pay off the debt in capital as it is stated by the loan contract. This makes it impossible for the local government to use the income from borrowings to finance debt repayments associated with former borrowings: the "new" borrowings (i.e. those appearing in the current year) are thus strictly earmarked for the financing of new investment expenses. This prevents the development of a "snowball" effect. This entails two consequences. First, the current balance in accounts of local governments needs to be positive in order to finance the debt repayment. Second, the income from borrowings is totally earmarked to cover investment outlays. Apparently, the local governments adjust the duration of their loans with the (long) duration of life of the public infrastructures they provide to the citizen. The duration ranges from two to 30 years, with a majority around 10-15 years. More precisely, the time horizon of debt repayment is globally disconnected from the period of time the present capital equipment can be used. The time horizon of the debt repayments results from the schedule written in the loan contract. There is no link between the two time horizons that result from quite different perspectives. The legal constraint on the balance of the current accounts deals only with the (annual) balance between the annual aggregate savings and the annual aggregate reimbursement of the capital borrowed. This is basically a short-term requirement that does not necessarily coincide with the economic perspective of the physical depreciation of the public capital equipment. The use of appropriate financial tools only partially corrects this bias, which gives only partial information between the two time horizons. Consequently, the accounting rule of balance in local public accounts used in France is only defined on the (contractual) horizon of the debt amortisation. It by no means refers to the physical depreciation of the public capital stock.

6.2.2 The Rule of *Ex Post* Balance in Accounts

At the end of the fiscal year, the executed budget is controlled by the CRC. If a deficit appears, which amounts to more than 5% or 10% of the current incomes (depending on the number of the population in the jurisdiction), the Regional Chamber of Accounts have to propose appropriate fiscal measures to the relevant local government.[2]

Under some reasonable assumptions, the surplus – positive or negative – at the end of the fiscal year equals the cash balance ("fonds de roulement") at the end of the year. This surplus thus summarises the fiscal surplus of the current fiscal year and those of the preceding ones. In this case, the deficit which corresponds to the legal definition of Art. 1612-14 is equivalent to a negative cash balance. Conversely, a decrease in the cash balance during the fiscal year does not necessarily lead to a deficit, insofar as the *cash balance* at the end of the fiscal year remains positive. A local authority could thus use its disposable incomes without any fear of facing a deficit. The control of the ex post annual accounts aims simply at preventing an excessive deficit of the *cash balance*. Two factors could increase this deficit. First, it could be that the short-term debts (expenses already registered but not yet paid) exceed in value the short-term credits (for incomes already registered but not yet received). This does not mean there is a structural deficit in the local finances. Second, and more frequently, a negative cash balance signals short-term difficulties in cash income due to a late mobilisation of financial resources with respect to the accounting of the expenses. De facto, local governments are allowed to borrow in order to finance the variations of their *"fonds de roulement"* within a given fiscal year. The permanent access to short-term cash facilities from the banks allows minimising the value of cash without any risk.

As the local governments have to deposit their disposable incomes to the Treasury free of any interest, they are induced to minimise their cash income.

The largest ones achieve this goal rather easily, as they are sure to prevent any incident while mobilising short-term credit facilities from the banking sector. However, the short-term loans must be fully reimbursed before the end of the fiscal year, or consolidated through medium term loans.

Thus, the control of the "actual equilibrium accounting rule" applies only to the level of the *fonds de roulement* and not to its variations over the fiscal year. This procedure raises several questions. It rests basically on the accuracy of the reported accounts. Manipulations are possible if the local authority knows precisely how it could raise money from additional short-term credits; in that case, the true value of the "short-term incomes to receive" before the end of the fiscal year must be questioned, and consequently the authenticity of the overall balance at the end of the year. However, a recent bill (22 June 1994) which gives the local representative of the central government the right to audit the accuracy of the local accounts has cancelled this possibility of cheating.

6.3   FISCAL SUSTAINABILITY OF THE LOCAL GOVERNMENTS

Management of the local investment policy varies extensively from one local authority to another. The determination of the optimal amount of expenditures in capital and borrowings results from a medium term programming procedure strongly linked with the political agenda, basically with the election horizon.

This medium-term fiscal planning exercise differs from ones that are realised in private firms. First, the exercise is global; all investment projects are considered together over the same time horizon. Second, the aim of this provisional scheme is basically financial. The criteria of the decision do not refer directly to any return on investment, economic or even social, but only to the sustainable solvability of the financed operation.

This medium-term prospective exercise of the fiscal conditions at the local level is not an easy one. The future is uncertain. Thus a risk diagnosis must be added to the prospective exercise. Before the decentralisation bills and the liberalisation of the access of local government to financial markets, the risk was limited. The ex ante controls exerted by the central state prevented any risk of insolvency. This is no longer true since the management of local debt rests exclusively on the control over the balance of accounts and, of course, the careful behaviour of the local representatives. As the legal constraints on these matters are not yet fully reliable (see above), the risk cannot be totally excluded.

In these conditions, the constraints derived from the equilibrium of the budget do not necessarily coincide with those derived from the need for solvency. They may differ in two respects. First, local governments have now control over the amount of the annual debt repayment. The controls exerted by central government, based on this figure, could be more or less bypassed. Second, the solvency constraint implies taking into consideration the financial situations of all the public or private/public entities that revolve around the same local authorities; the accounting rule based on the individual local government's budget constraint does not. The lack of fiscal consolidation thus leads to a systematic underestimation of the risk and, at least, to only a partial view of the actual fiscal and financial situation of the locality.

6.3.1 Correction of the Intertemporal Bias

As local governments can freely choose the duration and the procedure of amortisation of the loans they contract, and as central government stipulates that the amortisation of debt is financed out of the local current surplus (i.e. the gross savings), the auditing procedure is subject to an asymmetrical information context.

The legal constraint makes the ratio of debt to current surplus (which represents the time necessary to write off completely the present stock of debt with the gross savings accumulated year after year, and expected to stay for the future at that present level) to be less or at least equal to the ratio of debt to annual debt repayment, which represents the apparent duration of the remaining debt.

In reality, loans contracted by local authorities present diverse profiles of amortisation over time. So, due to the aggregation of "vintages" which represent the different loans, the apparent duration of the remaining debt is fairly unstable over time. Due to this uneven time profile, the need for annual current surplus ought to vary over time in the same proportion in order to secure the legal constraint. This could be impossible. Facing a dilemma between meeting the short-term budget constraint or the medium-term solvency one, the local authority is likely to choose the short-term constraint, at the expense of the potential budget imbalance for the future.

The correction of this bias is not straightforward. It needs first the discounting of the flows of annual debt repayment on the one hand, and the discounting of the flows of current fiscal surpluses on the other hand. Even if the flows of debt repayment result from several loans, which differ in terms of length, interest rates and repayment conditions, the accounts give a correct evaluation of the total. Conversely, the discounting of the flows of future current gross savings is less straightforward.

A second difficulty arises from the quality of the statistical data needed. The local authority knows the financial data related to the loans with certainty. This is not the case, however, for the expected gross savings, which are simply uncertain. No probability could be associated with these figures. So, the prevision exercise relies on the building of various scenarios, and de facto gives first place to the scenario of the "steady state".

Turning to the medium-term solvency requirement, it is necessary for the minimum time needed to accomplish the full amortisation of the debt to be less than the weighted average terms of the loans (if the annual gross savings remain constant over time and if they are exclusively devoted to the repayment of the debt). This condition could appear easy to formulate because both elements are expressed in terms of a number of years. In reality, once again a control based on such a figure would be difficult to assess. It is clear that if the control is based on a ceiling expressed in terms of a given number of years, the same figure must apply to every local authority. If it were not the case, the opportunity would be given to local governments to bypass the constraint by increasing the term of the loans, by postponing the repayment of the debt, and thus finally by increasing the risk. Choosing a unique figure would be much more simple, fair and efficient. But the assessment of the correct figure is difficult. In France, the Crédit Local de France chooses eight years, some independent experts prefer 10 years, and experts of the Ministry of Finance propose 15 years.

In short, a prudent local authority should save enough out of its current resources in order to fulfil simultaneously the short-term requirement and the medium-term one. In other words, the number of years necessary to accomplish the complete writing-off of the debt must be less than, or at least equal to, the lowest of these two constraints.

Figures 6.1 and 6.2 give an illustration of the respective situations of different categories of *communes* in terms of these two indicators. The chosen medium-term solvency target is ten years. The reported figures represent the average situation of the *communes* regrouped by regions and size of population. Even if the disparities of the individual situations are lessened by the aggregation procedure, the figures show a large heterogeneity of the local situations. With respect to these ratios, rural and urban-peripheral *communes* (with fewer than a 10,000 inhabitants) perform better than the *communes* with over 10,000 inhabitants.

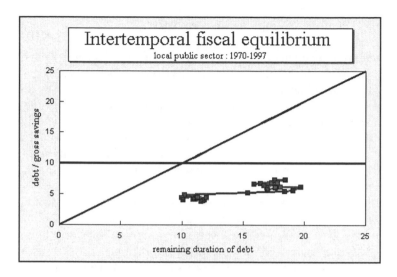

Source: DGCL, Guide des ratio des communes.

Figure 6.1 Intertemporal fiscal equilibrium: local public sector 1970-1997

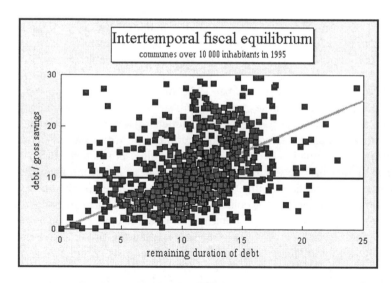

Source: DGCL, Guide des ratio des communes (the points correspond to average figures with respect to demographic scale and region).

Figure 6.2 Intertemporal fiscal equilibrium: communes over 10,000 inhabitants in 1995

6.3.2 Correction of the "Comprehensiveness Bias"

A comprehensive evaluation of the actual solvency of a local authority ought to take into account all the elements that affect or are likely to affect its financial state. This is no longer the case. The accounts subjected to the "balance of accounts equilibrium" rule are not fully comprehensive. They leave aside the accounts of the entities providing local public services by means of a delegation they receive from the local authorities. Their accounts are not fully integrated/consolidated with these of the local authority itself. This is also the case for the financial risks arising from this part of the (delegated) local public sector.

The budget of a locality is composed of a "core" and of several "subsidiary components". The core, the local authority itself, provides the main part of the local public services. But other responsibilities or projects are left aside and delegated abroad. A first example of the fiscal consequences of this externalisation process is the "attached budgets" (*budgets annexes*). They have to be fully consolidated with the main budget (*budget principal*) of the local government (under the law 92-125-6 February 1992).

Public bodies created by the communes jointly with other local governments give a second example. They are set up to provide some local public services on a larger scale. These public entities (*syndicats intercommunaux sans fiscalité propre*) are distinct from the local governments themselves. They have their own budget but are not allowed to levy taxes. Their incomes come only from the local governments in the form of specific grants. By law (6 December 1992, art. 13) it is compulsory for local governments to report these grants comprehensively in the main budget. In addition, at the end of the fiscal year, a document attached to the executed budget document must give detailed information on the fiscal state of these *groupements*. This situation is nevertheless not fully satisfactory. From a risk-taking point of view, there is a difference between attaching supplementary documents reporting the present state of related public bodies, and consolidating the budgets. A consolidation with the local main budgets, according to the individual fiscal contribution provided by the *commune* would be a much better way to fully appreciate overall the fiscal risk of the commune. It simply entails additional administrative costs of collection of the data.

A third example of incomplete recording of the potential fiscal risks is given by the case where a *commune* freely joins, with others, a "community of communes". This could take diverse forms including *communities of communes, districts, communautés urbaines*. These public bodies, which are not local governments as such (they do not elect directly a local assembly), can levy taxes on their own. The tax rate is decided by a community assembly which is composed of members of the constituent local governments' assemblies (directly elected at the commune level). A key point is that the taxes levied at the *communauté* level may not affect the levying of taxes by the constituent local governments themselves by the way of possible vertical tax competition.[3] If the cross-effect of the levying of community taxes on the local taxes is likely, and thus entails some consequences on the fiscal situation of the local authority for the present and the future, a full consolidation is needed. Diagnosis of the anticipated and present solvency of the community and the constituent members could not be made in isolation from one another. In the opposite case, vertical tax competition is unlikely and the consolidation of accounts is not needed. The respective solvency diagnoses can be realised separately.

Another case of incomplete comprehensiveness in the recording of fiscal risks within the local public sector, results from the financial operations made by the local authorities in order to protect themselves against the risk of default of public/private bodies on the loans for which they provided a borrowing guarantee. This guarantee given by the local government to the lender consists mainly in a guarantee of repayment, if necessary, of the loan contracted out by the private/public body. The legal framework requires the local governments to make special provisions for these operations.

These guarantees represent potential fiscal risks to the local governments, and these risks remained systematically underestimated in the past. Now, however, these operations are subject to two different sets of legal constraints. First, the demand for the borrowings guarantee of the local authority originating from private bodies (with the exception of the social housing sector) cannot be met if the cumulated amount of annual debt repayments (resulting from both the direct loans contracted by the local authority and those which are guaranteed) is above a ceiling of 50% of the current incomes of the local governments. The only exception relates to the guarantees given to private/public bodies aiming at the "intérêt général" (public interest). Moreover, the annual debt repayments guaranteed to a given individual cannot exceed 10% of the ceiling of potential guarantees resulting from the former condition.

These criteria and legal constraints could be seen as extremely favourable to private/public bodies that are seeking a borrowing guarantee. This is not exactly the case because these ceilings apply to all local debt repayments, both those resulting from the communes' own borrowings and those that are guaranteed to other bodies. If the own borrowings are large, the ceiling might be very restrictive with respect to private demands for guarantees.

The legal constraints have proved to be a useful safety net in the recent past, as some local governments faced a dramatic increase in the debt repayment they had to make for guaranteed loans. No compulsory proviso is required by law if the guarantee of debt repayment is given to bodies aiming at *the public interest* or acting in the social housing sector (or if the debt is warranted by a financial institution). Otherwise, the annual provision the local government has to make must amount to 2.5% of the remaining annual debt repayments, with a ceiling of 10% of the total of the guaranteed annual debt repayments. Clearly, the risk derived from the borrowing guarantee given to other public/private entities is tightly controlled, and limited.

Conversely, the risks derived from other types of delegated local public services (*concessions, affermage, marché d'entreprises de travaux publics*), or the support given by the local governments to the "*associations para-municipales*" and the risks derived from the involvement of local governments in large urban development projects (Gilbert and Guengant, 1996), are far from being comprehensively evaluated, or even clearly perceived by the local officers.

6.4 THE PRESENT STATE OF FRENCH LOCAL GOVERNMENTS' FINANCES

The present state of French local government finances could be viewed from two different perspectives. The first one, based on individual data, aims at describing the distribution of individual situations: some of the local authorities are in a favourable position, others are not. Analysing the findings of these individual studies in an aggregate way could lead to wrong or at least inappropriate conclusions. Conversely, a macroeconomic perspective has the advantage of giving a correct general view. But this view is only correct on average, leaving the microeconomic situations unrevealed. Turning to the questions of debt, solvency and fiscal imbalance, the macro and the micro perspectives give different and complementary pictures of the situation of the finances of the local governments.

Until the mid-1980s, French local government had extended access to loans at reduced rates, and the interest rates were normally negative in real terms. After this period, the cost of borrowed capital, net of inflation, became significantly positive and, moreover, higher than the local authorities were able to save out of their current resources. So the interest rate per unit of borrowed capital moved far above the net saving per unit of investment expenses (see Figure 6.3).

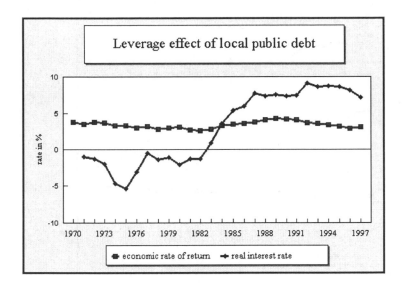

Figure 6.3   Leverage effect of local public debt

6.4.1 The Evolution over Time of Public Capital Expenditures

Facing now this " Modigliani–Miller leverage effect", local governments adjusted their demand for investment goods and their financing. First, local governments' own resources (equivalent to the "net savings" described above) partially substituted for debt finance. Only 28% of capital investment was financed by debt in 1990 as compared with 55% in 1982. Conversely, the share of capital investment financed out of current savings increased from 31% in 1982 to 54% in 1990. The remainder (18% to 20%) of the capital expenses were financed out of subsidies for capital investment granted to local government by the central state (see Figure 6.4).

Initially, until about 1992, the changing conditions on the financing side of capital investment did not reduce the rate of growth of capital expenditures. On the contrary, the capital outlays continued to increase to reach a high, in 1992, of 184 billion FRF (constant 1995). At the same time, the demand for loans decreased in order to limit the risks of future insolvency linked to the increase in interest rates and the rise in the volume of capital investment.

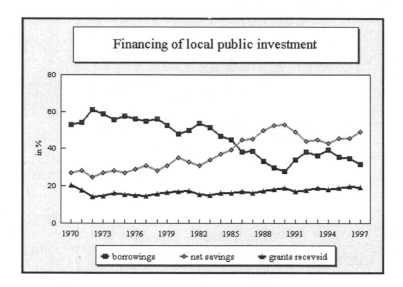

Figure 6.4   Financing of local public investment

Following this period, as the macro economic conditions worsened, they reduced in a sensible way the fiscal surpluses of local governments. Their contribution to the financing of capital investment reduced from 50% in 1991 to 42–43% in 1994–95. Conversely, the contribution of debt to the financing of investment rose from 33% in 1991, to around 40% in 1994–95. As the "leverage effect" reversed (it is by now negative), local governments could not use it in order to increase the capital investment volume. The control of the debt burden and the solvency requirement led them to cut their investment expenses. This situation clearly appeared on a macro level in 1992 (see Figure 6.5).

The decrease in capital investment outlays observed for 1993 was preceded by two other periods of decrease from the beginning of the 1970s (for 1977–78, and for 1983–84). However the length of the recent decrease period is much longer than the former ones. It seems that, provisionally, a reverse upward trend could start for 1997.

This rather unusual situation must not be viewed as the consequence of financial factors exclusively. Other key parameters, such as the macroeconomic situation or the electoral cycle, could as well influence the demand for local public investment goods in the opposite direction; if the macroeconomic situation were to improve; if the needs for new urban capital equipment and infrastructures (environment, urban transportation) were to be set as priorities on the political agenda; or simply if the need for replacement of used or obsolete public capital goods were taken seriously into account.

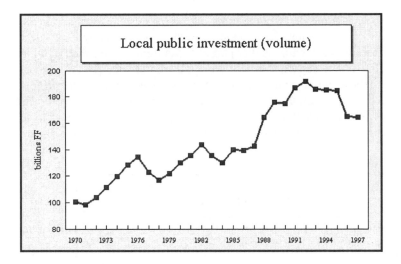

Figure 6.5   Local public investment (volume)

6.4.2 The Taming of Local Public Debt

The stock of public capital goods induces not only one, but two separate and cumulated needs for capital incomes; that is, future indebtedness. The first is a technical one. It comes from the accumulated need for current expenditures directly linked to the use and maintenance of public equipment. These expenditures which clearly appear in a sort of vintage plaster model of local public investment, are likely to be quasi-rigid in the short and the medium term. This causes the local (current) budgets to increase incrementally; which in turn fuels the increase in local tax rates, and thus finally lessens the gross savings available for the financing of future capital goods.

The second is a purely financial one. It comes from the accumulated fixed interest commitments and debt repayments. If the ratio of these annual debt repayments plus interest, to the recurrent current expenditures remains largely less than unity (122 billion FF vs 430 billion respectively for 1995), the annual debt burden is a key determinant of present and future fiscal equilibrium and sustainable financial solvency.

Turning to more of a macroeconomic perspective, two main conclusions arise. First, the evolution of the local public debt over time remains under control. The annual expenses for the debt burden are increasing at the same annual rate as the current incomes of the local governments: the relevant ratio has remained remarkably stable over time since the early 1970s, at around 16–17%. Moreover, the annual debt burden financial commitments have increased at approximately the same rate as the current fiscal surpluses: the relevant ratio is within the range 50-60%. As a consequence, debt servicing absorbs at present a smaller part of the current savings than it did in the early 1970s. The capacity of debt reducing (represented by the ratio of volume of debt to gross savings) stands at about five years for the present time, a much shorter term than the (weighted) average term of loans contracts presently held by local authorities (8–10 years). In addition, the stock of local public debt remains fairly stable over time with respect to GNP (see Figure 6.6).

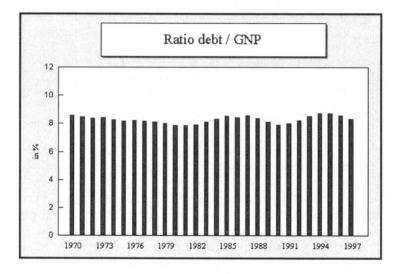

Figure 6.6   Ratio of debt to GNP

Turning now to for financing needs of the local public sector in total (*administrations publiques locales*), as they appear in the macroeconomic accounts, the figure stood around 1% of GNP in the early 1970s; then it decreased gradually to virtually vanish at the end of the 1980s (–16% for 1989). If a deficit appeared once again at the beginning of the 1990s, it seems that it will disappear for 1997.

6.5   LOCAL PUBLIC DEBT AND LOCAL PUBLIC FINANCE IN FRANCE IN THE MAASTRICHT TREATY PERSPECTIVE

The future of the EU addresses two separate questions to the French model of local public finances. First, are the local governments' finances actual threats to the qualification for and the participation of France in the euro? Moreover, do the present situation and the likely future of central government finances threaten the fiscal discipline imposed by the EMU rules? Consequently, might the control of the fiscal deficits imposed by the Treaty lead to a stronger pressure and a tighter control of central government on local public finances and finally a decrease of local fiscal autonomy?

In this European perspective, and that of the fiscal criteria associated with the Maastricht Treaty, local government finances hardly appear to be a major threat to the overall performance of French public finances and the qualification of France to the euro. For 1996, the current deficit of the public sector, in the Maastricht Treaty's conventional definition amounted to −4.15% of GNP (−325 billion FF); the central state deficit contributed −3.50% of GNP (−274 billion FF), the social security institutional sector −0.60% (−54 billion FF) and local public government +0.04% (+3 billion FF). At the same time the stock of the public debt reached 4,360 billion FF (55.7% of GNP). The local public debt amounted to 690 billion FF (8.8% of GNP). However, the comparison between central state statistical figures and local government ones is misleading. The deficit raised by the central state is partly due to fiscal transfers directed towards local governments. A part of these transfers is undoubtedly the direct consequence of the general disease that local governments suffer from due to the inadequate tax system. Survival of the overall local tax system, and moreover a status quo in the system of intergovernmental fiscal relations, implies costly compensations (75 billion FF, which represent 1% of GNP) granted by the central state to the local governments in order to (artificially) reduce local tax rates which would otherwise cause large economic distortions and unbearable fiscal disparities among local authorities.

A last problem could appear between the different tiers of government, due to the aggregate feature of the Maastricht convergence criteria. At present, the potential risk of difficulties between central government and the lower tiers of governments is rather low, due to the fact that France has still a (small) degree of liberty with respect of the 3% and the 60% norms. But, if this small margin of discretion were to vanish, a conflict between the different tiers of governments would certainly arise. There is at present no political debate on this question in France. On the one hand, the Maastricht Treaty allows each member a two-year delay in order to reduce deficits in excess. But on the other hand, the adjustment effort would have to be shared among central government, the social security sector, and the local authorities. Is it so certain? In the French context of decentralisation, the total weight of the adjustment to the European norms would most probably be borne by central government. But, on the contrary, if the fiscal efforts were

Local public finance in Europe

shared between central and local tiers of governments, it could be interpreted as a threat to the decentralisation process (see Figure 6.7).

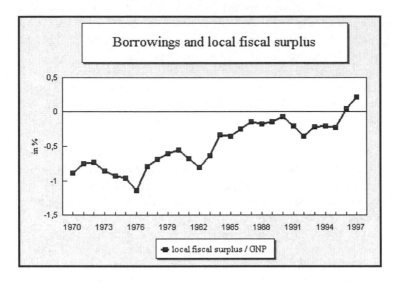

Figure 6.7   Borrowings and local fiscal surplus

6.6   CONCLUDING REMARKS

For the sake of international comparison, it is useful to go back to the French concept of "fiscal equilibrium of the local public accounts", with a special reference to depreciation rules and practices in the local public sector and to the legal requirements for the depreciation of the stock of capital. Apart from the capital equipment which is financed out of debt, and which has to be fully amortised, the legal requirements on the depreciation accounting rules are rather incomplete. Local governments are only committed to writing off renewable capital goods (such as motor vehicles). They are not tied to write off the fixtures. Thus local governments substitute financial amortisation with a physical one, even if the capital stock used in production and in local public services truly depreciates and is subject to obsolescence. But there is no reason for the financial amortisation of the debt and the physical depreciation of the capital equipment of the local governments to coincide. If the local governments were obliged to make depreciation allowances for physical depreciation, the rule of equilibrium in current and capital accounts would be changed in depth and would lead to a situation similar to that of Norway or of Switzerland, for example.

As for the future, compliance with the Maastricht Treaty criteria of 3% for the overall public sector deficit and 60% for the total public debt will call for a combined management of debt and current deficit between all tiers of governments. The concrete modes of this internal fiscal regulation process are not yet precisely defined but could entail important consequences for the decentralisation process in France.

NOTES

1. In the reverse case (art. L 1612-5 du CGCT) *"lorsque le budget d'une collectivité territoriale n'est pas voté en équilibre réel, la Chambre régionale des comptes, saisie par le représentant de l'Etat dans un délai de trente jours à compter de la transmission prévue, le constate et propose à la collectivité territoriale, dans un délai de trente jours à compter de la saisine, les mesures nécessaires au rétablissement de l'équilibre budgétaire et demande à l'organe délibérant une nouvelle délibération". "Toutefois, pour l'application de l'article L 1612-5, n'est pas considéré comme étant en déséquilibre le budget dont la section de fonctionnement comporte ou reprend un excédent et dont la section d'investissement est en équilibre réel, après reprise pour chacune des sections des résultats apparaissant au compte administratif de l'exercice précédent" (art. L 1612-6 du CGCT). De même, "à compter de l'exercice 1997, pour l'application de l'article L 1612-5, n'est pas considéré comme étant en déséquilibre le budget de la commune dont la section de fonctionnement comporte ou reprend un excédent reporté par décision du conseil municipal ou dont la section d'investissement comporte un excédent, notamment après inscription des dotations aux amortissements et aux provisions exigées" (art. L 1612-7 du CGCT).*
2. Article 1612-14 du CGCT states: *"Lorsque l'arrêté des comptes des collectivités territoriales fait apparaître dans l'exécution du budget, après vérification de la sincérité des inscriptions de recettes et de dépenses, un déficit égal ou supérieur à 10 pour 100 des recettes de la section de fonctionnement s'il s'agit d'une commune de moins de 20 habitants et à 5 pour 100 dans les autres cas, la chambre régionale des comptes, saisie par le représentant de l'Etat propose à la collectivité territoriale des mesures nécessaires au rétablissement de l'équilibre budgétaire, dans le délai de un mois à compter de cette saisine".*
3. A legal ceiling on cumulated local tax rates and those of the community expresses the threat of vertical tax competition amongst the community members.

REFERENCES

Gilbert, G. and A. Guengant (1996), "La prise en compte des retombées fiscales" in *L'aménageur urbain face à la crise*, Paris, Editions de l'aube, pp. 93–106.
Guengant A. (1998), *La gestion financière des collectivités locales*, Paris, Economica.

7. Local government borrowing in Germany

Gisela Färber

7.1 CONSTITUTIONAL REFORM OF PUBLIC SECTOR FINANCE IN 1969/70 AND THE DEVELOPMENT OF LOCAL DEBT

When in 1969/70, the big financial reform took place in Germany, there were some important issues dealing with local finance. At that time, local debt was estimated to be too high. Furthermore, an extremely unstable tax base throughout the economic cycle was criticised as being the reason for the undue pro-cyclical fiscal policy of the German municipalities. And with regard to the importance of local governments for infrastructure investment expenditures – they still account for more than two-thirds of public sector real investment expenditures – appropriate rules for local borrowing transactions should be established. This area of goals also determined the reform of local borrowing regulation in all German Länder.

Although in the field of local finance the Länder are free to install regulations for "their" local governments – except for certain principles of public budgeting fixed by federal law – they had agreed to follow common rules. Therefore, local borrowing regulations which count among the rules of local budgeting are very similar in Germany. After 1990, the year of German unification, the rules were also established in the five "new" Eastern Länder. Due to the still continuing differences concerning fiscal capacities as well as the fact that the public infrastructure in Eastern Germany shows a huge catch-up, the empirical development of local debt is to be analysed separately.

The chapter starts with information about the development of local debt and related indicators of local investment expenditures as well as about the special structure of creditors. After some short theoretical considerations about the legitimisation and the limits of local debt in section 7.2, section 7.3 then gives a brief summary of the legal framework of rules and criteria concerned with the limits of local borrowing. In section 7.4, I will show that behind the global indicators that on the first sight give no reason for worrying there are a lot of cities burdened by a considerable indebtedness due to the particular failures of the approval criteria. The final section rebuilds the contexts to the whole government sector and asks the question for the fiscal balance among federal, state and local governments which is also reflected by the problems of local debt.

7.1.1 The Development of Local Debt in Germany

After World War II, the German government sector was rather free of any debt because of the monetary reform in 1948 when all monetary credits and debts were devaluated by the ratio 10:1. However, in the context of establishing the new financial institutions of the public sector (the Bank of German Länder – in the 1960s changed to the German Federal Bank – the central banks of the Länder, other credit and insurance institutions), new debt of an amount of 17 billion DM was created for the federal and regional governments. Because most of the institutions were and still are owned by Länder governments, they had a share of two thirds of total public debt in 1950. Local governments did not hesitate to follow the two other government levels in increasing borrowing. In 1966, they had almost reached them: they had collected an amount of local debt of more than 33 billion DM; more than 30% of the total public debt.

However, the desired decrease of local government debt growth happened only in the late 1970s, when the second petrol crisis stopped all the dreams of re-establishing a stable economic growth by Keynesian employment programme. Until German unification in 1990, local government debt had thus reached an amount of 126 billion DM, but the ratio of total debt to GDP had decreased from 7.2% in 1975 to 5.2% in 1990 (see Table 7.1).

After German unification, local governments also increased borrowing – in absolute amounts as well as relative to GDP. The statistical indicators for the unified Germany however do not show that most of the growing debt lies in local governments in the new Länder which, meanwhile, have almost overtaken the West German municipalities regarding local debt per inhabitant (see Table 7.2).[1] This is a consequence of the huge investment expenditures necessary to repair the dilapidated infrastructure of the former GDR on the one hand, and the insufficient revenues from taxes and grants of the East German municipalities on the other. Compared with West German local governments, the share of investment expenditures which is financed by borrowing is much higher in East Germany although it recently has declined to near to the Western level.

Table 7.1   Public   sector   debt   1950-1999   (since   1991   including   East Germany)

	Federal	State	Local	Total	Federal	State	Local	Total	Federal	State	Local
		in millions of DM				In % of GDP				In % of total debt	
1950	7 290	12 844	500	20 634	7.5	13.2	0.5	21.2	35.3	62.2	2.4
1955	20 791	15 523	4 670	40 983	11.6	8.7	2.6	22.9	50.7	37.9	11.4
1960	26 895	14 695	11 169	52 759	8.9	4.9	3.7	17.4	51.0	27.9	21.2
1965	40 422	17 401	25 844	83 667	8.8	3.8	5.6	18.2	48.3	20.8	30.9
1970	57 808	27 786	40 295	125 890	8.6	4.1	6.0	18.6	45.9	22.1	32.0
1975	114 977	67 001	74 411	256 389	11.2	6.5	7.2	25.0	44.8	26.1	29.0
1980	235 600	137 804	95 208	468 612	16.0	9.4	6.5	31.8	50.3	29.4	20.3
1985	399 043	247 411	113 738	760 192	21.9	13.6	6.2	41.7	52.5	32.5	15.0
1990	599 101	328 787	125 602	1 053 490	24.7	13.6	5.2	43.4	56.9	31.2	11.9
1991	680 815	352 346	140 702	1 173 864	23.9	12.3	4.9	41.1	58.0	30.0	12.0
1993	902 452	433 840	172 859	1 509 150	27.9	13.4	5.3	46.6	59.8	28.7	11.5
1995	1 287 688	511 687	196 599	1 995 974	36.6	14.5	5.6	56.7	64.5	25.6	9.8
1997	1 421 573	595 471	202 120	2 219 163	38.8	16.2	5.5	60.5	64.1	26.8	9.1
1999	1 506 636	640 511	196 750	2 343 897	38.9	16.5	5.1	60.5	64.3	27.3	8.4

Source: Sachverständigenrat.

In West Germany, local borrowing had increased until 1993 due to the good economic situation – itself a result of the German unification boom. From 1994, the continuing recession caused sharp consolidation activities of local governments burdened both by growing expenditures resulting from long lasting unemployment (leading to social aid expenditures) on the one hand, and from declining tax revenues as well as from shrinking fiscal equalisation grants on the other hand. The considerable losses of current revenues in 1996 and 1997 from recession and tax reforms (introduction of tax reductions into personal income tax for child allowances, exemption of minimal living income from income taxation) and the abolition of the local assets tax in exchange of a local share of the revenue of the turnover tax in 1998 continued the decline of local revenue bases. Only in 1998, were tax revenues of an amount equivalent to those of 1993 expected. The revenues from grants and particularly from general fiscal equalisation grants however remained below the level of 1993.

The sharp decline of local borrowing in 1994 in West Germany can be interpreted as a prompt reaction to the setback of tax revenues. The decline of local real asset expenditures followed less sharply, but has been continuing until today. The statistical numbers however exaggerate the decline in local capital expenditures, because during that period the formal privatisation of many local enterprises from parts of local administration to independent enterprises in possession of the same local governments took place. As these privatised local enterprises were "equipped" with a certain amount of local debt which came about through formerly financing the enterprises' capital assets by local borrowing, the total amount of "old" local debt was decreased. But privatisation of the "old" local debt can be measured because the difference of local debt at the end of the year is no longer equal to the amount of new local borrowing. So the total amount of local debt is nowadays underestimated. As there is no exact information and no statistical data available on how many local administration assets and hence local debts have been taken out of local budgets, the effects of local budgetary consolidation and of the "flight from local budgets" cannot be exactly estimated. According to observations the latter effects should not be estimated to be very small, and could even be rather considerable.

In a long-term economic perspective, one of the most important problems concerned with local government borrowing is its pro-cyclical effect on economic development combined with the unstable real investment expenditures. As local governments are responsible for about two thirds of total government real investment expenditures it is obvious that they have a significant influence on the provision of infrastructure capital which is essential for the international competitiveness of German locations. Since the 1960s, local investment expenditures declined from about 40% to 16.6% of local expenditures in 1997. Resolved by the expenditures of the East German governments, the decline of investment expenditures continued until reaching 15.1% in 1998. The share of local expenditures financed by borrowing also shrank from +/–10% in the 1960s/early 1970s to 1–2% at the end of the 1980s, increasing again to 3–4% at the beginning of the 1990s. At the end of the 1990s, West German municipalities had a net redemption in 1999. There ought to be a faint hope that the decline of local investment expenditure has reached the bottom.

Corresponding to the long-term decline of investment expenditures since the 1960s (see Figure 7.1), the share of borrowing-covered expenditures also decreased, reaching a level of 1.5% in 1997. The local government sector however provided a much lower level of deficit finance than the two other federal tiers. The government as a whole even raised more credits than expended for real investment projects; at the end of the 1990s still more than 8% of total expenditures were covered by credits. Again remarkable differences between East and West German local governments are to be regarded. The East German municipalities account for a larger share of the per capita higher investment expenditures by credits (see Table 7.2). But they started to consolidate in the second half of the 1990s.

Table 7.2 Local government borrowing and debt indicators in West and East Germany

	Local governments old Länder				Local governments new Länder			
	Net borrowing	Real investment expenditures	Total expenditures	Total debt	Net borrowing	Real investment expenditures	Total expenditures	Total debt
	in billions of DM				in billions of DM			
1991	5.63	43.15	201.88	132.10	6.15	12.07	43.30	8.60
1992	7.60	46.79	221.56	139.16	5.67	18.68	56.49	17.69
1993	9.28	44.86	230.90	146.76	5.93	18.16	59.02	23.36
1994	3.08	41.87	235.05	153.38	4.20	17.47	59.18	32.24
1995	5.47	40.28	237.89	157.27	−1.27	16.13	60.75	36.83
1996	5.05	37.61	232.93	158.61	1.49	14.46	57.72	38.98
1997	3.02	35.83	226.86	160.16	1.71	13.41	54.16	38.69
1998	0.53	34.83	225.34	158.96	0.98	12.90	52.16	39.87
1999	−0.07	36.49	230.60	156.55	0.46	12.00	51.22	40.20
2000*	0.00	37.20	235.50	156.55	0.80	11.30	51.00	41.00
	DM per inhabitant				DM per inhabitant			
1991	87.87	673.48	3 150.93	2 061.84	386.55	758.64	2 721.56	540.54
1992	117.18	721.40	3 415.97	2 145.54	360.46	1 187.54	3 591.23	1 124.60
1993	141.61	684.57	3 523.58	2 239.58	379.16	1 161.13	3 773.66	1 493.61
1994	46.77	635.74	3 568.93	2 328.88	269.92	1 122.75	3 803.34	2 071.98
1995	82.45	607.18	3 585.92	2 370.67	−82.04	1 041.99	3 924.42	2 379.20
1996	75.85	564.88	3 498.50	2 382.25	96.57	937.14	3 740.76	2 526.25
1997	45.31	537.58	3 403.75	2 403.00	110.97	870.21	3 514.60	2 510.71
1998	7.95	522.43	3 379.96	2 384.30	63.75	839.16	3 393.07	2 593.59
1999	−1.05	547.17	3 457.84	2 347.47	30.00	782.52	3 340.07	2 621.46
2000*	0.00	557.64	3 530.21	2 346.73	52.25	738.08	3 331.16	2 678.00
	Net borrowing/real investment expenditures (%)		Share of borrowing of total expenditures (%)		Net borrowing/real investment expenditures (%)		Share of borrowing of total expenditures (%)	
1991	13.0		4.7		51.0		14.2	
1992	16.2		6.1		30.4		10.0	
1993	20.7		7.0		32.7		10.0	
1994	7.4		2.3		24.0		7.1	
1995	13.6		4.0		−7.9		−2.1	
1996	13.4		3.6		10.3		2.6	
1997	8.4		2.1		12.8		3.2	
1998	1.5		0.4		7.6		1.9	
1999	−0.2		−0.0		3.8		0.9	
2000*	0.0		0.0		7.1		1.6	

Note: * Results of the local government financial planning documents.

Sources: Deutscher Städtetag (2000), *Gemeindefinanzbericht 2000*, in Der städtetag 4/2000, p. 83, German Federal Bank, *Monthly Bulletin*, several editions.

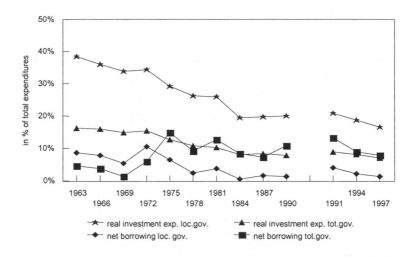

Source: Sachverständigenrat.

*Figure 7.1   Real investment expenditures and net borrowing of local
            (loc.gov.) and total government (tot.gov.) (share of total
            expenditures of the respective government level)*

7.1.2 Local Government Creditors

Creditors of local governments are quite different from those of Bund and
Länder. As Table 7.3 shows, local governments take the highest share of
their borrowing directly from the banking sector and only issue a very small
amount of direct bonds in the financial markets. Among the direct loans from
financial institutions, the loans from savings banks and their clearing houses
dominate by representing more than 60% of total local borrowing
transactions. The so-called local credits from saving banks and their
"mothers", the clearing houses of the Landesbanks, have that special
importance because local governments are the guarantors and owners of this
type of bank. They hold their accounts at their regional savings banks and get
borrowing conditions that often are out of competition against those of other
financial institutions. As the local savings banks often are too small to give a
bigger credit to their local government, the clearing houses of the
Landesbanks have taken over a bigger share of local credit business during
the last 40 years (see Schwarting, 1994, p. 29).

   Beside the general local borrowing activities, there are special credit
programmes established by federal government under control of the

Kreditanstalt für Wiederaufbau (KfW), a particular bank in the ownership of federal and state governments established after World War II to administer the European Recovery Programme (ERP) under the Marshall plan. Over the years the volume of ERP loans decreased and the federal government used the KfW for other special loan programmes. After unification a special programme for local government infrastructure investments was introduced to provide loans particularly for local governments in East Germany at reduced interest rates. Apart from the KfW programmes, local governments can also obtain reduced interest rate loans from the European Investment Bank as long as they fulfil the conditions of the respective programmes.

Table 7.3   Total amount and structure of government debt in Germany at the end of December 1999, millions of euro

End of 1999	Interest-free treasury bonds	Obligations treasury bonds *	Bonds	Direct loans from financial institutions	Loans from non-financial institutions		Debt from former government institutions		
					Social security institutions	Others (incl. foreign creditors)	From German unification	Compensation claims	Others **
Federal Government	11 553	206 454	379 808	67 872	60	2 568	476	45 175	104
West German Länder	150	40 979	2 054	226 022	23	4 979	0	0	1
East German Länder	891	12 750	767	37 602	0	189	0	0	0
West German local governments	0	153	680	78 726	53	1 898	0	0	0
East German local governments	0	51	335	20 138	124	78	0	0	0
Federal "shadow" budgets ***	0	32 408	111 083	78 432	82	3 471	0	0	1
Total government	12 594	262 163	418 871	450 111	281	10 200	476	45 175	105

Notes:
*   includes federal obligations and special federal treasuries.
**   mainly from the London debt treaty of 1948.
*** Kreditabwicklungsfonds & Erblastentilgungsfonds from German unification, German unification fund, European recovery programme fund, railway fund debt, compensation fund hard coal.

Source: German Federal Bank.

7.2　SOME THEORETICAL CONSIDERATIONS

Local government borrowing can be considered under federal aspects as well as under the aspects of "pure" public finance. The latter is concerned with effects of borrowing activities on allocation, distribution and stabilisation, the first with the intergovernmental relations in a federal state.

From the point of view of public finance and the various approaches favouring borrowing instead of taxation, there remains only one argument in favour of the first, particularly as the burdens of public debt in the form of interest payments have overloaded public budgets since the 1970s. The reasons lie in the increase in borrowing transactions since that time on the one hand, and in the high level of interest rates until the mid-1990s on the other hand. According to the DOMAR theorem (Domar, 1944), the most severe danger for the long–term financial scope of public budgets lies in the fact that the growth rate of GDP and also the corresponding growth rate of tax revenues are lower than the interest rates. Therefore there is no long term positive financial scope to be expected from borrowing.

Under the aspects of stabilisation policies, arguments for deficit spending have become weak (Postlep, 1993, p. 147). The reasons come from the political sphere on the one hand and from the globalisation process on the other. The deficit financed expenditure programmes in the recessions of the late 1960s and the 1970s undoubtedly had positive effects for employment. But governments were not able to cut back the expenditure levels of public budgets in the boom periods. They therefore contributed to inflation and a permanent increase in public debt and interest payments. Additionally, globalisation puts limits on the national effects of deficit financed employment programmes because an increasing share of the outcomes spreads across the national borders into other economies. The smaller a jurisdiction is, the stronger are the effects of employment programmes in favour of their neighbours. Local governments therefore have the least chance to create local employment by deficit spending. However it should be clear that they are not to follow a pro-cyclical fiscal policy which is still supposed to intensify private sector economic cycles.

Local governments have another argument for financing their investments in local infrastructure by borrowing – they can enlist finance for the infrastructure from those who will benefit from its use. If residents have to finance a local facility by tax revenues in the period of building there is an imbalance between the period of finance and the period of benefits. If people die or leave the jurisdiction they had the burden of taxation and definitely no benefits. Immigrating inhabitants benefit without payment. Debt financing opens the chance to distribute the financial contributions to the generations of residents who benefit from them (Tiebout, 1956). Local debt is therefore an instrument of optimal allocation of local goods if it consequently follows the rules of the pay-as-you-use principle (Ricardo, 1817/1951; Barro, 1989).

A final argument against an uncoordinated public debt policy in a federal system is concerned with bailing out. In general it cannot be excluded that one jurisdiction will suffer a budget emergency as a result of over-indebtedness. The danger becomes the smaller the more the inhabitants of a jurisdiction have to pay back all public liabilities by additional taxes. Only then do they have a strong interest to control the government not to take up too much borrowing. If they can enlist other jurisdictions and the respective taxpayers to pay for the consequences of their budget emergency; that is, if they can "bail out", their will to control will be comparably weak. However there are also few situations possible where jurisdictions come into budget emergencies for "external" reasons. For both cases a federal system has to provide rules which in the first place prevent jurisdictions from collecting so much public debt that they are no longer able to fulfil their constitutional responsibilities and, in the second place, provide for emergency situations. The smaller a jurisdiction is and the weaker its tax base, the more important are these constitutional rules of a "federal debt constitution".

7.3 LOCAL BUDGET AND BORROWING REGULATION BY STATE LAWS

Local budget and borrowing regulation has been established in all German Länder in an almost identical way. With certain regards, it is significantly different from federal and state government rules as these constitute the two tiers in the German federal constitution equipped with the legal status of state quality. Local governments are in this respect members or parts of the Länder and do not constitute a proper federal tier as far as legal aspects are concerned. In a functional sense, however, they do. And the German constitution (*Grundgesetz*) confirms the right of local autonomy for all local concerns in art. 28 (II). This autonomy is a limited one insofar as local budgets have to be approved not only by local parliaments but also by local control agencies of the states. This budgetary control focuses on keeping the general rules of local budgets, particularly the borrowing rules.

German local governments do not only provide local public goods from their own democratic voting procedures, they are also obliged to administer and execute many responsibilities which are determined by federal and state laws often in rather strict regulations. Therefore local governments – and in particular district governments which constitute the most common type of associations of municipalities and were in former days established as the lowest level of state administration (and are still until today in some Länder)

– have a double function of autonomous self-administration on the one hand and compulsorily providing public goods against the background of establishing equal living conditions all over Germany (art. 72 (III) GG) on the other hand.

In some Länder – particularly in East Germany where state constitutions and the state's local constitutions were established recently after unification, but also in some "old" German Länder (e.g. in Bavaria) – referenda can be held for several purposes. Even East German mayors can be voted out by a referendum. But no referendum is possible against local parliamentary decisions about local taxes and budgets.

7.3.1 Subsidiarity for Borrowing Finance in the States' Local Constitutions

There are general rules concerned with covering local investment expenditures by different types of revenues:

1. Borrowing is only permitted to finance investment expenditures. They are budgeted separately from current expenditures and receipts in the capital account. Repayment of credit due and interest payments from local debt *must* be financed from current account revenues. Particular accounting procedures are undertaken to secure these basic rules (see section 7.3.2).
2. Local governments are obliged only to use borrowing finance after all other sources of revenues have been exhausted. Before raising credits, revenues from general reserves and from actual current revenues must be used.

In former days, local borrowing was even regarded as an insult to a city's or a mayor's honour (Schwarting, 1985, 623). At this time, investment projects began with a period of building up financial reserves from current revenues – separately for each project. Since 1970, local governments only have been obliged to hold reserves:

- to secure their general liquidity reserve with an amount of about 1–2% of the volume of the current account (general reserve);
- to equalise the cyclical amount of tax revenues; and
- to finance investment projects the financial volume of which is comparatively large for the respective local budget.

Local governments are obliged to draw up a rolling mid-term (5-year) investment programme outlining the volume of investment projects and the destined financial coverage. In this plan, they can begin to build up reserves in advance and to schedule special transactions within the capital account. Although critical arguments are stated against reserves that keep current financial resources out from taxpayers' actual use, there is agreement that reserves are necessary to smooth out pro-cyclical local investment behaviour and to prevent local governments from a dramatic decline of investment expenditures when recession sharply reduces local tax revenues. Therefore, the decline of local capital expenditures happens only in the second or third year of a recession. Against this background, nobody requires today a total pre-financing of investment projects with regard to the volume of local investment expenditures necessary to maintain a certain level of modern local infrastructure. Nor is borrowing finance rejected with regard to the pay-as-you-use principle of their long-term use of local infrastructure.

Actual revenues either from current accounts or from capital accounts finance most local investment projects. The latter are to be divided into local capital charges from the potential users – mostly the land and house owners (e.g. of sewers, sewage purification plants and streets), and capital grants from federal and state budgets. Among these, only a few are given without any special condition. Most of them are distributed for certain purposes and with special conditions on reception or use (e.g. local traffic, kindergartens, schools, fire engines, and so on). They are regulated by the respective state ministries (also responsible for the determined distribution of federal grants programmes) which often require a certain share of local finance as an award condition.

Finally, if all other sources of local finance have been used to cover investment expenditures, local governments can get a permit to borrow credits. State regulatory boards give the permits for the budget that is due to be executed, after a strict check of local budget propositions to ensure interest payments and redemption will not restrict future budgetary responsibilities. Borrowing is to be forbidden if the obligations from the former and the actually planned debt funding lead to an "endangering of the permanent ability of a local government to fulfil its responsibilities". Particular procedures are used to control that undetermined legal expression (see section 7.3.3).

Since 1970, borrowing permits have been given for the total planned borrowing volume. Only local governments under special state control due to budget emergencies have to ask for each special raising of a new credit. Special allowances are also needed in the case of a general federal limit of public borrowing intended in the stabilisation policy law to depress public demand during a boom period. A distinction is to be made between new credits (net borrowings) and the rediscounting of repayments due. The latter do not need to be passed in the local budgetary law, so a permit from the state control agency is not required (Ade, 1992, p. 42).

In order to execute the local borrowing limits, a special documentation of transaction has been established in the context of local budgets that is the same for all local governments in Germany. The proper control of local borrowing allowances also follows exactly the same criteria all over Germany.

7.3.2 Current and Capital Account Regulation

All local budget laws require formally balanced budgets both for current and for capital accounts. There is a formal way to register the financial transactions concerned with debt finance between current and capital accounts that should guarantee a proper control of local borrowing activities. All local government transactions concerned with deficits and borrowing are strictly under state control. Without these special state agencies' approval, a local budget cannot come to legal force.

Unlike in the two budgetary accounting procedures of federal and state governments, local governments are obliged to establish a current and a capital account in an expenditure and revenue accounting system. The first contains all "current" and in the economic convention consumption expenditures and receipts, the second all transactions concerned with investment (real estate and long-term equipment purchases or sales, which are called "real investment") and financial investment transactions containing subsidies and loans to third parties for investment purposes[2] (for details see Figure 7.2). Both accounts are connected by so-called contribution from one account to the other. So the amount of expenditure respective to receipt transactions in both accounts is higher than the aggregated amount.

In general, the current account has to provide an excess of revenues (particularly taxes, refunds for activities on behalf of other governments, and general fiscal equalisation grants) over current expenditures. This excess is designated to cover the debt reimbursements due in the budgetary period and the borrowing costs (discount, commissions, credit fees) which are listed in the capital account. The idea is that the repayments of debt must be financed from current receipts. It should be emphasised that the German system does not calculate amortisation or depreciation on the local assets to be covered by current receipts.[3] There is only the financial principle that all expenditures resulting from borrowing in former budgetary periods must be covered by receipts of the current account. Most Länder therefore require that local governments obtain a *compulsory contribution* from current to capital account to cover the debt instalments and borrowing costs. There are also *voluntary contributions* from current to capital account when municipalities and districts finance investment expenditures of the actual budgetary period or the increase of reserves by current revenues. These "contributions" are calculated as expenditures in the current account and – at the same size – as receipts of the capital account.

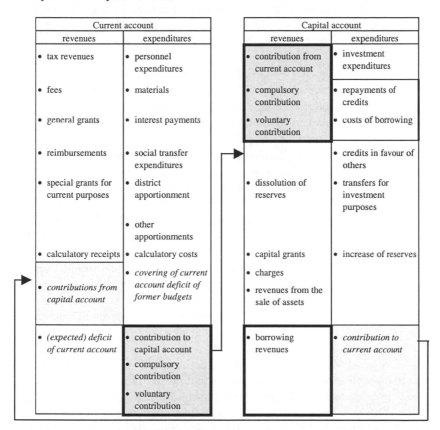

Current account		Capital account	
revenues	expenditures	revenues	expenditures
• tax revenues	• personnel expenditures	• contribution from current account	• investment expenditures
• fees	• materials	• compulsory contribution	• repayments of credits
• general grants	• interest payments	• voluntary contribution	• costs of borrowing
• reimbursements	• social transfer expenditures		• credits in favour of others
• special grants for current purposes	• district apportionment	• dissolution of reserves	• transfers for investment purposes
	• other apportionments		
• calculatory receipts	• calculatory costs	• capital grants	• increase of reserves
• *contributions from capital account*	• *covering of current account deficit of former budgets*	• charges • revenues from the sale of assets	
• *(expected) deficit of current account*	• contribution to capital account • compulsory contribution • voluntary contribution	• borrowing revenues	• *contribution to current account*

Figure 7.2   General local budget frame of current and capital accounts

Most Länder apply the extremely restrictive version of the local borrowing regulation in the above described definition of a compulsory contribution from current to capital account. Some Länder however (e.g. Baden-Württemberg) only oblige local governments to install a compulsory contribution to capital account in the cases where the regular revenues of the capital account (without borrowing revenues) are not sufficient to cover capital expenditures. Rhineland-Palatinate and Thuringia determine the compulsory contribution from current to capital account as the amount of debt repayments and borrowing costs minus those revenues of the capital account which are not destined for special purposes. Additionally and in general the total contribution to capital account should be sufficient to cover a necessary increase of reserves and at least enough to cover the depreciation of those local administrations units which are financed by special user fees (Schwarting, 1994, p. 71). These latter rules give a bigger scope of interpretation both for local governments and for local control agencies of the states.

Problems arise when municipalities cannot balance the current account. This happens when tax revenues fall short during economic crisis; when state governments consolidate their budgets by cutting back local fiscal equalisation grants; when the current expenditures increase faster than the current receipts; or when the compulsory contribution from current to capital account increases due to former borrowing transactions. The latter also influence current expenditures in form of interest payments. So local debt can lead – among other factors – to a deficient current account. Although local financial law requires a balanced current account, for short-term deficits the state control agencies can give their approval of the local budget. Local governments then have to prove that they cannot close the deficit by increasing other revenues or cutting back current expenditures. In many cases, the expensive federal and state regulation of local administration responsibilities (e.g. the increase of social assistance expenditures[4]) together with problems of structural economic change and high regional unemployment are due to the local deficits of current account. Sometimes local expenditures cannot be adjusted to match declining receipts as fast as necessary.

In all these cases of temporary current deficits, state control agencies will and are allowed to approve local budgets, but mostly imposing conditions to ensure that the deficit will be a temporary one. In case the current deficit continues and the reasons for it are of a structural nature (e.g. due to special compulsory expenditures which are far above average because of a high local unemployment rate or extremely low tax revenues in a rural region), most Länder pay special grants (*Bedarfszuweisungen*) to equalise these deficit providing factors. If a local government has caused the current account deficit through use of proper political decisions, state control agencies negotiate the mid-term covering of it by cut backs of other current expenditures or by special revenues from the sale of local assets and immovable property which are then accounted for as contributions from capital to current account to change them from revenues of the capital account to those of the current account.

A deficit of the current account has to be balanced in the budget at the latest in the second year afterwards.[5] That means the current revenues of the next budget or the one after that must be used to cover the deficit.[6] The rule is secured by the express introduction of the position "covering of current account deficits of former budgets" in the respective current account. Meanwhile the deficit is financed by short-term credits which do not count among the borrowing revenues of the capital account.

Current account deficits are supposed to be exceptional. The legal rules indicate that only the case of collapse of tax revenues – initially by recession,[7] meanwhile also by federal tax reform – legitimates the approval of the state agency for a municipal current account deficit. It is obvious that the rule comes from the theory of anti-cyclical fiscal policy of Keynes. Local governments should not be enforced to reduce their expenditures at the moment when recession breaks out. If the deficit results from (too high) expenditures which in a medium perspective exceed the current revenues then the state agencies have to negotiate how to close the gap by cutting back current expenditures.

7.3.3 Local Borrowing Limits

The limits of borrowing to finance investment expenditures in the capital account are in contrast derived from budgetary arguments and are not connected with those of fiscal policies. The idea of limiting the annual amount of borrowing aims at "maintaining the future ability of a local government to fulfil its legal responsibilities". Although local governments cannot go bankrupt, the budgetary burdens from former borrowing procedures should not carry so much weight that they restrict the scope of future budgets, particularly not the necessary balancing of the current account.

Local borrowing limits are closely connected with the medium term, a 5-year financial planning process (Michaelsen, 2000, p. 99). Local governments are obliged to provide a 5-year investment programme beginning with the running fiscal year (t_{-1}), the period to be planned (t_0) and three further fiscal years (t_1-t_3). It is part of the medium term financial planning process. Although these plans do not possess any legally binding force, they are documents projecting financial developments and budgetary priorities. Apart from general statistical purposes of the total government sector,[8] the data are used to control whether the amount of borrowing in the budgetary period to be planned would lead to chronic current account deficits as described above, or whether the additional compulsory contributions to the capital accounts will be covered by future current revenues.

The concrete rules to determine local borrowing limits differ from Land to Land (Michaelsen, 2000, p. 102) and can be outlined as more or less simplified simulations of the financial consequences of the credits which are due for approval. For the actual, for the planned and for further three budgetary periods, tax revenues deduced from the total government sector tax estimations plus other regular revenues are compared with the estimations of "necessary" regular local expenditures. These expenditures are mostly expenditures of the current account and are bound by legal regulations (e.g. social aid expenditures), and by contracts (e.g. for local public servants who cannot be dismissed, or for interest payments); they are nearly as high as the total current expenditures of the financial plans. Two positions of the medium term current accounts are influenced by the borrowing volume to be tested. The compulsory contribution to the capital account will be increased by the credits in the actual planning period, if repayments or instalments are to be paid during the following three years.[9] The interest payments on the additional credits increase the "necessary" current expenditures. The general decision rules then are the following:

- No problems result from the planned borrowing volume if the estimated current account provides a surplus after the compulsory contribution to the capital account. The budget can be approved.
- If the current account was deficient in the last planning period and the planned borrowing volume leads to a negative value of the current account balance, it indicates "danger" and decreasing financial scope. In this case the budget cannot get the state agency's approval or the municipality is asked to review its budgetary planning.

In Schleswig-Holstein and Rhineland-Palatinate, the procedures for calculating the so-called "free top" are explicitly regulated. In Schleswig-Holstein, it is the difference between the surplus of the current account on the one side and the expenditures for borrowing costs and repayments on the other side. The procedure applied in Rhineland-Palatinate is a bit more complicated and detailed; for example not taking into consideration revenues from special low fiscal capacity grants or the transfers from capital to current account. If the value of the so-called "free top" is negative, it is an indicator that expenditures for other purposes have to be reduced in favour of repayments of credits.

In case of a negative value of the "free top", the responsible state control agency negotiates with the respective local government how to close the financial gap. This procedure is rather easy if the deficit only comes from high investment expenditures, such as, say, from a special investment project for attracting a new enterprise to the local area or from building a new spa infrastructure in order to have more paying guests for the local hotels and spa enterprises, because modifications of the investment programme and its financial covering are discussed. The negotiations become difficult if a negative "free top" comes from chronically deficient current revenues or comparatively high compulsory current expenditures and if there is no financial scope for additional transfers to capital account for future credit repayments.

The most rigorous action that can be taken against local governments which are not yet able to service their debt from current revenues is the introduction of a state commissioner instead of the local mayor or the city director. During the commissioner's regime, local self-administration rights are only valid in a very restricted manner. The commissioner's main role is to develop and execute a rescue plan for the local budget and to re-establish financial balance. As local governments are not able to go into liquidation and even most of the local government property cannot be distrained for sale to pay the creditors, state governments have to take the economic consequences of local debt, that is, to repay it in the end if the local government is not yet able to do it itself. This is finally the reason why local autonomy concerned with borrowing is legally restricted.

7.3.4 Local Government Borrowing and the Maastricht Criteria

Since the European member states signed the Maastricht Treaty in 1993, the discussion has emerged how to share the newly established borrowing limits among the federal tiers in Germany. Until today, federal and state governments have not found any solution. One important reason is the severe problems of public debt resulting from the huge unification costs. However the discussion which took place between Bund and Länder gives some interesting information about the relative position of local governments in the German federal system (Schwarting, 2000, p. 3).

The federal government opened the discussion in 1996 by requiring a share of the 3% borrowing limit according to its share of total government borrowing. Using the actual data on public debt this would mean that the federal government could take up net credits of about 64% of the total permitted borrowing of the public sector. In 1997 the limit had an amount of nearly 109 billion DM from which federal government could have taken over almost 70 billion DM (1.93% of GDP). State and local governments in contrast would have had the "right" only to cover borrowings of less than 40 billion DM or 1.07% of GDP.

The other solution offered by the federal government was to share the borrowing limit according to the share of public expenditures among federal and state governments. Under this agreement the federal government would have been authorised to exploit about 40% of the borrowing limit, almost 44 billion DM in 1997. With regard however to the reform of the family allowances from federal expenditures to tax reduction, that amount would have shrunk to 40 billion DM. Since that time, the discussion about sharing the Maastricht borrowing limits has not been continued. It is however expected that it will be taken up again during the negotiations about the reform of the state equalisation system.

With regard to local governments it is remarkable that the total debate was led without direct participation of their representatives, even without explicitly discussing the problem of how to share the borrowing limit of state governments between them and their local governments. It can be supposed that in the case of an agreement between federal and state governments, this problem would have been solved in the same way as the enforced participation of local governments in the costs of German unification, which means decreeing to them a certain share. But the true problems do not lie in the vertical sharing of the borrowing limit but in the horizontal sharing as regards the Länder's sharing out of the borrowing limit among the Länder and the local governments. What about those state and local governments suffering from budget emergencies for whatever reasons (it mostly happens due to the regional effects of structural economic crisis), that are not able to cut their deficits back within a short term consolidation period? Should they be punished by additionally having to pay their share of the financial sanctions, which were agreed among the European Ministers of Finance without sufficient participation by the lower levels of governments in the federally organised nations? What about the principle of "good faith" of the members of the German federal constitution against each other, which also counts for financial concerns?

Apparently, the established rules of the German fiscal constitution do not provide a functional agreement about the federal implementation of the Maastricht borrowing limits among the German government tiers. Maybe, if the fundamental reform of the fiscal constitution had come shortly after 2000, federal and state governments would have found an agreement. Actually, the shrinking public borrowing ratio – as a result of economic recovery and some slight consolidation efforts – to a planned amount of 1% of the GDP took the political pressure out of the discussion.

7.4   PROBLEMS OF LOCAL BUDGET AND BORROWING REGULATION

The official documentation of total local government debt apparently signals no problems concerned with local borrowing. But there are large differences of local debt per inhabitant among different cities. The "champion" of local debt still is Frankfurt/M with an amount of almost 8,532 DM per inhabitant at the end of 1998 (see Table 7.4). At the end of 1994, Frankfurt/M had an amount of local debt of 9,810 DM per inhabitant. The least indebted local government among the cities at the end of 1998 was Rinteln with only 41 DM per inhabitant, in 1994 it was Delbrück with an amount of DM 15 per capita. Table 7.4 shows that the ranking changed during the period 1994–1998, as well as the amount of debt per inhabitant: Frankfurt/M shows a decreasing volume of local debt, Bonn a remarkable increase. In general, statistics indicate that there is an increase of local debt per inhabitant with the growing number of citizens.

An econometric analysis of local debt data to get further empirical evidence about the parameters of local borrowing however soon leads to difficulties. The data base is not very homogeneous because of the differences of local finance regulation among the Länder and the differing status and responsibilities of district free cities, municipalities which are members of districts and the districts themselves. The access to the necessary statistical data is additionally given only for the district free cities. A simple correlation analysis of selected data of German cities however provided the following findings which unfortunately are – due to regional differences and the previously mentioned institutional erosion of the local government sector (see section 7.4.3) – of a very low statistical validity:[10]

- The volume of debt per inhabitant is positively correlated with the local fiscal capacity from revenues of local business and property taxes as well as with the total per capita tax revenues. This means that high own revenues give a strong base for getting approval to raise credits because these cities have the financial means to service local debt.
- Debt per inhabitant is slightly negatively correlated with the per capita general grant revenues from state budgets. As general fiscal equalisation grants are conditioned on a low fiscal capacity and/or high "fiscal needs" it is clear that the amount of grants mostly indicates small financial scope in the current account of a municipality.

Because of the difficulties of undertaking a valid empirical analysis, this chapter can only emphasise some "qualitative" fundamental problems concerned with local borrowing which have emerged during the 1990s. The most important are:

1. the traditional critical arguments against the applied borrowing criteria,
2. chronic deficits of many current accounts which according to the established approval criteria for local borrowing should lead to a refusal, but often do not,
3. highly indebted local governments evading the area of state controlled borrowing by accounting techniques and so-called shadow budgets.

Table 7.4   Total debt in DM per inhabitant of city governments on 31 December 1998 and 1994

	Average	Highest	Lowest	Average	Highest	Lowest
		on 31.12.1998			on 31.12.1994	
Total cities	2 416			2 593		
More than 500 000		Frankfurt/M	Stuttgart		Frankfurt/M	Dortmund
	4 333	8 532	2 451	4 345	9 810	2 502
200 000–500 000		Bonn	Rostock		Bonn	Halle/S
	3 014	5 941	1 134	3 128	4 664	754
100 000–200 000		Koblenz	Reutlingen		Neuss	Reutlingen
	2 205	3 686	755	2 614	4 701	681
50 000–100 000		Hanau	Bad Homburg		Hanau	Delbrück
	2 202	5 964	438	2 253	6 022	15
20 000–50 000*		Würselen	Rinteln		Marktredwitz	Weißenb/By
	1 462	5 247	41	1 537	3 379	359

Note: * only selective documentation of cities.

Source: *Statistisches Jahrbuch Deutscher Gemeinden*, 1995, 1999.

7.4.1 Critical Arguments Against the Criteria of Local Borrowing Limits

The statistical indicators of local debt show few reasons for apprehension in general, at least in comparison with the state of indebtedness of federal and state governments. Local debt, which had increased to 7.2% of GDP until 1975, decreased again in the 1980s and continued doing so during the 1990s in West Germany. Only certain East German local governments seem to be in danger of becoming over-indebted, not because of their high debt, but because of their extremely low local fiscal capacity. Some cities and smaller villages have already come under the governance of a state commissioner. The most famous among these was the municipality of Weimar.

However, there are lots of problems with the criteria of approbation and the consecutive effects of local borrowing. Fundamental arguments are provided with regard to allocative and stabilisation goals of local finance:

- The systematic over- or under-estimation respectively of tax revenues of local and state governments during the economic cycle provides incorrect information about the medium term financial situation. In recessionary periods, the "free top" tends to be too small. During boom periods it shows the capacity of a local government to pay for interest payments and redemption as being too high. Because of that phenomenon, borrowing is sharply restricted in recessions, and generously permitted during booming economic development. Both enforce an undue economic development.

- The tax estimation, first provided for unified Germany twice a year, is more difficult to assess at the decentralised regional level. The average growth rate of tax revenues is usually spread very unequally: local governments can suffer from the bankruptcy of certain industrial enterprises located in the area, yet without any loss of tax revenues in the neighbouring cities. Also, different regional growth rates across Germany leave their mark on different regional tax revenues, which are not equalised by any local fiscal equalisation system. As a result, there is insufficient security that a local government will in the future have the estimated revenues that were the base of the borrowing permit.

- The projections of whether additional credits would lead to deficits of the current account are vulnerable against certain special arrangements. If the borrowing contract imposes annual instalments of a constant amount, the indicators show the resulting decline of the financial scope. If the credit contract schedules repayment of the whole debt at the end of the period of validity, repayments are not indicated in the projected three future budgets. The financial consequences of borrowing are then underestimated and give false information to the responsible state control agency.

- As credits which rediscount due debt repayments are not as strictly controlled as net borrowing, the pay-as-you-use principle is not realised. The net value of the local assets cannot be evaluated. The local borrowing control does not count all future financial obligations from local debt. The true financial situation of a local government is often covered up. Many critics therefore require the establishment of a local accounting system similar to private enterprise balance sheets.[11]

- Besides the officially declared local debt, severe problems of hidden debts and the evasion of the borrowing criteria emerge by way of "accounting tricks". For example, borrowing proceeds not used for investment expenditures could be booked ad interim into the reserves of the capital account, then dissolved and put as "revenues" by way of transfers from the capital to the current account. In doing so, some cities implicitly have used revenues from borrowing to finance current expenditures. If state control agencies do not see through the arrangements and restrict the necessary budget approval, these cities get over-indebted in the long run.

- There is also no distinction made between borrowing taken for investments into economic development (e.g. the development of new industrial areas) and general investments for public goods necessary for private consumption or an excess capacity of schools, kindergartens or theatres. But the distinction is important. The first sort of investment expenditures might be rather "profitable". Operational costs with the latter might lead to increasing deficits of the future current budgets.
- In calculating the "free top", no deduction is made for the future maintenance of local infrastructure facilities. This factor however must be taken into consideration in the future use of the local infrastructure. Additionally, other future investment expenditures necessary to operate the project which now should be financed by borrowing, must be deducted from the "free top". Many local governments have suffered the hard experience that all the infrastructure facilities built up during the 1960s and 1970s today need a high sum of additional expenditures to maintain their value and actual use. But there is no revenue left today to maintain the asset value of this local infrastructure.

By way of the practised borrowing limits, problems of the decline of local infrastructure facilities might on the one side be enforced. On the other side, cities located in regions suffering from long-lasting economic problems are in the end not protected from over-indebtedness compared with the increasingly deficient fiscal capacity. However, the problems are not only concerned with local debt, but with the general decline of local finance in the federal fiscal constitution of Germany.

7.4.2 Chronic Deficits of Current Account and Local Disinvestment Politics

In the 1990s, local governments have suffered a remarkable erosion of their revenues base. Tax revenues stagnated because of the economic development and federal tax reforms;[12] grant revenues from local fiscal equalisation which are compulsorily part of the tax sharing system between state and local governments were reduced to make municipalities share in the costs of German unification. High unemployment rates burdened local current accounts; as did compulsory social aid expenditures. The resulting fiscal pressure led to important cut-backs in local budgets which however were in many cases not sufficient to balance the current accounts. Since 1995, many cities have undertaken a broader consolidation of their budgets, starting by cutting back investment expenditures and finally continuing by cutting back expenditures of the current account. The process of consolidation was and still is burdened by former current account deficits which at that time were considered to be temporary, but later built up additional factors working against the balance of the current account.

Table 7.5 shows certain indicators of selected city budgets in 1998. Column 1 indicates the expected current account deficit, column 4 the total contribution from current to capital account, column 5 the compulsory contribution. It becomes obvious that many cities were not able to finance additional investment expenditures from current revenues. The covering of the compulsory contribution from current to capital account was going along with current account deficits which were themselves partly caused by the obligation to cover current account deficits of former budgets (column 2), and partly by new current deficits in the budgetary period 1998.[13] Many German cities have suffered from deficient current accounts not only in 1998, but also for longer periods, which is indicated by the amount of cover required for current account deficits of former budgets. The "net" current deficit which does not exist in a legal sense but can implicitly be calculated is then the difference between columns 2 and 3 of Table 7.4. The current account of Hannover, for example, was planned to be deficient by 215 million DM, more than 8% of the revenues of the current account, and 133 million DM were caused by a current account deficit of the 1996 (or 1997) budget which had to be covered in 1998. It is not surprising that the contribution from current to capital account just covers the compulsory one and not more.

Column 6 of Table 7.5 indicates that many cities have been trying to decrease their current deficit by contributions from the capital account either by dissolving reserves (column 7) or by sale of assets (column 8). This means that current account deficits are reduced by using means of the capital account or even by selling existing local assets. Hannover has resolved reserves of 400 thousand DM to finance current expenditure. Freiburg i.Br., for example, had a balanced current account, but was not able to cover the compulsory contribution to capital account (0 instead of 15 million DM). Freiburg however planned a contribution from capital to current account of an amount of more than 39 million DM which was financed by dissolution of reserves and by sale of assets. It therefore had in column 3 an obtained investment rate of −54.2 million DM. Both cities were not able to maintain the net value of their local assets − which is indicated by the negative value of the obtained investment rate − and finance current expenditures by the dissolution of local infrastructure, immovable property and the local "family jewels".

Table 7.5   Current account deficits of selected cities 1998 (in mill. DM; according to budgetary plans)

	1	2	3	4	5	6	7	8	9
City	Current account deficit	Covering of current account deficits of former budgets	Obtained investment rate*	Contribution to capital budget	Compulsory contribution to capital budget	Contribution to current account	Financed by dissolution of reserves	Sale of assets, other revenues	For information: revenues of current account
Kiel	−39.8	0.0	−0.7	36.1	36.1	0.7	0.7	0.0	1 088.4
Hannover	−214.7	132.6	−0.4	45.5	45.5	0.4	0.4	0.0	2 527.9
Göttingen	−109.0	58.1	0.0	23.4	23.4	0.0	0.0	0.0	575.4
Dortmund	−110.4	72.5	−73.7	84.5	84.5	73.7	73.7	0.0	2 708.6
Düsseldorf	−74.3	123.8	−75.5	306.0	294.4	87.1	87.1	0.0	3 825.5
Bonn	0.0	0.0	−53.7	74.4	74.4	53.7	38.7	15.0	1 629.6
Neuss	−17.3	28.9	0.0	16.1	16.1	0.0	0.0	0.0	363.3
Frankfurt/M	−691.1	0.0	−29.8	21.1	21.1	29.8	22.6	7.3	4 987.2
Wiesbaden	−121.2	69.0	−68.3	35.3	35.3	68.3	68.3	0.0	1 273.0
Offenbach/M	−317.0	235.8	1.0	23.5	22.5	0.0	0.0	0.0	429.7
Hanau	−65.4	28.4	−1.9	16.6	16.6	1.9	1.9	0.0	333.4
Mainz	−162.0	89.0	−3.3	22.1	22.1	3.3	0.0	3.3	615.0
Trier	−43.4	34.1	−4.7	11.0	11.0	4.7	0.1	4.6	352.7
Speyer	−28.1	13.0	−0.8	4.2	4.2	0.8	0.0	0.8	141.3
Stuttgart	0.0	0.0	−82.7	194.9	277.3	0.2	0.2	0.0	3 488.2
Mannheim	0.0	0.0	−27.6	5.1	32.7	0.0	0.0	0.0	1 457.1
Freiburg i.Br	0.0	0.0	−54.2	0.0	15.0	39.1	15.9	23.3	861.5
München	0.0	0.0	−236.3	28.5	170.3	94.6	94.6	0.0	6 344.5
Schweinfurt	0.0	0.0	−36.1	0.0	16.5	19.6	16.5	3.0	248.7
Saarbrücken	−337.1	227.9	0.0	24.8	24.8	0.0	0.0	0.0	739.1
Potsdam	0.0	0.0	−29.7	6.4	6.4	29.7	0.0	29.7	585.9
Frankfurt/O	0.0	0.0	−88.0	1.8	1.8	88.0	0.0	88.0	357.8
Leipzig	0.0	0.0	−10.2	91.1	91.1	10.2	10.2	0.0	1 797.8
Chemnitz	−19.1	0.0	0.4	17.9	17.5	0.0	0.0	0.0	880.6
Halle/S	0.0	0.0	−35.9	14.2	14.2	35.9	35.9	0.0	1 025.9
Gera	−54.4	0.0	0.0	5.0	5.0	0.0	0.0	0.0	303.4

Note: * contribution to capital account, minus compulsory contribution, minus contribution from capital to current account.

Source: Deutscher Städtetag, *Gemeindefinanzbericht 1998*, in Der Städtetag 3/1998, p. 185.

Table 7.5 also illustrates the different legal rules of German Länder. While the Northern, the South Western and the new East German Länder require that the compulsory contributions to the capital account are explicitly covered – which sometimes leads to imbalances of current accounts – Bavaria and Baden-Württemberg demand a balanced current account, but do not require the compulsory contribution to the capital account. The material result is however equal. The South German cities were also unable to finance credit repayments from current revenues, but formally they do not show deficient current accounts. This background however explains the sharp decline of local net borrowing in the late 1990s.

The continuing deficits of current accounts indicate severe problems of local finance in Germany. They are partly related to problems of the federal financial politics of Bund and Länder which – because of the often criticised interdependence of the German fiscal constitution – always influence the financial situation of municipalities too. Partly the deficits can be regarded as an expression of municipal resistance against a declining (local) government sector. Their best chance to maintain their financial status against the powerful position of the respective Länder is to declare they are unable to cut back expenditures, which can best be expressed by a deficient current account. As the borrowing criteria cannot be seen as "hard" decision criteria but only as a base for more or less political negotiations – it is obvious that there are many critical local budgets which are only approved because it is politically impossible to refuse the approval! – it is clear that the necessary adaptations and reductions of credit finance will only happen in a medium perspective.

7.4.3 Evasion of Borrowing Limits by Privatisation

Since the beginning of the 1990s, there has been a new wave of outsourcing administrative enterprises from local budgets to separate economic entities, giving these newly funded local enterprises a certain part of the local debt to take with them. The procedures of the so-called "formal" privatisation are undertaken particularly in the field of big local enterprises; that is, water provision and sewage purification enterprises, local traffic enterprises, and refuse disposal enterprises actually receiving about 80% of the total amount of local fees plus high proceeds from selling services under quasi-market conditions.[14]

The enterprises concerned, formerly parts of the local administration, are now established as independent enterprises owned by the local government and equipped not only with a company capital mostly consisting of the material capital formation and buildings, but also with part of the local debt.

It is just difficult to determine the appropriate share of local debt caused by the not yet repaid amount of credits of local investment expenditures. The formally privatised enterprises are still guaranteed by local governments because of the fact that they provide services due under the legal local responsibilities and are still under the regime of the state legislation regarding calculating fees and prices. They present few risks for creditors and take over local borrowing under the advantageous conditions which local governments receive particularly from their local savings banks. The material equipment of these local enterprises is not to be impounded by creditors because it serves to provide local public goods. However, local governments are legally liable for these enterprises and remain responsible for deciding on the amount and the structure of fees and prices.

From this perspective, it is profitable for a local treasurer to equip these local enterprises "going private" with a high volume of local debt. This procedure becomes easy if there is no calculation of from what financial sources the investment expenditures had been financed. There is a strong likelihood that among the considerable "freeing" from debt most of the big cities have seemingly undertaken during the last years, most of it was not a substantial redemption but only an outsourcing of debt to local enterprises now under private law. About the latter phenomenon, there is no statistical information available.

There are only indicators about the volume of that sort of "privatisation" of local debt and public personnel. As an example, the city of Saarbrücken is equipped with about 7,000 civil servants and employees, of which only 2,600 are members of the local administration and about 4,500 are employees of the privatised local enterprises. From 1990 to 1994, the volume of administrative debt of Saarbrücken declined from 658 million DM (3,517 DM per capita) to 632 million DM (3,338 DM per capita). The debt from administration-related enterprises increased from 0 to 227 million DM. The decline of local debt in Frankfurt/M from 1994 to 1998 (see Table 7.3) is also not the result of net repayments but comes only from privatisation of local enterprises.

The debt of the local enterprises under private law is not registered in the official local statistics. Neither do the economic transactions of local enterprises under private law fall under the normal state control, respectively under the budgetary right of the local parliaments. However, losses have to be covered by the owner which still is the municipality. The more local enterprises are set under competition by European deregulation, the higher become the risks for the local budgets. Actually there is huge economic pressure on local governments to take over additional sureties for these enterprises. No state control agency considers these transactions outside the local administration in the narrower sense. The transactions which provide similar financial risks for future local budgets such as direct local borrowing are beyond political control. It should not be denied that many cities might have even bigger problems from that hidden local debt than from their official public budgets.

7.5   STATE INDEBTEDNESS INSTEAD OF LOCAL DEBT? PERSPECTIVES OF REFORM BY REBUILDING THE GERMAN FISCAL CONSTITUTION

Although many German municipalities have collected a considerable amount of local debt, it should be stated that many more have undertaken a relatively restrictive borrowing policy. With regard to the pay-as-you-use principle of local debt and the long life of local infrastructure, the suspicion might come up that too many projects were pre-financed by taxes and grants. Taking the bad state of the local infrastructure into the calculation, the decline of net borrowing and the decline of real investment expenditures show dangers for the future competitiveness of the German economy.

It should however not be overlooked that local investment expenditures are only partly financed by proper local means. A considerable share is covered by grants from state budgets (Dornbusch, 1997, p. 130), a minor share also from federal budgets. Against this background, the question must be asked whether the under average share of local governments in total public debt does not result (also) from state grants which – as so-called "financial" investment expenditures – were financed themselves by credits. This procedure is legal according to the federal constitution and state budgetary laws. Unlike under local regulation however, federal and state governments are not obliged to repay public debt from current receipts – neither to economise an amortisation. They therefore compile annual net borrowings year after year without any regard to the still existing value of public infrastructure. The passion of state governments to pay capital grants instead of general grants (in favour of current accounts) to municipalities cannot be explained only by the so-called "golden rein" (Zimmermann, 2000, p. 225), but also by the fact that these can be financed by raising debt instead of using tax receipts.

Therefore the theoretical question should be raised whether the total government debt would be lower if local governments had financed local investment expenditures by their own means, even if they had received the same amount of grants but in the form of general grants instead of – conditional or unconditional - grants in the capital account. At least state governments could not yet argue that their volume of debt would not only result from their "own" politics, but also from local infrastructure. And it shows that the interdependence of the German fiscal constitutions, which is meanwhile called a "system of organised irresponsibility", is not only valid for public expenditures and tax receipts, but also for public debt.

From this perspective, the only solution to state and local government debt is a total reform of the fiscal constitution equipping both with considerable autonomies in the field of taxation. Recently, federal legislation has provided another local tax "reform", abolishing the capital asset tax as part of the local trade tax which is traditionally vested with an autonomous right of determining a local multiplier of the tax rate. Local governments receive a share of VAT instead, which is uniform all over Germany and not vested with an instrument of local tax autonomy. State governments do not have any right of tax autonomy. Only by this right are governments able to decide on their budgets in a responsible way and, within that context, on the volume of borrowing and debt they can meet. But one cannot avoid noticing that particularly state governments lack the necessary courage to become more independent from the federal decisions about their level of public finance. It should be clear as well, however, that there is no other way out of the crisis for the German government sector. And they have to do it before the burden of official and hidden state and local debt has reached a level where the pain of the interest payments really throttles the already reduced local self-administration.

NOTES

1.　The total debt indicators differ slightly from those of Table 7.1 which come from different statistical sources. The increase of total debt does not equal net borrowing because of certain other local debt transactions whether concerned with exporting debt in the context of privatising local enterprises or taking over local debt, e.g. from the Eastern local housing sector.
2.　Capital transfers in favour of outsourced independent local enterprises are treated as financial investment expenditures as well as those in favour of private enterprises.
3.　The positions "calculatory costs" and "calculatory receipts" are from the point of view of real budgetary transaction "fakes". They indicate costs which do not correspond with *expenditures* in the budget. They occur in those administrative entities which cover more than 50% of their expenditures by fees. The German local financial system distinguishes calculatory amortisation, calculatory interest payments and calculatory rents. These calculatory costs lead to problems in balancing the current account. Therefore accounted calculatory receipts present the same amount as calculatory costs in the budget.
4.　Social assistance expenditures which local governments have to spend according to the narrowly defined rules of the respective federal law increased from 3 billion DM in 1970 to 51 billion DM in 1995 – 17 times the amount of 1970 relative to a growth rate of GDP of about 650% during this period.
5.　The time lag of covering current account deficits comes from the "technical" necessity that at the time when a local budget has to be decided – in general before the beginning of the respective fiscal year – the current account deficit of the current fiscal year is not yet determined because of the unfinished budget period. Therefore it is in general the second fiscal year after the one that closes with a current account deficit when the deficit has to be covered by current revenues of that fiscal year.
6.　In some Länder, there are slightly different rules for balancing deficits of current account for districts. For example, in Lower Saxony, districts can provide current account deficits according to the same rules as municipalities. In Rhineland-Palatinate however, districts must not have this type of deficit. They have to increase the rate of the district apportionment, which gives them a certain share of their municipalities' current revenues, until the deficit is balanced.

7. Local fiscal equalisation systems in Germany do not contain elements of equalising losses of receipts due to recession. They only equalise differences between fiscal capacity and "fiscal needs" which are determined by the size of population and certain special factors like the number of pupils, the expanse of local area, and others.

8. The data are used to provide an overview of the total budgets of the German government sector which is then used for co-ordination of general fiscal policy recommendations by the Financial Planning Council and the Council for Fiscal and Economic Policy Co-ordination. In both councils the three local government organisations are represented, alongside federal and state government members and other important institutions (e.g. the German Federal Bank).

9. If the repayments are due after that period, e.g. in the case where the repayment is contracted at the end of a borrowing period longer than three years, the indicator fails.

10. The statistical results might have been better again if the data from independent local enterprises, the so-called local shareholder property, would have been included particularly because recently most larger cities have begun to separate dependent local enterprises in their administration from independent shareholder properties, giving them a certain amount of debt to their opening balances (see also section. 7.4.3). Unfortunately, there are no general data available.

11. See Lüder, 1998.

12. All important local taxes, e.g. the trade and property tax as well as the personal income tax of which local governments receive a share of 15%, are under federal legislation.

13. The latter case is indicated by a current account deficit which is larger than the covering of former current account deficits.

14. The difference between fees and proceeds as considerations for services produced by local enterprises is the fact that in the case of fees citizens are obliged to enlist the local services, but in the case of proceeds they are free to take them or not. For example, in the case of purification of sewage there is a general obligation to plug into the local drainage system, but nobody is forced to join a public bus or tram.

REFERENCES

Ade, K. (1992), "Die finanzielle Leistungsfähigkeit der Gemeinden – ein unbestimmter Rechtsbegriff mit Beurteilungsspielraum?", *Der Gemeindehaushalt* no. 2, p. 40.

Barro, R.J. (1989), "The Ricardian Approach to Budget Deficits", *Journal of Economic Perspectives*, vol. 3, p. 37

Deutsche Bundesbank, *Monatsberichte* (monthly bulletins), Frankfurt/M., several editions.

Deutscher Städtetag (2000), "Gemeindefinanzbericht", *Der Städtetag* 4/2000.

Deutscher Städtetag, *Statistisches Jahrbuch Deutscher Gemeinden*, Stuttgart a.o., several editions.

Domar, E.D. (1944), "The 'Burden of Debt' and the National Income", *The American Economic Review*, vol. 34, p. 798.

Dornbusch, Hans-Ludwig (1997), *Gemeindehaushalt – Haushaltsrecht und Haushaltsanalyse*, Institut Finanzen und Steuern, *IFSt-Schrift* No. 358, Bonn.

Lüder, K. (1998), *Konzeptionelle Grundlagen des Neuen Kommunalen Haushaltswesens*, Stuttgart.

Michaelsen, J. (2000), *Die materiellen Kriterien zur Bestimmung der Schuldendienstgrenze gemeindlicher Haushalte*, Frankfurt/M a.o.

Postlep, R.-D. (1993), *Gesamtwirtschaftliche Analyse kommunaler Finanzpolitik*, Baden-Baden.

Ricardo, D. (1817, 1951), "Funding System", in Sraffa, P. (ed.) *The Works and Correspondence of David Ricardo*, vol. IV, Pamphlets and Papers, 1815–1823, Cambridge, p. 149.

Sachverständigenrat zur Begutachtung der gesamtwirtschaftlichen Entwicklung: *Jahresgutachten*, Stuttgart a.o., several editions.

Schwarting, G. (1985), "Grundsätze für die Kreditaufnahme der Gemeinden", Püttner, G. (ed.) *Handbuch der kommunalen Wissenschaft und Praxis*, 2nd. edition, Berlin et al., p. 621.

Schwarting, G. (2000), *Kommunale Kreditwesen - Haushaltsrechtliche Grundlagen - Schuldenmanagement - Neue Finanzierungsformen*, 2nd edn, Berlin.

Tiebout, C. (1956), "A Pure Theory of Local Expenditures", *Journal of Political Economy*, vol. 64, p. 416.

Zimmermann, H. (2000), *Kommunalfinanzen*, Baden-Baden.

8.   Local borrowing: the Italian case

Angela Fraschini

8.1   INTRODUCTION

The aim of this chapter is to analyse the capacity of indebtedness of the Italian local authorities (communes and provinces) in the light of the rule of balanced budget.

At present, by law local authorities can raise revenues from loans only to finance capital expenditures, specifically for public works (long-lasting infrastructures). On the contrary in the past, particularly during the period immediately following the tax reform implemented in 1973,[1] local authorities were allowed to have a current deficit that, under certain conditions, was financed by loans. At the local level there was a "softening" of the budget constraint,[2] due to several reasons, among which

> the mismatch between own resources and functions at local level (...) the large overlapping of functions among the different levels of government, which reduced accountability of the local politicians and induced local governments to free-ride against each other (...) the inability of central government to commit to a precise policy concerning local finance, defining functions, own resources and grants to local governments in a coherent framework and maintaining that framework consistently (...) the lack of transparency in accounting procedural at the local level and in the formulas for intergovernmental transfers (...) the lack of an adequate system for political representation at the local level which often resulted in the selection of local politicians who were hardly responsive to local preferences (Bordignon, 1999, pp. 2-3).

The heavy recourse to debt financing was due to the imbalance between current revenues and expenditures, that in its turn derived in part from the increasing separation of spending and taxing decisions,[3] and quickly led to a local financial crisis.[4] The interpretations of that crisis are well known, and both the revenue side and the expenditure side of the budget were considered. The causes of the financial difficulties dated back to (a) the non-buoyant taxes available to local governments, (b) the reduction of revenue in real terms fostered by the tax reform of the early 1970s, (c) the "not accountable" behaviour of the local politicians who did not worry about the expenditure's financing, (d) the growth of local current expenditure to meet the demand of new social services and to improve the existing services.

In 1976 current revenues financed only 70 per cent of local current expenditures and on January 1977 the accumulated debt[5] was about 23,488 milliard lire (11% of GDP), of which 52.6 per cent was due to the financing of current budget deficits. In addition, more than two-thirds of new loans were destined to repay previous debt.

So, to reclaim the financial situation, in 1977 Act n. 62 consolidated local authorities' loans and fixed a limit for short-term loans (cash advances),[6] restricting the period (not to exceed three months) and the amount (not to exceed 3/12 of current revenues assessed during the preceding accounting period). In 1978, on the basis of Act n. 43, local authorities were freed from the burden of previous debts, with central government being responsible for the amortisation of funded debts.[7] Consequently, the current part of the budget had to be balanced and local authorities could borrow only to finance capital outlays. Moreover, afterwards some constraints were placed on the contracting of loans; in fact, Act n. 155/1989 established that in order to obtain the loans local authorities were obliged to turn first to the Deposits and Loans Fund (*Cassa Depositi e Prestiti*) and only in the event of a negative response were they authorised to turn to other banking companies. In the latter event, however, the Treasury Ministry determined the maximum applicable interest rate.

The constraints on the raising of loans had the aim of making the local authorities' debt level compatible with that of the public sector as a whole, as well as placing the borrowing authorities in the condition of being able to amortise their debt and the accrued interests which, on the other hand, could not exceed 25 per cent of current revenues of the budget (Fraschini, 1993).

The analysis begins, in the next section, with a short description of the structure of local government in Italy. Section 8.3 examines the present rules relative to balance, borrowing and its repayment. Section 8.4 deals with the local authorities' bonds, and Section 8.5 concludes the chapter.

8.2   THE STRUCTURE OF LOCAL GOVERNMENTS

Italy is a unitary state, even if the constitution recognises that the regions have a legislative, administrative and financial autonomy. There are four levels of government: the central government (*Stato*), the regions (*Regioni*) (20 in number), the provinces (*Province*) (103 in number at present) and the communes (*comuni*) (about 8,100 in number at present).[8]

The regions are established as autonomous units with powers and functions specific to them, in accordance with the principles laid down in the constitution itself. The legal structure of the regions is not uniform: the autonomy enjoyed by five of them (the regions with special statute[9]) takes particular forms and is subject to particular conditions,[10] whereas the other 15 (the regions with ordinary statute, established in 1970[11]) are subject to uniform general legislation. The ordinary regions have legislative power in the matters listed in article 117 of the constitution.[12] They perform administrative functions in the same specified matters (often through the provinces and the communes to which the region delegates some functions). They exercise supervision over a few acts of the local authorities (i.e. budgets, statutes, regulations within the competence of the communal and provincial councils – but organisational competence and book-keeping autonomy are excluded).

The provinces and the communes (named local governments) are administrative autonomous bodies within the terms of the principles laid down in the general national legislation that specifies their functions. The communes are the more important of the two bodies and they provide many services, mainly:

(a)   *social, educational and recreational services* (municipal police, social care for the elderly, nursery schooling, pre-school and compulsory education, sports facilities, local museums and theatres, education in handicrafts and professions, and public housing, in connection with other special bodies);

(b)   *economic development services* (tourism and hotels, trade fairs, mineral and thermal waters, quarries and mines, handicrafts, agriculture and forestry);

(c)   *land and territorial services* (communal road construction maintenance and building, urban transport, aqueducts and sewerage, refuse collection and disposal, gas distribution and (in some cases) electricity production and supply, cemeteries, environmental controls, together with the provinces) (Pola, 1996, pp. 4–5).

To continue, according to Act n. 142 of 1990 (Rules of local autonomies), at present the communes perform all the administrative functions concerning the population and communal territory mainly in the sectors of social services, territory utilisation and economic development, except for the functions that are expressly attributed by state or regional laws to other authorities. Furthermore the communes manage some services that are in the competence of the state (ballot, general register, statistics and levy). Further administrative functions related to services that are within the central government's competence can be assigned to the communes by the law that also regulates the relative financial relations securing the required resources.

The basic functions of the provinces are those delegated to them by the region in which they are situated (including health, hygiene, public works, regulation of fishing and hunting, public transport) and those directly allocated to them by the national and regional legislation in several fields, including ground defence, protection and improvement of the environment and of water and energy resources, improvement of cultural goods, flora and fauna protection, natural parks, organisation of waste disposal at provincial level, control of air and noise emission, water pollution control and education. It is clear that this list is not exhaustive.

For the last few years local governments have been under reform. Recently, the process of decentralisation has undergone acceleration with the entering into force of Act n. 59 of 1997[13] and the implementing legislative decree n. 112 of 1998.[14] The latter confers administrative functions to the regions and to the local governments in the following fields:

(a)   *economic development and productive activities* (relating to: agriculture and forestry, craftsmanship, industry, energy, mines and geothermic resources, rules of the chambers of commerce, trade and fairs, tourism and the hotel industry);

(b)   *territory, environment and infrastructures* (relating to: territory and city planning, natural and environmental protection, pollution control and waste management, water resources and ground safeguard, public works, road conditions, transport, civil protection);

(c)   *services to the person and to the community* (relating to: health protection, social services, education, training, cultural goods and activities, sport);

(d)   *regional and local administrative police, authorisation system.*

Unlike the previous process of decentralisation, carried out with presidential decree n. 616 of 1977, that minutely determined the functions to be transferred to the regions and to the local governments, the present procedure follows the opposite path: in each of the above fields the functions reserved for central government are specified,[15] whereas all the other functions are conferred upon the regions and the local governments. In their turn each region had six months[16] from the issuing of decree n. 112 (31 March 1998) to determine by regional law the administrative functions that fall into the unitary practice at regional level, conferring all the other functions to local governments. In case of default of the single region, central government issues legislative decrees for the division of functions between the region and the local governments and these decrees will be valid until the regional law comes into force.[17]

The new model of decentralisation is founded on the principle of subsidiarity and is respectful of demographic, territorial and structural diversities that characterise local governments. But given the conferment of functions through a "cascade mechanism", at present it is not easy to draw a map of the functions that will be performed by local governments under this regime (1 January 2001). Moreover the central government has not yet determined and transferred to them all the resources (financial resources, human resources and goods) that are needed to carry out the new functions.

8.2.1 Local Fiscal Structure

The main elements of local government financing in Italy are:[18]

(a)   *own resources* (taxes, fees and user charges), that represent about 40% of current income, about 29% of total receipts and finance about 43% of current expenditures. The main tax at communal level is ICI, a property tax on houses, agricultural land and building sites,[19] whose estimated revenue was 17,650 milliard lire in 1999, equal to 49% of the local governments' own resources;

(b)   *current grants*, that represent about 38% of current revenues and finance about 40% of current expenditures, whereas capital grants represent about 89% of capital receipts and finance about 58% of capital expenditures. Both grants represent about 42% of total receipts and finance about 41% of total expenditures. Most of the grants are distributed as block grants based on objective criteria taking into account population, territory, economic and social conditions, imbalance due to local taxation. There are also matching grants and equalisation grants;

(c)   *borrowing*, that represents about 3.7% of total receipts;

(d)   *other forms of income* (sale of goods and services, capital income, financial entries), that represent about 29% of total receipts.

Table 8.1 and Figure 8.1 show the local government finance account, by economic category.

In 1999 total local government revenue amounted to around 5.8% of GDP; if we also consider the total revenue of the regions the above value rises to 14.2%, lower than that of other European countries (Norway, for example).

*Table 8.1   Local   government   finance   account   (cash)   -   absolute   data
              (milliard lire) and percentage composition, 1999*

	1999	%
	Current income	
Income from taxes	36 176	29.2
Sale of goods and services	10 902	8.8
Income from capital	5 315	4.3
Grants	34 020	27.5
Other forms of income	3 775	3.1
	Capital account	
Grants	17 636	14.3
Other forms of income	2 214	1.8
	Financial entries	
Collection of credits	3 773	3.0
Other financial entries	9 906	8.0
Total	**123 717**	**100.0**

Source: Relazione generale sulla situazione economica del Paese, 1999; own calculations.

As shown in Table 8.2, at present local governments derive a substantial part of their resources from their own taxes and their fiscal autonomy has been further increased from 1999 with the entering into force of a communal and a provincial surtax on IRPEF (personal income tax) .[20] During the last two decades the tax-levying capacity of local authorities has increased jointly with the decrease of the grants' weight from the central government. While in 1980 grants to local governments represented 75% of their own revenues, much higher than the average of other OECD countries, at the beginning of the 1990s they were almost equal to the international average (see Table 8.3). With due caution that is required by comparisons with quite different institutional systems, it is interesting to note that in Italy the reduction in financial dependence of local authorities from the central government was substantial (from 75% to 46%), whereas in other countries considered in the table the differences were not so remarkable. Therefore, one can say that it took 20 years to correct the "mistake" made by central government in the ambit of the fiscal reform of the 1970s, that is, the abolition of the local tax-levying autonomy.

**Percentage composition of local government's
finance account - 1999**

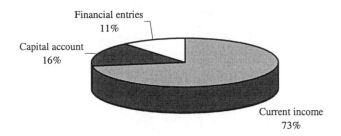

Financial entries
11%

Capital account
16%

Current income
73%

*Figure 8.1   Percentage composition of local government's finance account –
1999*

The principles that have been invoked to justify a return of tax-levying
autonomy to the Italian local governments (in particular the communes) were
like those invoked in other countries:[21]

(a)   the *principle of accountability*, which would ensure that decisions
        taken by local administrators reflect the preferences of the citizens,
        avoiding such irresponsible behaviour as offering services at local
        level beyond the optimal amount because the cost of such services
        is borne by central government;

(b)   the *benefit principle*, which takes into account the fact that the
        advantages from the services provided by the local authorities – in
        particular the communes – are primarily enjoyed by those residing
        in a particular locality and that, therefore, the beneficiaries should
        bear the cost for such services.[22]

Table 8.2   *Local government current revenues (cash) – percentages,*
             1987–1999

Years	Own Taxes	Grants central gov.	others	Non-tax income	Total
1987	12.7	67.6	5.7	14.0	100
1988	13.7	64.9	5.6	15.8	100
1989	17.1	57.9	6.3	18.7	100
1990	18.0	56.9	7.6	17.5	100
1991	18.2	57.2	6.9	17.7	100
1992	21.3	51.5	7.3	19.9	100
1993	27.6	44.6	8.0	19.8	100
1994	37.6	33.9	7.8	20.7	100
1995	37.9	33.8	8.6	19.7	100
1996	40.2	34.3	6.8	18.7	100
1997	41.5	29.8	7.5	21.2	100
1998	37.3	30.6	10.9	21.2	100
1999	40.1	26.8	10.9	22.2	100

Source: Relazione generale sulla situazione economica del Paese, v.y.; own calculations.

Table 8.3   *Ratio of grants from central government*
             to local government own resources

Countries	Grants / Own resources % 1980	1990
Italy	75.0	46.0*
Belgium	64.4	55.5
Denmark	51.8	42.9
Finland	31.6	34.0
France	41.2	34.8
Spain	9.8	27.8
Sweden	25.3	19.7
Ireland	74.6	70.0
Luxembourg	35.9	n.a.
Netherlands	81.1	78.6
Norway	38.0	40.2
United Kingdom	46.7	58.9
Average	**45.2**	**46.2**

*Note: * Datum referred to 1993.

*Source: Ministero dell'Interno (1996).

8.2.2 Local Public Expenditures

Currently, about 68% of total local government expenditures are revenue spending, whereas capital expenditures are about 24%. In 1999 total expenditures amounted to 125,030 milliard lire (equal to 5.9% of GDP), of which 84,882 milliard lire (about 4% of GDP) represent revenue spending and 30,619 milliard lire (about 1.4% of GDP) are capital expenditures (see Figure 8.2). The most part of capital expenditures is devoted to public works that are mainly financed by capital grants from central government and by borrowing. In fact, it has been argued (De Magistris, 1998) that public works expenditure depends on the amount of grants and that there is a substitution effect between grants and loans; in other words, local authorities decide to contract new loans when grants are lacking. Moreover, the sources of financing and the planning capacity of local authorities, mainly communes, can be considered the principal determinants of the investments' variability in real terms.

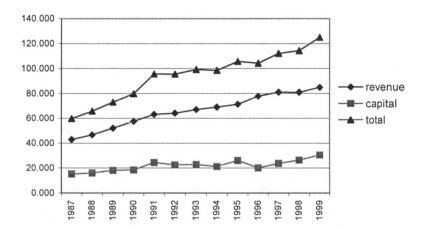

Figure 8.2   Local government expenditures – cash (milliard lire)

8.2.3 Local Borrowing

At 1 January 1999 (last available data), local government debt (short-term and long-term) amounted to 70,769 milliard lire (3.3% of GDP), of which 91.1% was for public works, whereas in 1977 (the first year of "controlled evolution" of local government expenditures) it amounted to 23,488 milliard lire (equal to 11% of GDP) of which around 53% was to balance the budget, 24% was to finance public works, around 20% for cash advances and 3% for other aims.

Table 8.4 (illustrated in Figure 8.3) and Table 8.5 show, respectively in absolute value and in percentage terms, local government short- and long-term debt by category of loans in the last two decades. Since 1978 the majority of the debt has been for public works, whereas cash advances almost disappear in recent years as a consequence of the adopted measures to reclaim the financial situation of local governments.

Table 8.4   *Local government borrowing (stock) at 1 January, absolute data (milliard lire) and percentage, 1977–1999*

Years	Public works	Other aims	Cash advance	Total	% GDP
1977	5 749	604	4 778	23 488*	11.0
1978	6 944	998	845	8 787	3.5
1979	8 424	1 021	362	9 807	3.2
1980	10 841	1 299	285	12 425	3.2
1981	14 853	1 358	349	16 560	3.6
1982	18 352	1 508	236	20 096	3.7
1983	22 862	1 701	535	25 098	4.0
1984	29 004	1 779	505	31 288	4.3
1985	35 120	2 221	370	37 711	4.7
1986	40 628	3 671	342	44 641	5.0
1987	46 953	4 180	227	51 360	5.2
1988	51 629	4 171	289	56 089	5.1
1989	56 766	4 895	230	61 891	5.2
1990	62 950	4 996	317	68 263	5.2
1991	62 969	6 287	291	69 547	4.9
1992	63 666	6 119	298	70 083	4.7
1993	62 962	5 825	347	69 134	4.4
1994	61 372	5 258	270	66 900	4.1
1995	59 513	4 581	155	64 249	3.6
1996	59 289	4 625	76	63 990	3.4
1997	54 848	5 514	31	60 393	3.1
1998	61 549	5 180	17	66 746	3.2
1999	64 447	6 299	23	70 769	3.3

Note: * In the total are included 12,357 milliard lire to balance the budget.

Source: *Relazione generale sulla situazione economica del Paese*, v.y.; own calculations.

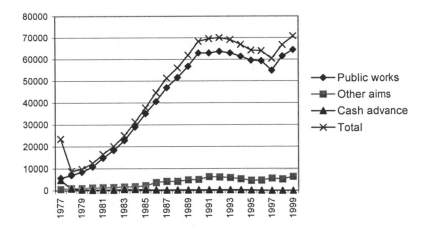

Figure 8.3 Local government borrowing (stock), absolute data (milliard lire)

In 1978 the strong reduction of local borrowing, both as a percentage of GDP and in absolute value, is the result of the restrictions and rules imposed on local governments to get out of the financial crisis. As already said, first of all local authorities were freed from the burden of previous debt by making central government responsible for the amortisation of funded debts, the current part of the budget had to be balanced (therefore no more borrowing to balance the budget was allowed, but some local governments avoided that restriction by creating off-budget debts[23]), and the borrowing had only to finance capital outlays. In the following years some constraints were placed on the contracting of loans, (see section 8.1) with the consequence of a continuous reduction (from 1990 to 1997) of the borrowing's ratio to GDP. In 1998/99 there was a slight increase in that ratio due to the growth of borrowing to finance public works.

It is also worth stressing the different composition of the local borrowing that, after 1978, is mainly due to public works (particularly for transport and communications, public housing, school buildings), being forbidden the financing of current expenditures through indebtedness, as already mentioned.

Local public finance in Europe

Table 8.5   *Local government borrowing at 1 January, percentage,*
               1977-1999

Years	Public works	Other aims	Cash advance	Total
1977	24.5	2.6	20.3	100*
1978	79.0	11.4	9.6	100
1979	85.9	10.4	3.7	100
1980	87.3	10.4	2.3	100
1981	89.7	8.2	2.1	100
1982	91.3	7.5	1.2	100
1983	91.1	6.8	2.1	100
1984	92.7	5.7	1.6	100
1985	93.1	5.9	1.0	100
1986	91.0	8.2	0.8	100
1987	91.4	8.2	0.4	100
1988	92.0	7.5	0.5	100
1989	91.7	7.9	0.4	100
1990	92.2	7.3	0.5	100
1991	90.6	9.0	0.4	100
1992	90.8	8.7	0.4	100
1993	91.1	8.4	0.5	100
1994	91.7	7.9	0.4	100
1995	92.6	7.1	0.3	100
1996	92.7	7.2	0.1	100
1997	90.8	9.1	0.1	100
1998	92.2	7.8	0.0	100
1999	91.1	8.9	0.0	100

Note: * In the total is included 52.6% to balance the budget.

Source: *Relazione generale sulla situazione economica del Paese*, v.y.; own calculations.

From 1990 the growth rate of borrowing slows down and after 1993 the residual debt starts to decrease, with refunding being greater than new borrowing. This is in line with the trend of expenditures for public works, that since 1989 have shown a reduction mainly due to both the exhaustion of special laws issued by central government to support specific local public works, and the reform of 1992 (legislative decree n. 504). On the basis of that reform central government gives local authorities limited capital account grants and both the capital expenditures and the burden of the indebtedness fall totally on the same local authorities. On the contrary, during the period 1978–85 the investments of local authorities were almost entirely financed by central government and during the period 1986–92 central government's financial intervention was remarkable. The financing at zero price of local authorities' investments is not an incentive to make the best choices, since the change of the factor prices can have caused a distortion in the use of the factor combination and therefore one cannot exclude a certain over-capacity of local authorities. Moreover, the subsidised financing of the investments can cause the underestimation of the operating expenses and this is another negative effect in efficiency terms. In fact, during the 1980s there were several cases (concerning especially the smaller communes) of public works that were built but never used (see Piperno, 1998). Besides, during the period 1985–1998 many local authorities did not utilise, totally or partially, the loans granted by the Deposits and Loans Fund, with the consequence of the non-execution of the planned works. This resulted in the appropriation of resources to spend on the local social communities' needs (Corte dei Conti, 1998, cap. III).

Local public debt and the stability pact
Local public debt contributes to the calculation of the Maastricht Treaty's parameters. Nevertheless, the rules ("deficit less than or equal to 3 per cent of GDP" and "total debt less than or equal to 60 per cent of GDP") initially were applied to the whole public sector and not to the sub-sectors. It was only with the Act n. 448/1998 (an act geared to the financial act of 1999) that the regions and the local authorities had to conform to the realisation of the objectives of public finance that the country adopted with adhesion to the Stability Pact for Europe (Fraschini, 1999).

The sub-national levels of government bind themselves to reduce progressively the deficit financing of their own expenditures and to reduce their debt ratio to GDP.[24] In 1999 the reduction of the deficit had to be equal to, at least, 0.1% of GDP, whereas in the two successive years the requirement is that the annual deficit ratio to GDP remains constant. With regard to the reduction of the debt ratio to GDP, the reference datum is that relative to 31 December 1998 and the reduction must be considered as a tendency during the three years. In other words, increases of the ratio are allowed in each year, provided that such increases are counterbalanced during the same three years. For the authorities that respect the Stability Pact there is a "prize", consisting of a reduction of the interest rate on the loans granted by the Deposits and Loans Fund.

8.3 THE PRESENT RULES

In this section we analyse the rules relative to balancing the budget, local borrowing and its repayment.

8.3.1 Balance

The national legislator with Act n. 142 of 1990 (rules of local autonomies)[25] reaffirmed for local authorities the principle of a balanced budget, with regard to the current account and the total budget, and subsequently this rule was confirmed with legislative decree n. 77 of 1995 (local authorities' financial and book-keeping rules), which was updated and modified by a legislative decree approved on 12 September 1997.

According to the current legislation, the balance assumes two dimensions: the first refers to the total budget (financial balance), the second refers to the current account and the debt repayment (economic balance). The economic balance is defined in the following way:

$$eb = ce + aq - cr$$

where: eb = economic balance
        ce = current expenditures, including interests
        aq = amortisation quota of debt repayment
        cr = current revenues.

In fact, the above algebraic sum can also be negative; in other words, the amount of current revenues can be higher than the amount of current expenditures and amortisation quota of debt repayment. If so, the surplus can be used to finance investments.

The main reason for the financial balance is to be sought in the action of co-ordination and control exercised by central government over local public expenditure, according to the principle that a budget deficit must be the responsibility of central government.

On the contrary, the rationale for the economic balance is to guarantee the repayment of the debt in a pay-as-you-use finance scheme. As it is well known (see, for example, Musgrave, 1959), that scheme requests the division of the budget accounts into a current and a capital part and the deficit in the current account is not compatible with efficient budgeting. On the other hand, the financing of long-lasting infrastructure through borrowing allows that the citizens who enjoy the services pay for their provision. Therefore, debt financing of capital expenditure allows distributing costs across all (current and future) users of capital improvements. In other words, capital expenditure must be financed from loans in order to secure intra- and inter-generational equity and to promote optimal spending level (King, 1984, ch. 8).

8.3.2 Borrowing

The legal framework splits borrowing into two types:

1. *short-term loans*, which can be used only for temporary deficiencies of cash and have the aim of allowing the payment of urgent and undelayable expenses that otherwise could not be made, with negative repercussions on the working out of local public services. In other words, short-term loans cannot be considered as additional resources in respect of those estimated in the budget, but as a tool that allows the payment of expenses that could not otherwise be paid due to a lack of liquidity. Short-term loans are subject to the limits indicated above (duration not beyond three months and amount not exceeding 3/12 of current revenue assessed during the preceding accounting period) and must be paid off in the same financial year as they are contracted;

2. *long-term loans*, which must finance investment expenditures and off-budget debts[26] and are subject to several ties, among which is the earmarking of resources. Other constraints on the borrowing capacity of local governments,[27] also fixed by the central government, are the following:

    (a) the annual interest expenditures (net of state and regional grants on interest accounts) cannot exceed 25% of current revenues[28] of the statement relative to the penultimate financial year preceding that when borrowing is decided;

    (b) the statement of the penultimate financial year must be passed;

    (c) the budget of the year when the loans are deliberated must be passed.

Act n. 403 of 1990 abolished the previous constraint according to which to obtain the loans local authorities were obliged to turn first to the Deposits and Loans Fund. The aim of that constraint was to contain the local authorities' interest expenditures since the interest rate applied by the Deposits and Loans Fund was lower than those applied by the banking companies.

Other ties are imposed by law (Act n. 144/1989) on the moneylending contracts drawn up with corporations – apart from the Deposits and Loans Fund, the National Sport Finance Corporation (*Istituto di credito sportivo*) and the National Institute of Security for Civil Servants (*Istituto Nazionale di Previdenza per i Dipendenti dell'Amministrazione Pubblica – INPDAP*).[29] These contracts must be stipulated in public form and must contain the following clauses and conditions (among others):

(a) length of amortisation not shorter than ten years;

(b) instalment of amortisation including, from the first year, the amortisation quota and interest;

(c)   exact indication of the nature of the expenditure to be financed with the loan;

(d)   assignment of the loan on the ground of the expenditure records or on the ground of the state of works progress;

(e)   respect of the maximum interest rate (applicable to the loans), periodically determined by the Treasury;

(f)   possibility of borrowing to finance public works devoted to public services only if the contracts provide for the realisation of projects "on stream" and at a specified price that cannot be increased.

Economic financial plan

The above-mentioned rules constitute the budget discipline, limiting in advance the possibility of deficit spending or borrowing.

Since the last decade, especially, the local authorities' current expenditures induced by investment expenditure have assumed an increasing importance, due to the huge amount of local governments' loans that central government took upon itself (totally or partially). The national legislator with Act n. 155/1989 subjected the granting of loans to finance local investments to the approval of the financial plan.[30] The plan can therefore be seen as a form of budget responsibility that intervenes, under definite conditions, for individual investment decisions.

With the drawing up of the plan the local authority must demonstrate the real payment capacity either of the instalments of loans' amortisation or of the higher operating expenses resulting from the investment, showing they have the resources to meet the above-mentioned expenditures. In other words, taking notice of the investment costs appearing from the project's economic table, one determines the amount of the instalment of amortisation and the expenditures for the public work's management; on the bases of these quantities one must individualise the corresponding amount in the budget. Therefore, the cognitive purpose of the financial plan allows the choice of the project and the valuation of the financial impact; in these circumstances the local authority knows for certain the total costs it will have to bear.

According to the legislative decree n. 504 of 1992 (reorganisation of local authorities' finance) the above financial plan must be integrated with a further economic financial plan, meant for the assessment of the economic financial equilibrium of both the investment and the management service, in order to determine user charges taking also into account the investment's expected receipts. According to the legislative decree n. 528 of 1993 the economic financial plan exclusively concerns new public works (devoted to public services for which a user charge must be paid) whose general project involves expenditure higher than a thousand million lire. In this case the financing of the investment is subject to the drawing up and acceptance of the economic financial plan on the part of a banking company (listed in a decree of the Treasury Ministry[31]) or of the Deposits and Loans Fund for the investments financed by the same Fund. Finally, Act n. 724 of 1994 also imposed on the investments financed by bond issue the duty to draw up an economic financial plan.

The aim of the economic financial plan is to determine a user charge for the public service sufficient to ensure the economic and financial recovery of the investment's burdens. Those burdens can be covered either by the sale of a greater quantity of the public service (when the investment allows an additional supply of the pre-existing service) or by increases of the user charge applied to the quantities of the service already supplied (when the investment does not allow an increase of the existing service capacity).

8.3.3 Repayment of Borrowing

The repayment of borrowing is compulsory and current revenues must cover the corresponding expenditure. In fact, the annual instalment of amortisation, composed of interest and principal, contributes to form the economic balance, as defined above. In this way, the debt repayment is self-financed and local authorities cannot borrow to repay previous loans, thus avoiding the risk of accumulating debt.

Since more than two-thirds of local indebtedness is financed by the Deposits and Loans Fund, we refer to the rules of amortisation applied by this agency to the loans at fixed interest rate.[32]

The beginning of the amortisation starts from the first of January of the year following that when the loan has been granted (the same rule is applied by the banking companies). With Act n. 539 of 1995 local authorities can ask for the beginning of the amortisation from the first of January of the second year following that when the loan has been granted. In this case, on 31 December of each year of pre-amortisation the borrower must pay the interest at the same rate of amortisation.

The duration of the amortisation is generally 20 years (no more), in order to reduce the impact of the periodic payment on the local authority's budget and to promote investments, but the borrower can ask for decennial amortisation which is, in any case, compulsory for the purchase of motor vehicles, moveables, informatic projects and loans of which the amount is not above 20 million lire.

The instalments comprise both principal and interest, they are constant, half-yearly, deferred and paid every year on 30 June and 31 December.

The half-yearly instalment is calculated as follows:

$$R = C \, x \, i/1 - (1+i)^{-n}$$

where: R = half-yearly instalment
        C = borrowed capital
        i = half-yearly rate of interest
        n = number of the half-yearly instalments of repayment.

The rate of delayed interest is equal to the current interest rate applied by the Deposits and Loans Fund increased by five percentage points.

8.4 LOCAL AUTHORITY BONDS

On the basis of Act n. 142 of 1990, local authorities can issue bonds;[33] nevertheless the Act does not regulate in detail these means of financing since it is a general law on the rules of local autonomies. The detailed normative tools have been established by article 35 of Act n. 724 of 1994, according to which the bond issue must finance investments exclusively. Moreover, the issuing local authority must not be in a situation of financial trouble, the statement relative to the penultimate financial year must not result in a deficit and the budget of the year when the bond issue is deliberated must be passed. The bond issue's amount must be equal to the value of the investment's executive project to which it refers. Naturally, the interest rates on bonds concur to the determination of the limit of above-described indebtedness.

In the matter of bond issue the subsequent ministerial decree n. 152 of 1996 established the following rules:

(a) the bonds' term must exceed five years;
(b) the issue must finance investments and cannot finance current expenditures;
(c) the issue is subject to the approval of the economic financial plan, of the executive plan and of the redemption plan relative to the investment, which the local authority intends to carry out;
(d) the coupons' yield (quarterly, half-yearly or yearly, at variable or fixed rate) cannot exceed the gross yield of analogous government bonds by more than one point;
(e) any guarantee to be charged to the central government and/or the regions is excluded.

The resolution of a bond issue on the domestic market exceeding 100 milliard lire must be communicated to the Bank of Italy for prior consent, whereas the placing of foreign currency loans on the foreign market must be authorised by the Treasury.

With regard to the tax treatment, a withholding tax equal to 12.5%[34] is applied and the levy belongs to the issuing local authority. Moreover, 0.1% of the amount collected at the moment of placing must be paid to the Treasury.

The bond issue from local authorities represents an important step towards a greater autonomy and efficiency of their financial policies; nevertheless it involves associated expenses that do not arise for loans, that is bond expenses and operating costs. Therefore, the local authority has an advantage to issue bonds when the interest rate differential (loans–bonds) is not eroded by the associated expenses connected with the bond issue.

At the beginning of 1998 (last data available) the bond issue from communes is limited: the most substantial issues are still those of Rome and Naples, for which amounts are 100 milliard lire and 195 million dollars respectively. The bond issues from provinces began at the end of 1997 with 100 milliard lire from the Province of Milan, 71.25 milliard lire from the Province of Verona and 28.1 milliard lire from the Province of Bergamo. The most promising issuers certainly are the regions: Sicily issued international eurobonds amounting to one milliard dollars, Tuscany issued bonds amounting to 450 milliard eurolire, Sardinia issued floating rate eurobonds amounting to about 500 million dollars and 200 milliard lire, Piedmont issued bonds amounting to 18.2 milliard lire, whereas Latium is going to issue bonds amounting to one milliard dollars.

During 1998 the bond issue from communes and provinces amounted to about 1,150 milliard lire, of which 363 milliard lire were issued by the commune of Turin, 71 milliard by the province of Verona and 60 milliard by the province of Milan.

8.5 CONCLUDING REMARKS

Analysis of balanced budget requirements and debt limits at local level reveals that the constraints have been effective in reducing the ratio of local government borrowing to GDP (from 11% in 1977 to 3.3% in 1999) and in modifying the composition of local public debt in favour of public works (from 25% of the total in 1977 to 91% in 1999). Nevertheless, during the 1980s there were several cases (concerning especially the smaller communes) of public works that were built but never used. Besides, during the period 1985–1998 many local authorities did not utilise, totally or partially, the loans granted by the Deposits and Loans Fund, the consequence of which was the non-execution of the planned works and the resulting appropriation of resources to spend on the local social communities' needs.

NOTES

1. For a short description of the main measures concerning local governments see Fraschini (1989).
2. According to Kornai (1986, p. 4), "The 'softening' of the budget constraint appears when the strict relationship between expenditure and earnings has been relaxed, because excess expenditure over earnings will be paid by some other institution, typically by the State. A further condition of 'softening' is that the decision-maker expects such external financial assistance with high probability and this probability is firmly built into his behaviour". The main focus of Kornai's paper is on the firm; nevertheless the concept can be applied to local governments as well, as the author does on page 23. For a recent analysis of the relationship between organisations of government involving some fiscal decentralisation and the degree of the soft budget constraint see Qian and Roland (1998).
3. For analysis concerning the effect of the separation of spending and taxing decisions in federal systems see, for example, Winer (1983).
4. Nevertheless, the financial crisis that hit local governments badly after the tax reform of the early 1970s had a more remote beginning, starting in the early years after the unification of 1861. See Fraschini (1988).
5. According to the definition given by the Bank of Italy, local public debt is the amount of local authorities' liabilities; a concept of "gross public debt – capital = net public debt" does not exist in Italy.
6. Local governments engaged in short-term loans to cover temporary operating deficits due to the mismatch between expected revenues and scheduled expenditures, caused mainly by the delay in the allotment of central government grants.
7. That measure, that can be associated with the writings of Keynes, reflects one of the principles of fiscal federalism stated by Musgrave, according to which the budget deficit is reserved to the central government.
8. About 68% of the total are located in the North-Centre and the remaining 32% are located in the South. About 73% of the total have a demographic dimension less than 5,000 inhabitants (about 71% of these communes are located in the North-Centre) and only three communes (Rome, Naples and Milan) have over 1 million inhabitants.
9. The five special regions are (in alphabetical order): Friuli-Venezia Giulia, Sardegna, Sicilia, Trentino-Alto Adige, and Valle d'Aosta. Of the five special regions, four were given their statutes in 1948 (Sicily had its own statute operating since 1946, before the promulgation of the Constitution), while Friuli-Venezia Giulia received its statute in 1963 after the resolution of the problem of Trieste with Yugoslavia.
10. The functions and the assignment of resources are not uniform, but each single statute, which has the same rank as constitutional laws, establishes them. The special statutes were passed in the form of constitutional legislation by the Constituent Assembly and by the national parliament for the case of Friuli-Venezia Giulia.
11. The 15 ordinary regions are (in alphabetical order): Abruzzo, Basilicata, Calabria, Campania, Emilia-Romagna, Lazio, Liguria, Lombardia, Marche, Molise, Piemonte, Puglia, Toscana, Umbria, and Veneto.
12. Article 117 of the Italian Constitution assigns powers in 19 different areas to the regions. These are: the arrangement of offices and administrative bodies that are under the control of the region; communal boundaries; urban and rural police forces; fairs and markets; public assistance and health and hospital care; handicraft and professional education and scholastic assistance; local museums and libraries; urban planning; tourism, hotel and catering industry; regional public transportation; regional communications, aqueducts and public works; navigation and inland ports; mineral and thermal waters; quarries and

peatbogs; hunting; fishing in inland waters; agriculture and forestry; handicraft and other matters set out in constitutional legislation. The fact is that the regions suffer many constraints imposed by central government. For example, most of the grants from central government are conditional and moreover the same central government gives the regions very strict guidelines on how to spend the money in particular sectors, leaving them very little room to exercise their legislative power. A prime example is the health sector (see Bordignon, 1999).

13. The Act n. 59 of 1997 is a law of delegation with which, furthermore, the Italian Parliament fixes some principles that must guide the Cabinet in issuing decrees related to the assignment of functions to regions and local governments. The first principle, to which a great importance is attributed, is that of subsidiarity, an old principle rooted in the 15th century and recently held in the Maastricht Treaty. About the principle of subsidiarity and the assignment of powers to governing bodies located at different jurisdictional tiers, see Breton et al. (1998).

14. This decree has been modified and supplemented by the legislative decree n. 443 of 1999. For a short description of the recent decentralisation of powers from the centre to regional and local authorities see Breton and Fraschini (1999).

15. For example, with regard to craftsmanship the following functions are reserved to the State: (a) protection of the production of clay goods; (b) possible co-financing, in the national interest, of regional development programmes in support of craftsmanship. All the other functions not reserved to the State are conferred to the regions.

16. That term was subsequently fixed on 31 March, 1999.

17. In fact nine ordinary regions (Piemonte, Lombardia, Veneto, Marche, Lazio, Molise, Campania, Puglia and Calabria) did not respect the term of 31 March 1999 to issue the regional laws implementing decree n. 112/1998. Therefore with the legislative decree n. 96/1999 central government provided for division of the administrative functions between the defaulter regions and their local authorities.

18. Cash data refer to 1999. The Italian public accounting system distinguishes between the budget of "entitlements" and "obligations" (*bilancio di competenza*) and the cash budget (*bilancio di cassa*).

19. ICI was introduced in the Italian fiscal system by legislative decree n. 504/1992 and first implemented in 1993. The communes can choose the tax rate in a given interval (at present between 0.4% and 0.7%) and they have a certain degree of autonomy in determining tax deductions and in monitoring the tax base. Among the other local taxes there are: the tax for garbage collection and disposal (TARSU), the advertising tax, the surcharge on the central government tax on electricity consumption, fees for public billposting, fees for occupying municipal space and public areas (TOSAP), fees for municipal concessions, urbanisation charges, and the surtax on personal income tax.

20. The communal surtax on IRPEF was introduced by legislative decree n. 360/1998, whereas the provincial surtax was introduced by Act n. 133/1999. The rate is composed of two parts: the first is the same for all local authorities (communes and provinces) and is fixed by central government; the second part of the rate (concerning only the communes) is variable, within the limits determined by the national legislator (that is, the variation cannot exceed 0.5 percentage points, with an annual increase not greater than 0.2 percentage points), and discretionary (that is, each commune can freely decide the application of that part of the rate).

21. For example Great Britain (see HMSO, 1976 (Layfield Report) and the DoE, 1986).

22. For the application of the benefit principle see, for example, Musgrave and Musgrave, (1984).

23. As it is known, balanced budget requirements may stimulate the use of off-budget items. The result is that "the fiscal effects of government grow harder to assess and grow less amenable to control and oversight through the budget process" (Nice, 1986, p. 135).

24. The technicalities to calculate the local authorities' deficit (for the purpose of the Stability Pact) have been recently established with a decree of the Treasury Ministry, issued on the 1 August 2000.

25. The rules of the Act are now absorbed by the Code of Local Authorities (*Testo unico delle leggi sull'ordinamento degli enti locali*) (legislative decree 18 August 2000, n. 267).

26. The off-budget debts are listed in article 37 of legislative decree n. 77 of 1995. They include: instantly executory judgement or judgement beyond recall; recapitalization of joint-stock companies formed to produce local public services; expropriation procedures for works of public utility; and orders not imputable to administrators, officers or employees of the local authority. Before choosing borrowing, local authorities must verify the possibility of using other resources (surplus, sale of real property and so on) to cover off-budget debts. The amortisation of loans to finance off-budget debts follows the same rules as long-terms loans to finance investments. The rules of the legislative decree n. 77 of 1995 are now absorbed by the Code of Local Authorities (legislative decree n. 267 of 2000).

27. The limit to the borrowing capacity of the 15 ordinary regions is more stringent and it is fixed as follows: the total amount of the annual principal and interest repayment must not exceed 25% of the regional tax revenues, which include own taxes and quotas of taxes belonging to the Treasury and devolved to the regions. For the special regions (Valle d'Aosta, Trentino-Alto Adige, Friuli-Venezia Giulia and Sardinia) the respective statutes establish the quantitative limit, while the statute of Sicily does not provide for any limit.

28. Excepted *una tantum* revenues and adjusting entry of the expenditures. The reason for the exclusion is to avoid a swelling of the indebtedness capacity, as the former have a character of exceptionality and the latter are mere book-keeping means. In order to calculate the limit to borrowing it must exclude from the current resources also state and regional grants on the interest account.

29. The ties are imposed on private banking institutions to guarantee a uniform treatment for every local authority.

30. As a matter of fact, the approval of the financial plan (from the local authority's council) is compulsory for whatever investment, independently of the means of covering (article 13 of Act n. 38/1990). So for self-financed investments, or for those financed by loans whose amortisation is totally at charge of central government and/or the regions, the financial plan only concerns the operating expenses resulting from the investment.

31. Decree 19 April 1993, published in *Gazette* 24 April 1993, n. 95.

32. The Deposits and Loans Fund also grants loans at variable interest rates. See the decrees of the Treasury Ministry issued on 7 January 1998 and 16 February 1999.

33. In other countries the issue of local authority bonds dates back to more remote time. For example, in the United Kingdom the Local Government Act of 1963 authorised the issue of "local authority bonds" by any local authority.

34. The withholding tax does not apply to the local bonds subscribed by legal entities. This measure should increase local authorities' ability to obtain new debt.

APPENDIX 1   CHRONOLOGY OF THE ITALIAN ACTS CONCERNING LOCAL GOVERNMENTS (QUOTED IN THE TEXT)

Act/Legislative decree/Presidential decree/Treasury Ministry decree		Measures
1977	A. n. 62	1) Local loans are consolidated.
		2) Short-term loans (advances of cash) are limited to three months; the amount cannot exceed 3/12 of current revenues assessed during the preceding accounting period.
1977	P.d. n. 616	Administrative functions are transferred to the ordinary regions and
1978	A. n. 43	1) Local governments are freed from the burden of previous debts; the central government is responsible for the amortisation of funded debts.
		2) Current budget must be balanced.
		3) Local borrowing is allowed only for capital outlays on conditions that: a) amortisation and interest can be paid within the current balanced budget; b) interest payments must not exceed 25% of current revenues of the budget.
1989	A. n. 144	Several ties are imposed on the money-lending contracts drawn up with corporations other than the Deposits and Loans Fund, the National Sport Finance Corporation and the National Institute of Security for Civil Servants.
1989	A. n. 155	1) In order to obtain the loans local governments are obliged to turn first to the Deposits and Loans Fund; only in the event of a negative response (within 45 days from the request) are local governments authorised to turn to other banking companies.
		2) The granting of loans to finance local investments is subject to the approval of the financial plan.
1990	A. n. 38	Financial plan is compulsory for all investments independently of the means of covering.
1990	A. n. 142	1) Requirement of a balanced budget for the current and total budgets.
		2) Local authorities can issue bonds.
1990	A. n. 403	Abolition of the constraint introduced by Act n. 155/1989 (see above 1)).
1992	L.d. n. 504	1) Reorganisation of local authorities' finance.
		2) Financial plan must be integrated by a further economic financial plan, meant for the assessment of the economic financial equilibrium of both the investment and the management service.
1993	L.d. n. 528	1) Economic financial plan exclusively concerns new public works (devoted to public services for which a user charge must be paid) over a thousand million lire.
		2) Acceptance of the economic financial plan on the part of a banking company or the Deposits and Loans Fund is needed.
1993	M.d. 19 April	List of banking companies that can accept the local authorities' economic financial plan relative to projects involving expenditures higher than a thousand million lire.
1994	A. n. 724	1) Economic financial plan is also imposed for financing by bond issue.
		2) Bonds issue must finance investments only.

1995	L.d. n. 77	1) Financial and bookkeeping rules for local authorities. 2) Balanced budget rule is confirmed. 3) List of off-budget debts.
1995	A. n. 539	Beginning of amortisation from the second year following the grant of the loan.
1996	M.d. n. 152	Rules for issuing bonds at local level: a) bonds' term must exceed five years; b) issue must finance investments only; c) issue is subject to the approval of the economic financial plan, of the executive plan and of the redemption plan relative to the investment; d) coupons' yield cannot exceed by more than 1 point the gross yield of analogous government bonds; e) no guarantee by the central or regional governments.
1997	A. n. 59	Principles are fixed that must guide the Cabinet in issuing decrees related to the assignment of functions to regions and local governments.
1998	L.d. n. 112	Administrative functions are conferred to regions and local governments in the following fields: a) economic development and productive activities; b) territory, environment and infrastructures; c) services to the person and to the community; d) regional and local administrative police, authorisation system.
1998	L.d. n. 360	Issuing of the communal surtax on IRPEF.
1998	A. n. 448	Extension of the Stability Pact for Europe to the regions and local governments.
1998	M.d. 7 January	Characteristics of the loans at fixed interest rate granted by the Deposits and Loans Fund.
1999	M.d. 16 February	Characteristics of the loans at variable interest rate granted by the Deposits and Loans Fund.
1999	L.d. n. 96	Division of administrative functions between the defaulter regions and their local authorities is provided by central government.
1999	A. n. 133	Issuing of the provincial surtax on IRPEF.
1999	L.d. n. 443	Modification and integration of the functions conferred to regions and local governments with the legislative decree n. 112/1998.
2000	M.d. 1 August	Technicalities to calculate the local authorities' deficit for the purpose of the Stability Pact.
2000	L.d. n. 267	Code of Local Authorities

REFERENCES

Bordignon, M. (1999), *Problems of Soft Budget Constraints in Intergovernmental Relationships: The Case of Italy*, W.P. Istituto di Economia e Finanza dell'Università Cattolica del Sacro Cuore, Milano.

Breton, A., A. Cassone and A. Fraschini (1998), "Decentralization and Subsidiarity: Toward a Theoretical Reconciliation", *University of Pennsylvania Journal of International Economic Law*, vol. 19, n. 1, 21–51.

Breton, A. and A. Fraschini (1999), "Vertical Competition in Unitary States: The case of Italy", *ICER Working Paper Series*, n. 20/99.

Corte dei Conti (1998), *Relazione 1998*.

De Magistris, V. (1998), "Un modello econometrico per l'analisi dei comportamenti finanziari dei comuni dal '70 al '93", *Amministrare*, n. 3, 441–473.

DoE (1986), *Paying for Local Government*, HMSO, London.

Fraschini, A. (1988), "The Local Governments' Deficit", *Rivista di diritto finanziario e scienza delle finanze*, n. 4, 510–517.

Fraschini, A. (1989), "Local Autonomy, Accountability and a New Local Tax: the Italian Debate", *Policy and Politics*, vol. 2, 155–163.

Fraschini, A. (1993), "Financing Communal Government in Italy", in J. Gibson and R. Batley (eds), *Financing European Local Governments*, Frank Cass, London, 79–93.

Fraschini, A. (1999), "Finanza locale: autonomia e vincoli", in L. Bernardi (ed.), *La finanza pubblica italiana. Rapporto 1999*, Il Mulino, Bologna, 211–230.

HMSO (1976), *Local Government Finance: Report of the Committee of Enquiry (Chairman F. Layfield)*, London.

King, D. (1984), *Fiscal Tiers. The Economics of Multi-level Government*, George Allen & Unwin, London.

Kornai, J. (1986), "The Soft Budget Constraint", *Kyklos*, vol. 39, Fasc. I, 3–30.

Ministero dell'Interno (1996), *Rapporto sulla finanza degli enti locali e sui trasferimenti 1994*, Roma.

Ministero del Tesoro, del bilancio e della programmazione economica, *Relazione generale sulla situazione economica del Paese*, v.y.

Musgrave, R. (1959), *The Theory of Public Finance*, McGraw-Hill, New York.

Musgrave, R.A. and P.B. Musgrave (1984), *Public Finance in Theory and Practice*, McGraw-Hill, New York.

Nice, D.C. (1986), "State Support for Constitutional Balanced Budget Requirements", *The Journal of Politics*, vol. 48, Issue 1, 134–142.

Piperno, S. (1998), "Un quarto di secolo di finanza comunale in Italia (1971-1996)", *Amministrare*, n. 3, 347–393.

Pola, G. (1996), "Local Public Finance in Europe: The Case of Italy", mimeo.

Qian, Y. and G. Roland (1998), "Federalism and the Soft Budget Constraint", *American Economic Review*, vol. 5, 1143–1162.

Winer, S.L. (1983), "Some evidence on the effect of the separation of spending and taxing decisions", *Journal of Political Economy*, n. 1, 126–140.

9. Local government budgeting and borrowing: Norway

Lars-Erik Borge and Jørn Rattsø

9.1 INTRODUCTION

The organisation of the local public sector in Norway attempts to combine local democracy with an agency role in welfare services. Local governments are an important part of the welfare state and run about two-thirds of public service production.[1] Municipal and county governments are responsible for education from kindergartens to high schools, primary health care and hospitals, as well as care for the elderly, cultural services and infrastructure. Since equalisation of services in these areas is a central goal of the welfare state, service provision is subject to centralised financing and regulation. The local governments have been integrated into the welfare state by national laws defining social reforms combined with matching grants. The legal and financial framework established for the local public sector must be understood in this context.

The local governments also represent a tradition of local democracy and self-rule. They are an independent political structure with a local council elected by proportional representation as the highest authority. The mayor and the deputy mayor together with leaders and members of political committees are elected by and from the local council. Their authority is negatively defined – a local government can get involved in any activity not forbidden by law. In terms of service production, they enjoy most discretion in cultural services and infrastructure, but they also influence important "local" aspects of the welfare services, such as location of institutions (schools) and quality of service (like teacher intensity in schools).

The two key financial controls in the Norwegian system are a balanced budget rule and a procedure for loan approvals. The balanced budget rule implies that current revenues in local governments must finance current spending inclusive of debt servicing. Investments are to a large extent financed by loans, and there is an approval procedure for total loan financing.

The emphasis on loan financing of investment is assumed to stimulate inter-temporal efficiency. The central government controls are motivated by fiscal discipline, both between central and local governments and within local governments. Because of the moral hazard problems associated with centralised financing, controls are established to limit the use of deficits and debts as strategic instruments to obtain additional central grants. Given the centralised system of financing, discipline based on financial markets is not considered a viable option. Since Norway is not a member of the EU, adjustment to the Maastricht rules has not been an issue.

The controls also are seen as responses to decision problems at local level. Local voters may find it tempting to finance current spending by borrowing or sale of property. They can enjoy a high level of service provision in the short term, and by moving out of the community after a few years, they avoid the costs in terms of debt repayment or a public infrastructure that is run down. This has not been an important concern since mobility is low. More important, the welfare services represent redistribution and local politics must balance strong external interest groups and internal producer interests (professions). The centralised controls are a counterweight to the spending pressure resulting from redistributive welfare services.

According to Owens and Norregaard (1991), central governments in most OECD economies control the level of local government loan financing and in some countries even the purposes for which loans can be raised directly or through state banks. Compared with their overview, Norway looks like a less dirigiste regulation regime. The system is meant to encourage decentralised accountability and priority within a system of centralised financing with hard budget constraint. Ter-Minassian and Craig (1997) classify the Norwegian regime as "administrative control", as opposed to "market discipline", "co-operative control" or "rule-based control", and emphasise the approval procedure for total borrowing. The distinction between the four categories is not clear-cut in practice. As will become clear, we see the Norwegian design as a mixture of co-operation, rules and administrative control. The established rules and co-operation reduce the necessity to apply administrative intervention.

The chapter is organised as follows. Section 9.2 gives a brief overview of the financing of the local public sector. The regulations in place are presented in section 9.3. The system has produced deficits and debts as described in section 9.4. The working of the system at central government and local government levels is discussed in sections 9.5 and 9.6. The final section summarises some recent debates about changing the regulations.

9.2   THE FINANCING OF THE LOCAL PUBLIC SECTOR

Compared with most countries, the financing of local governments in Norway is very centralised. The centralisation implies limited local discretion in financing service provision. Local discretion is seen as a threat to the equality principles of the welfare state, both in terms of paying for services and receiving equal service supply. The main elements of the financing are:

* Grants represent about 40% of the revenues. Most of them are distributed as block grants based on objective criteria, but a variety of earmarked grants are in place to promote the detailed ambitions of national politicians. A residual grant amount is distributed annually based on a 'judgement' of the economic conditions in each locality.
* Most tax revenue is income tax and wealth tax shared with central government. Tax rules are determined in the national parliament and local tax rates are limited to a narrow band. All local governments apply the maximum rate (since 1979) and in this situation the tax revenue works as a block grant, except that local governments can influence the tax base over time.
* Property tax is not available to all local governments (in practice 200 of 435 municipalities have it), since it is restricted to urban areas and certain facilities (notably power stations). In addition, the property tax rate is limited to a narrow band. User fees are of rising importance. They are regulated by law and are limited to cover costs, but the share of costs covered and the cost levels do vary.
* The wage scale of local public employees is set in national bargaining with the trade unions. The Association of Local Governments (KS) negotiates on behalf of the local governments, but in close contact with the national government. Wage adjustments locally are limited to small amounts allocated for local bargaining and flexible use of the national pay scale. Teachers, who are employed by local governments, bargain directly with the national government over pay, workload and service regulations such as class size.

Total local government revenue amounts to around 17% of GDP, and Table 9.1 gives an overview of the major revenue sources. Local taxes account for 45% of total revenue, but behind this average figure we find considerable variation. The proportion of taxes in total revenue varies from 10 to 75% across the municipalities and from 25 to 60% across the counties. The local revenue sources, local taxes and user charges, amount to nearly 60% of total revenue. This figure is high compared with many other European countries, and may mislead an external observer into thinking that the Norwegian system of financing is rather decentralised. To get a proper understanding of the system, the central regulation of the local taxes stated above must be taken into account.

Table 9.1   Sources of income, municipalities and counties, %, 1998

Local taxes	44.8
Grants	39.7
User charges	11.7
Other	3.8
Total	100.0

Source: Advisory Commission on Local Public Finance.

In addition to financial controls, welfare services are regulated in detail by law. The regulations involve coverage (for example all children in primary school), standards (for example class size) and working conditions (for example children per employee in day care). Rights defined by law have grown more popular. Local governments must satisfy these rights, which are important in social support and health care.

Centralised financing is the result of the growing local government responsibility for national welfare services. Central government is seen as responsible for financing of the welfare services through grants and regulated income tax revenue sharing. The grant system includes tax equalisation and needs equalisation to promote equalisation of service standards. Local discretion to set user fees and property tax is marginal compared with the amounts channelled through grants and income tax. Local governments look to central government when they want to raise their revenue levels.

The financial conditions of the local public sector are decided by national parliament as part of the annual national budget. Prior to each fiscal year, central government announces a desired growth of total local government revenue, and of tax revenue and block grants separately. Parliament then sets maximum income tax rates and grants according to this overall revenue target. The distribution of block grants among local governments is also decided prior to the fiscal year. Based on these national decisions, local governments produce their own budgets.

The determinants of the growth of income tax revenues and grants during 1900–1990 are investigated by Borge and Rattsø (1997). They apply a standard demand model of local public services extended to include political structure. Local revenues are shown to be very income elastic; the elasticity with respect to the gross domestic product is 1.4. Given the size of the sector, the determination of the revenues is typically seen in relation to stabilisation policy. The analysis finds that macroeconomic booms have a negative impact on the growth of the local public sector. This is consistent with the view that central government uses the local public sector as a tool in a Keynesian-type stabilisation policy. National politics are also important. Both the ideology and strength of central government influence the growth of local revenues. Socialist oriented central governments tend to expand the sector, while strong governments, measured by coalition type, duration and fragmentation of parliament, are able to hold back on spending pressures.

9.3   THE REGULATORY FRAMEWORK OF THE LOCAL PUBLIC SECTOR

The Norwegian regulatory framework is based on a principle called "wealth preservation". The system has three main components. First, current expenditures cannot be financed by loans or sale of property. Second, loan financing is limited to investments and debt is preferably repaid in tandem with the economic depreciation. Third, central government can limit loan financing in local governments not obeying wealth preservation. The municipal debt crisis of the 1920s is often seen as the historical background for this "wealth preserving" principle.

At the local level, decision-making is organised around the annual budgets. These are regulated by the Local Government Act, and the main requirement is operational budget balance. In the budget, current revenue must cover current expenditures, interest payments and regular instalments of debt repayment. Loan financing of current spending is not allowed. The final budgets are controlled and approved by central government. Central government is represented by a regional commissioner in each county overlooking the local government finances. If a proper formulation of the budget implies an operational deficit, it will not be approved and is sent back to the local government for revision.

A balanced budget *ex ante* does not rule out an actual deficit when the account is settled. Income tax revenue during the year and expenditures linked to rules (like social support) may deviate from the budget. Actual deficits are allowed to be carried over, but as a main rule they must be "repaid" within 2 years.[2] In agreement with central government, the local council can extend the period to four years if faster repayment would have serious consequences for local service provision.

The balanced budget regulation is consistent with the "golden rule" that borrowing is limited to investment purposes. Benefit taxation promoting inter-temporal efficiency is encouraged since investments are allowed to be financed by loans. The rule may reduce inter-temporal flexibility, and service provision may be unstable when current spending is strongly linked to current revenues. However, local governments typically hold "rainy-day" funds to smooth out shifts in revenues, although this is not required. Compared with other countries, Norwegian local governments have wide discretion in investment policy, given the constraint that interest payments and debt instalment are included in the operational budget balance. Local governments know that larger loan-financed investment means future debt service covered by current revenues. It is probably more important that investments imply starting up of new service production that requires future spending for labour and materials.

In addition to annual budgets, local governments are required to work out a revolving long-term economic plan. This plan is part of another control system linked to loan financing: it must cover at least the next four years and provide a realistic forecast of revenues, expenditures and priorities in this period. The plan also includes a survey of debt, interest payments and instalments. If planned loan financing is inconsistent with the economic balance projected in the long-term economic plan, the local government must reduce its borrowing and investment activity. In addition to investment in fixed capital, loans may be raised for the conversion of older liabilities and for liquidity purposes. Liquidity loans must be discharged before the account for the fiscal year is settled. However, if there is an operational deficit, liquidity loans may be carried over and repaid over the same period as the deficit.

There are very few examples of local governments experiencing serious economic imbalances since World War II. When local governments are not able to fulfil their obligations, central government will take control of their finances. Local governments are not allowed to go bankrupt, and they will be bailed out by central government. Local governments do not speculate in this bail out, but they do use their "weak financial situation" as an argument for additional grants. The working of the system in this respect is evaluated by Rattsø (2000).

9.4   THE PERFORMANCE OF THE LOCAL PUBLIC SECTOR

The regulatory framework outlined above seems to work in terms of controlling debt accumulation and investment level. Table 9.2 displays the development of GDP, current local public revenue, investment and net debt during the years 1980–1998. In the 1980s revenues were strongly pro-cyclical. Revenue growth declined during the recession in the early 1980s and picked up again in the credit–led boom of the mid-1980s. After the drop in the oil price in 1986, the Norwegian economy went into a quite deep recession, which also hit the local public sector. In the 1990s the local public sector again was used in stabilisation policy, and revenues were more counter-cyclical. Revenue growth picked up in the early 1990s, while the recession continued, and was low in the boom years of 1995 and 1996. Primary education was extended to include 6-year-olds in 1997, bringing with it high revenue growth when the economy was still booming.

Table 9.2   GDP growth, revenue growth, investment and debt in the Norwegian local public sector, 1980–1998

Year	GDP growth [a]	Revenue growth [a]	Investment [b]	Net debt [c]
1980	5.0	4.6	17.7	43.5
1981	1.0	5.0	15.2	43.5
1982	0.2	2.6	13.2	41.8
1983	3.5	1.1	12.7	44.0
1984	5.9	4.3	11.4	42.3
1985	5.2	6.6	10.0	38.2
1986	3.6	1.8	12.0	35.4
1987	2.0	−0.1	13.5	40.2
1988	−0.1	2.8	13.6	46.0
1989	0.9	1.7	11.8	48.2
1990	2.0	3.3	9.8	45.4
1991	3.1	4.6	9.9	42.0
1992	3.3	4.9	9.2	42.5
1993	2.7	1.9	8.7	41.4
1994	5.5	3.4	8.7	37.3
1995	3.8	−1.5	9.5	35.9
1996	4.9	0.9	9.6	33.4
1997	4.3	4.1	12.1	29.8
1998	2.1	0.0	11.8	30.8
Average	**3.1**	**2.7**	**11.6**	**40.1**

Notes:
[a] Real growth (%).
[b] Gross investment as share of current revenue (%).
[c] Net debt as share of current revenue (%).

Sources: Statistics Norway and Advisory Commission on Local Public Finance.

The development of investment and debt shows the same pattern as revenues. Investment increased and debt was reduced during the boom in the mid-1980s. In 1986, the debt–revenue ratio was 35%. In the recession following the drop in the oil price in 1986, investment fell and debt increased sharply. The debt–revenue ratio was nearly 50% by the end of 1989, and with a real interest rate in double digits many observers feared that a debt crisis was emerging. However, a real crisis never appeared. The local governments were "saved" by a more expansionary fiscal policy and by lower interest rates. During most of the 1990s investment activity was low and the debt–revenue ratio gradually declined, to about 30%. Investment activity increased in 1997 and 1998, mainly driven by reforms initiated by central government within primary education and care for the elderly.

The financing of investments is documented in Table 9.3.[3] It appears that borrowing finances 45% of investments on average. There is substantial year-to-year variation. During the short period covered, the share of investments financed by borrowing varied from a low of 35% in 1996, to a high of over 53% in 1991. The operating surplus amounted to 35% of investments on average, varying from 17% in 1998 to 65% in 1994.

Table 9.3   Fixed capital investment, net borrowing and operating surplus, municipalities and counties, 1991–1998

Year	Investment (% of current rev.)	Net borrowing (% of investment)	Operating surplus (% of investment)
1991	9.3	53.4	25.6
1992	8.7	45.8	34.5
1993	7.6	49.8	33.2
1994	7.9	39.4	64.7
1995	8.5	45.8	38.0
1996	8.8	35.9	33.6
1997	11.2	43.2	40.6
1998	11.2	38.9	17.3
Average	**9.2**	**44.0**	**35.9**

Source: Advisory Commission on Local Public Finance.

The share of investments financed by borrowing varies substantially across the local units. In Table 9.4, we provide some information about the variation among the municipalities. In the period 1991–1998, the share of investments financed by borrowing was 44% on average, and one third of the municipalities had a borrowing rate between 40 and 60%. Nearly 20% of the municipalities financed a very small share (less than 20%) of their investments by borrowing. Although borrowing must be approved by the state, we observe quite high borrowing rates, even using an average over seven years. More than 10% of the municipalities had a borrowing rate above 70%. A high borrowing rate is not necessarily of concern if investment activity is low and/or revenues are high. However, the 18 municipalities with a borrowing rate above 80% did not have particularly low investment activity or high revenues. They only financed a large share of their investments by borrowing, and their borrowing-revenue ratio was twice the national average.

Table 9.4   Proportion of investments financed by borrowing, municipal averages [a], 1991–1998

Borrowing (% of inv.)	<20	20–40	40–60	60–80	80+
No. of municipalities (%)	18.2	24.7	32.2	20.7	4.2

Note: [a] Based on data for 429 municipalities. The capital Oslo, which is both a municipality and a county, and municipalities that are consolidated during the period under study, are excluded.

Source: Own calculations based on data from Statistics Norway.

The relationship between municipal revenue, operating surplus, investments and borrowing is investigated in Table 9.5.

Table 9.5   Correlation matrix for revenues, operating surplus, investments and borrowing; all variables are measured in per capita terms; municipalities [a], 1991–1998.

	Revenue	Operating surplus	Investments	Borrowing
Revenues[b]	1.00			
Operating surplus	0.49	1.00		
Investments	0.48	0.63	1.00	
Borrowing	−0.10	−0.24	0.11	1.00

Notes:
[a] Based on data for 429 municipalities. The capital Oslo, which is both a municipality and a county, and municipalities that are consolidated during the period under study, are excluded.
[b] Revenues include block grants and regulated income and wealth taxes.

Source: Own calculations based on data from Statistics Norway.

The correlation coefficients are based on average values over the years 1991–1998. First, there is a strong positive correlation between revenues and operating surplus, which is consistent with the more comprehensive econometric study by Borge (1996). Large revenues mean that more internal funds are available for fixed capital investment. Second, municipalities with revenue and surplus above average invest more than the average community, but they also borrow less. Consequently, good economic conditions are associated with a low borrowing-revenue ratio.

9.5 EXPERIENCE AT NATIONAL LEVEL

Central government's annual decision about income tax rates and grants balances a trade-off between revenue structure and revenue distribution. The decision is taken as part of the (*ex ante*) national budget process. The share of taxes in local government revenue varies substantially across the country (see section 9.2), and the mix of income tax revenues and block grants has important distributional consequences. An economic boom with high growth rate of local taxes will benefit local governments with a large share of taxes in total revenue. Local governments strongly dependent on grants will not take much part in the boom, particularly if grants are reduced in boom years. To avoid large differences in the revenue growth of local authorities, central government has aimed at an equal growth rate of taxes and block grants. In the 1990s, when the growth of the tax base exceeded the desired growth of total local government revenue, this was accomplished by reducing the maximum local income tax rates allowed. This policy was politically controversial, since it was seen as interventionist and reducing local autonomy.

Since Norwegian taxpayers pay their local taxes directly to the local government, central government cannot control the actual local tax revenues prior to the fiscal year. Local tax revenue is predicted on the basis of tax rates and tax rules together with a forecast for the development of the tax base. Predicted and actual growth of local tax revenue is displayed in Table 9.6, and there is a clear under-prediction bias. During the period 1986–1999, central government underestimated the growth rate each year except 1989 and 1999. This bias will also carry over to the local level since local governments usually apply the national government's predicted growth of total taxes in their own budgets. Central government will not accept budgets based on a higher growth rate.

The main reason for the systematic underestimation of the growth of local tax revenue is related to the annual construction of the national budget by central government. General wage growth is consistently underestimated in the national budget. Central government's prediction of nominal wage growth is seen as a guideline for wage bargaining and inflation expectations. It follows that predicted wage growth is biased downward. This bias has consequences for the prediction of tax revenue in general. It is an example of good intentions (keeping wage growth low) with unfortunate consequences (under-prediction of revenue).

Table 9.6   *Growth in nominal tax revenue (income and wealth taxes) for the local public sector; actual and predicted; %, 1986–1999*

Year	Predicted	Actual	Actual–Predicted
1986	6.6	12.7	6.1
1987	6.6	10.2	3.6
1988	6.4	8.7	2.3
1989	3.8	3.2	–0.6
1990	3.8	4.9	1.1
1991	3.5	4.2	0.7
1992	1.5	1.6	0.1
1993	3.7	4.6	0.9
1994	4.6	9.9	5.3
1995	–1.5	1.1	2.6
1996	1.3	6.4	5.1
1997	3.3	6.0	2.7
1998	0.8	4.5	3.2
1999	3.3	3.0	–0.3

Source: Advisory Commission on Local Public Finance.

During the fiscal year, central government gradually adjusts the estimated growth in local tax revenue. At this stage, the tax rates are already set. The government is caught in a "trap" with little room to manoeuvre. If central government wants to hold back a boom, the block grant must be reduced. Revenues for grant dependent local governments will be much affected, precisely those local governments that have little benefit from the tax boom. On the other hand, if central government wants to neutralise the distributional implications of the tax boom, it must increase the block grant in tandem with growth in local tax revenue and accept an even higher growth in total local government revenue. Usually it chooses a middle-of-the-road policy, which is to do nothing. Central government accepts that the growth of total local government revenue is higher than desired and that income distribution is shifted in favour of "tax rich" urban communities. The year of 1996 represents an exception from this "rule". Then central government decided to reduce the block grant when the growth of local taxes turned out to be higher than expected. This policy was very controversial, particularly because many grant dependent communities in the northern part of the country had a very low, or even negative, tax revenue growth.

202   Local public finance in Europe

9.6   EXPERIENCE AT LOCAL GOVERNMENT LEVEL

Local government budgets and borrowing must be approved by central government. Information about the exercise of these controls for municipalities is shown in Table 9.7. Regional commissioners in each county handle the controls. Most budgets and applications for borrowing are approved. The approval rate for budgets increased during the period 1994–1998, and was well above 90% in 1997 and 1998. The approval rate for borrowing has been stable and around 97% on average. The figures should not necessarily be interpreted as showing a lack of impact of the control instruments. First, the municipalities usually communicate informally with the regional commissioner before budget and borrowing applications are submitted. The staff of the commissioner supervise the local governments in their handling of finances, in particular the small municipalities. Budgets and borrowing applications are adjusted in this informal process. Second, the few budgets and borrowing applications that are rejected may be important for achieving financial balance in the municipalities under consideration.

Table 9.7   Control of municipal budgets and borrowing, 1994–1998

Year	Budgets		Borrowing	
	Approved	Disapproved	Approved	Disapproved
1994	374 (86%)	61 (14%)	1 413 (95%)	68 (5%)
1995	373 (86%)	62 (14%)	1 359 (97%)	48 (3%)
1996	389 (89%)	46 (11%)	1 237 (98%)	27 (2%)
1997	410 (94%)	24 (6%)	1 124 (96%)	42 (4%)
1998	406 (93%)	29 (7%)	1 188 (97%)	38 (3%)

Source: Ministry of Local Government.

The regional commissioners only control the municipal budgets *ex ante*. *Ex post*, when the account is settled, an operational deficit is not a rare event, as documented in Table 9.8. During the period 1980–1998, 15% of the municipalities managed to have an operating surplus every year. Nearly 40% of the municipalities had a deficit on more than three occasions, and as many as 15% had a deficit more than six years. On average, 18% of the municipalities had a deficit each year, but there was substantial variation from year to year. In 1985, only 5% of the municipalities ran a deficit, whereas more than 25% had a deficit in 1980 and 1987.

Table 9.8   The number of years with an operational deficit; municipalities^a,
        1980–1998

No. of years with a deficit	0	1–3	4–6	7–9	10–13
No. of municipalities	63	198	103	51	10
No. of municipalities (%)	14.8	46.6	24.2	12.0	2.4

Note: ᵃBased on data for 425 municipalities. The capital Oslo, which is both a municipality
        and a county, and municipalities that are consolidated during the period under study,
        are excluded.

Source: Own calculations based on data from Statistics Norway.

Although many municipalities ran deficits in this period, we cannot conclude that the balanced budget rule has no impact on actual budgets. The budget deficits and the number of communities with a budget deficit could well have been larger without this rule. Since all Norwegian local governments face the same regulations, the impact of these regulations is hard to evaluate.

The international literature about the empirical effects of balanced budget rules is limited. Poterba (1995) and Inman (1997) survey the recent literature on US States. They form an interesting case because the shaping of the balanced budget rules varies widely across states. The study by Bohn and Inman (1996) is particularly interesting because it helps to identify exactly what attributes of the balanced budget rules are of importance for the actual deficit. The empirical analysis indicates that the most important aspect is whether the balanced budget requirement is imposed *ex ante* or *ex post*; that is, whether deficits are allowed to be carried over or not. Effective rules do not allow deficits to be carried over to the next fiscal year. Rules that require a balanced budget *ex ante* and allow deficits to be carried over seem to be ineffective. Although it is not obvious that these findings can be carried over to other institutional contexts, they do suggest that the balanced budget rule facing Norwegian local governments may have a minor impact. In a study of local government responses to shocks, along the lines of Poterba (1995), Rattsø (1999a) shows that investment level is the main shock-absorber in Norway. The rigidity of current spending and revenue is consistent with the US evidence that responses to shocks are constrained by regulations.

Penalties for violating the budget rules are emphasised by Inman (1997) in the context of EMU and the Maastricht Treaty. If violators must pay large penalties, the balanced budget rules are likely to be more effective, even if they are imposed *ex ante* and not *ex post*. In the case of local governments, a reduction in intergovernmental grants is a possible penalty. Is there any evidence of such a penalty for Norwegian local governments? The answer is a clear no. The balanced budget rule is not linked to any penalty. If grants are affected by past deficits, the change is in the opposite direction. This is confirmed by Fevolden and Sørensen (1983) in a study of a part of the block grant that is distributed annually based on a judgement of the economic condition in each locality. They find that high debt servicing costs (interest payments and instalments) are rewarded by more grants.

An analysis of aggregate local government investment throws some light on the inter-temporal decisions taken. Rattsø (1999b) studies whether the recent stagnation of investment reflects a sensible response to future revenue growth and demographic shift, or myopic spending responding to pressure groups. The analysis applies an inter-temporal optimisation model with rational expectations and concludes that unexpected changes in GDP and unemployment have been important determinants of investment. Although the last word has not been said, the study is a support for the forward looking model.

How do the municipalities manage to run deficits when the law requires balanced budgets? In general there are two possible explanations. First, revenue or expenditure shocks during the fiscal year may turn a balanced budget into a deficit. Second, submitted budgets may be balanced by deliberate overestimation of revenues and/or underestimation of expenditures.[4] It is hard to judge to what extent the observed deficits are the result of shocks and to what extent they are the result of creative budgeting. However, if they were the result of revenue shocks one would expect revenues to be more volatile in municipalities that run deficits frequently. This hypothesis is evaluated by Borge (1996). He differentiates between municipalities that did not have any deficits in the period 1981–90, and municipalities that had a deficit in at least one year. It appears that the volatility of revenues, measured by the standard deviation of the revenue growth rate, is almost identical in the two groups. Moreover, the two groups did not differ with respect to revenue level per capita or average growth rate. Revenue shocks seem to be of little importance for violation of the balanced budget rule and, although expenditure shocks are not analysed, it is not unreasonable to conclude that creative budgeting in the form of overestimated revenues and/or underestimated expenditures may play a significant role.

Borge (1996) also conducted an empirical analysis of municipal budget deficits. Both economic and political determinants seem to be of importance. The effect of a short-run or transitory revenue increase is to reduce the budget deficit. Moreover, the impact of a permanent revenue increase is less than that of a transitory revenue increase. According to the estimates, the response to a transitory grant reduction is to reduce current spending by 60%

of the revenue loss and to increase the operating deficit by 40% of the loss. On the other hand, a transitory reduction in local taxes increases the operating deficit by 80% of the revenue loss. This difference is as expected because a change in local tax revenue is more of a surprise than a change in grants from central government. However, the difficulty of predicting the growth of the local tax base cannot explain why the long-run effects differ. According to the estimates, a permanent reduction in local tax revenue increases the deficit by nearly 40% of the revenue loss, compared with around 20% for a permanent reduction in grants.

Strength of political leadership is of importance for the budgetary outcome. Political strength is measured in several ways, and strong political leadership is characterised by majority control, little party fragmentation in the local council and small ideological differences within the ruling coalition. Whatever measure is applied, the message is that municipalities with a weak political leadership tend to have large budget deficits. Political strength has a substantial impact on budget responsibility at local level.

9.7 REFORM DEBATE

Central government control of the local public sector has been growing with the integration of local governments in the welfare state. The cumulative effect of this growing control to promote welfare services and secure equal provision across the country has led to frustrations concerning local democracy. Accordingly, there have been attempts at decentralisation since about 1980. A major reform of the grant system took place in 1986, and most conditional grants were replaced by block grants. The liberalisation of the credit market during the 1980s meant that control of local public investment through state banks was eliminated. The discussion about further reforms to improve the trade-off between equality and accountability is addressed by Borge and Rattsø (1998). Here we concentrate on the more narrow design of the regulatory framework.

Norway had a major reform of the Local Government Act in 1993 based on preparatory work of a commission and an active public debate. The reform basically addressed organisational issues, and local governments were given more freedom in organising their decision-making and service production. The framework of economic controls was not changed much. Operational budget flexibility was increased slightly, allowing the budget to be balanced by the use of rainy-day funds. Previously, surpluses from earlier years were earmarked for investment purposes. Furthermore, the period of "repayment" of an actual deficit was extended by accepting four years in special circumstances. Finally, a revolving long-term economic plan was made mandatory. The changes were meant to encourage local governments to focus more on the long-term consequences of their actions.

The commission that prepared the new Local Government Act proposed to abolish central government approval of local borrowing. The commission argued that approval is ineffective in terms of avoiding an economic crisis in individual local authorities, and that the economic competence at local level is substantially increased. Elimination of the approval procedure was seen as a way of increasing budget responsibility in local governments. A minority of the members of the commission wanted to keep the control on local borrowing. This minority argued that refusal of borrowing requests was the only effective instrument available to influence local governments with substantial fiscal imbalances. Moreover, since national government is held responsible for key welfare services such as education and health care, local governments may use borrowing strategically to extract more grants. Carlsen (1994) analyses this strategic aspect of local borrowing within a game-theoretical approach. The proposal to abolish central government approval of local government borrowing did not receive much support, and was strongly opposed by the Ministry of Finance and the regional commissioners. When the new Local Government Act was decided, parliament maintained the present system of control on local borrowing.

At the turn of the century the Ministry of Local Government proposed changing the central control of local budgeting and borrowing, taking a step towards increased reliance on market discipline. The previous system of administrative control described here will be maintained only for local governments that have violated the balanced budget rule in previous years. For the others, budgets and borrowing no longer need to be approved by central government. The main arguments for the proposal were that credit institutions get stronger incentives to check local finances before they levy a loan, and that resources spent on control and advice can be more effectively targeted towards local governments in financial imbalance. Some regional commissioners opposed the proposal, arguing that the current system of administrative control helped to achieve financial balance in the local public sector. It is also argued that local governments will face higher interest rates in the future, as credit institutions will consider loans to be more risky when they are not approved by central government.

Another debate has addressed the system of tax payments. The neighbouring countries, Sweden and Denmark, have chosen a system where local taxes are collected nationally and distributed to the local governments. The Danish and Swedish systems allow for more central control over local tax revenue prior to the fiscal year. A proposal by the Ministry of Finance to change to a more centralised system has been opposed vigorously by the local public sector and their Association of Local Governments. Such a reform most likely will reduce the growth of total revenue since central government will distribute local tax revenues prior to the fiscal year. The permanent underestimation of the revenue growth under the present system, as documented in Table 9.6, can be avoided. The alternative system is also seen as an important step towards more central control by effectively turning local taxes into a block grant. This point is also emphasised by Inman and Rubinfeld (1997, p. 47): "To avoid the moral hazard of having local governments view such transfers as 'blank checks' from the central government, the amount of such grants should be firmly tied to a publicly reviewed and locally decided tax rate." In Sweden and Denmark the centralised system of tax payment is combined with more local discretion to set tax rates.

9.8   CONCLUDING REMARKS

The financial situation of Norwegian local governments is and has been sound during the post-World War II period. No financial crises or mismanagement on any grand scale have been observed. The present system is seen as successful in this respect, and no major reforms of the regulatory framework are considered.

In a broader context, however, there is serious concern about the organising and financing of the welfare services run by the local public sector. Administrative federalism with strong vertical fiscal imbalance implies that the responsibility for the decentralised welfare services is not clearly set at the local level. Unclear accountability and spending pressure towards the centre may allow both allocative and cost inefficiencies. The vitality of the local democracy is the other side of this concern. Local politicians are hard pressed dividing a given pie among strong interest groups. The standardisation of the service provision and the rights defined by law has reduced the room to manoeuvre. The agency role of the local governments clearly contradicts the desire for local accountability and self-rule.

Reforms motivated by reorganisation of welfare services and stimulation of local democracy may influence the regulatory framework in the future.

NOTES

1. We use the concept "local government" to describe both levels of the local public sector, municipalities and counties.
2. The surpluses in the following two years must be large enough to cover the deficit.

3. The investment figures in Table 9.3 differ somewhat from the figures in Table 9.2. The reason is that Table 9.2 is based on the national accounts, whereas Table 9.3 is based on the local government accounts.
4. Inman (1983) discusses how US cities are able to violate the balanced budget law by clever book-keeping.

REFERENCES

Bohn, H. and R.P. Inman (1996), "Balanced budget rules and public deficits: Evidence from the U.S. states", *Carnegie-Rochester Series on Public Policy*, 45 (1–4), 13–76.

Borge, L-E (1996), "The political economy of budget deficits: A study of Norwegian local governments", mimeo, Department of Economics, Norwegian University of Science and Technology.

Borge, L-E and J. Rattsø (1997), "Local government grants and income tax revenue: Redistributive politics in Norway 1900-1990", *Public Choice*, 92, 181–197.

Borge, L-E and J. Rattsø (1998), "Reforming a centralized system of local government financing: Norway", in J. Rattsø (ed.), *Fiscal Federalism and State–Local Finance: The Scandinavian Approach*, Edward Elgar, Cheltenham.

Carlsen, F. (1994), "Central regulation of local government borrowing: A game-theoretical approach", *Environment and Planning C: Government and Policy*, 12, 213–224.

Fevolden, T. and R.J. Sørensen (1983), "Spillet om skatteutjevningen" (The tax equalization game, in Norwegian), *Tidsskrift for Sammfunnsforskning*, 24, 59–76.

Inman, R.P. (1983), "The anatomy of fiscal crisis", *Business Review* (Federal Reserve Bank of Philadelphia), September/October, 15–22.

Inman, R.P. (1997), "Do balanced budget rules work? U.S. experience and possible lessons for the EMU", in Siebert Horst (ed.), *Quo Vadis Europe?* Mohr, Tübingen.

Inman, R.P. and D.L. Rubinfeld (1997), "Rethinking federalism", *Journal of Economic Perspectives*, 11, 43–64.

Owens, J. and J. Norregaard (1991), "The role of lower levels of government: The experience of selected OECD countries", in J. Owens and G. Panella (eds), *Local Government: An International Perspective*, North-Holland, Amsterdam.

Poterba, J.M. (1995), "Balanced budget rules and fiscal policy: Evidence from the states", *National Tax Journal*, 48, 329–336.

Rattsø, J. (1999a), "Fiscal adjustment with vertical fiscal imbalance: Empirical evaluation of administrative fiscal federalism in Norway", mimeo, Department of Economics, Norwegian University of Science and Technology.

Rattsø, J. (1999b), "Aggregate local public sector investment and shocks: Norway 1946–1990", *Applied Economics*, 31, 577–584.

Rattsø J. (2000), "Vertical fiscal imbalance in a welfare state: Norway", in J. Rodden et al. (eds), *Soft Budget Constraints in Multi-tiered Fiscal Systems*, The World Bank, Washington, 2000.

Ter-Minassian, T. and J. Craig (1997), "Control of subnational government borrowing", in T. Ter-Minassian (ed.), *Fiscal Federalism in Theory and Practice*, The International Monetary Fund, Washington.

10. Capital expenditures and financing in the communes in Switzerland

Bernard Dafflon

10.1 INTRODUCTION

This chapter focuses on capital expenditure decisions and borrowing at the local level in Switzerland. With 2,903 communes at the end of 1998 and an average of 2,545 habitants per commune, one important issue in local government finance is the budgeting for and financing of capital expenditures. First, capital expenditures are uneven in nature and in small municipalities, which are the majority in Switzerland, a large investment in one year may preclude similar expenditures in subsequent years. But priority and coherence with long-term planning programmes are not self-evident in the decision-making process. Second, financing investment solely from the current revenues is impossible. Therefore the golden rule of a "balanced budget" must be revisited with the necessary distinction between current and capital budgets. Explicit rules are needed for long-term borrowing. Furthermore a distinction between replacement and new investment projects is necessary if the maximum term of the loan must correspond to the length of the life of the asset: the fiscal capacity available at any point in time cannot be assigned exclusively to new projects. Third, capital expenditure decisions are far from simple in practice, since it is difficult to identify and quantify the benefits and costs associated with them. Fourth, not only are the initial construction costs to be considered, but all future costs (that is, debt servicing, maintenance and operating costs) as well as non-market costs must be taken into account.

In most of the 26 Swiss cantons, these issues have been partly answered through constitutional processes linked to the budgeting process of the communes, and through the control by cantonal supervisory bodies over local capital budgets and subsequent borrowing by local governments. The following sections will try to explain how these institutions function. After a brief presentation (section 10.2) of the growth of the public sector between

1970 and 1998, its deficits and the evolution of the public debt, section 10.3 explores the main tenets of budget orthodoxy at the local level. Section 10.4 deals with the application of the "golden rule" at the communal level and the control of capital budgeting in the Canton of Fribourg, one of the twenty-six Swiss cantons. The consequences and results of this control are explained in section 10.5.

10.2   LOCAL PUBLIC FINANCES: AN OVERVIEW

10.2.1   Size and Growth of the Local Public Sector

The size and growth of the public sector over the period 1970 to 1998 are presented in Table 10.1. Total public expenditures jumped by 45 per cent in 28 years, from 22 per cent of GDP in 1970 to 32 per cent of GDP in 1998. Three decades are considered. The rate of growth was important between 1970 and 1980 in relative and absolute values for the three levels of government. In the 1980s, the share of public expenditures to GDP remained stable at around 26-27 per cent. It increased in proportion after the beginning of the 1990s, partly because the economic situation deteriorated and partly because unemployment benefits and social aid increased above average. In 1998, total public expenditures amounted to 143,459 millions SFr or 32 per cent of GDP. Despite the increase, this proportion is still low compared with other European countries.

The rates of growth of public expenditures for each layer of government followed a different trend over the three periods. Between 1970 and 1980, communal expenditures increased at a higher rate than the total average (Table 10.1, column 6: 141% > 131%); between 1980 and 1990 this was the case for the cantons (column 9: 88% > 84%); and between 1990 and 1998 for the confederation (column 12: 49% > 39%). The share of the communes in total public expenditures corresponded to 29 per cent in aggregate value between 1970 and 1990. It decreased from 29 to 27 per cent in the more difficult 1990–1998 period. Creeping centralisation towards the confederation to the detriment of the communes is perceptible (Table 10.1, column 13).

Table 10.1   Growth of the public sector 1970–1998 [a]

1	1970 SFr.	%[c]	1980 SFr.	%[c]	G[d]	1990 SFr.	%[c]	G[e]	1998 SFr.	%[c]	G[f]	G[g]
	2	3	4	5	6	7	8	9	10	11	12	13
Confederation[b]	7 834	32	17 532	32	124	31 616	31	80	46 962	33	49	499
Cantons	9 533	39	21 926	39	130	41 116	40	88	57 170	40	39	500
Communes	6 840	29	16 476	29	141	30 245	29	84	39 327	27	30	475
Total	24 207	100	55 934	100	131	102 977	100	84	143 459	100	39	493
% GNP	22		26			27			32			

Notes:
a public expenditures, in million of Swiss francs (SFr), current values, nominal;
b without social security;
c percentage share of each level of government in total public expenditures;
d growth rate in % over the period 1970–1980;
e growth rate in % over the period 1980–1990;
f growth rate in % over the period 1990–1998;
g growth rate in % over the period 1970–1998.
The growth rate formula is $[SFr_t^j - SFr_{t-1}^j] / SFr_{t-1}^j$ where j represents the government tiers and t the reference year: for example $[17532\ _{1980}^{Confederation} - 7834\ _{1970}^{Confederation}] / 7834\ _{1970}^{Confederation} = 1.2379$, that is 124% written in column 6 first cell.

Source: *Finances publiques en Suisse 1998*, AFF, 18/2000, Berne, pp. 2–3.

10.2.2   Deficits and the Evolution of Public Debt

The results for the current and capital accounts of the three layers of government for the period 1980–1998 are recorded in Table 10.2. A negative sign in columns 2, 3 and 4 indicates that the annual result for the administrative account[1] is a deficit. Since amortisation is not included in the net administrative result, total indebtedness of each layer of government corresponds to the accumulated deficit. At the local level, the result was negative for the last 11 years (from 1988 to 1998), but this includes investment. If one considers separately current expenditures and investment, the corresponding statistical data show that the total annual amount of communal investments is always higher than the annual total deficit, which means that the result for the current account is a surplus. In 1998, for example, the deficit was –557 million SFr for a total 5,178 million SFr investment: the cash flow calculated from these figures covered about 90 per cent of the local gross capital expenditures.

Table 10.2, columns 6, 9 and 12 contain the governments' financial obligations to external organisations and individuals. Liabilities are recorded at the amount ultimately payable (initial amount less past annual instalments). Only financial claims are recorded; physical assets such as land, building, infrastructure and machinery, though recorded in the balance sheet, are not taken into account in the net debt. There are no actuarial liabilities (in the sense of the statistical estimate of future costs coming from obligations for the employees' pensions and insurance) recorded in the balance sheet since these insurance schemes are managed outside government through independent institutions. In the same vein, contingent liabilities (for which a government is not currently responsible, but for which it may be if some future event occurs – such as the bankruptcy of the beneficiary of the government's guarantee) are not recorded in the balance sheet. In some cantons, the communes have a legal obligation to give their contingent liabilities on a separate list attached to the balance sheet.

Table 10.2   Deficits and the evolution of public debt 1980-1998, in million of SFr.

Year	Current + capital accounts				Public indebtedness (= net debt)[2]										
					Confederation			Cantons			Communes			Total	
	Conf.	Cant.	Comm.	total	SFr.	%	Δ real	SFr.	%	Δ real	SFr.	%	Δ real	SFr.	Δ real
1	2	3	4	5	6	7	8	9	10	11	12	13	14	15	16
1980	–1 071	–163	458	–776	24 394	34		22 213	31		26 000	36		72 607	
1981	–173	–342	119	–396	24 677	34	–5.03	22 990	31	–2.84	26 000	35	–6.12	73 667	–4.75
1982	–424	–631	–387	–1 442	24 968	33	–4.25	24 542	32	1.02	26 500	35	–3.55	76 010	–2.36
1983	–855	–733	–318	–1 906	25 249	32	–1.79	25 814	33	2.15	27 000	35	–1.05	78 063	–0.26
1984	–448	262	55	–655	27 736	34	6.77	26 908	33	1.32	27 000	33	–2.80	81 644	1.66
1985	–696	262	141	–293	29 266	35	1.98	27 555	33	–1.03	27 000	32	–3.35	83 821	–0.77
1986	1 968	388	313	2 669	28 198	34	–4.39	28 218	33	1.62	27 500	33	1.07	83 916	–0.65
1987	1 041	506	558	2 105	27 671	33	–3.23	28 737	34	0.43	27 500	33	–1.39	83 908	–1.40
1988	1 248	446	–73	1 621	26 073	31	–7.52	29 723	36	1.51	27 500	33	–1.86	83 296	–2.57
1989	885	–183	–248	454	25 101	30	–6.62	30 062	36	–1.89	28 000	34	–1.24	83 163	–3.16
1990	–779	–1 852	–822	–3 453	38 509	39	45.55	30 535	31	–3.63	29 000	30	–1.74	98 044	11.85
1991	–4 044	–3 781	–2 151	–9 976	43 915	40	7.66	34 983	32	8.16	31 000	28	0.92	109 898	5.82
1992	–5 040	–4 159	–2 629	–11 827	55 296	43	21.10	40 759	31	12.05	33 750	26	4.71	129 805	13.59
1993	–9 740	–5 390	–1 195	–16 325	65 970	45	15.48	46 971	32	11.55	35 000	24	0.38	147 941	10.32
1994	–6 918	–3 707	–893	–11 519	73 269	46	10.07	51 649	32	8.98	36 000	22	1.94	160 918	7.80
1995	–4 694	–1 964	–840	–7 499	79 936	47	7.19	53 436	31	1.64	37 000	22	0.97	170 372	4.02
1996	–5 773	–2 202	–496	–8 471	86 011	48	6.77	56 817	32	5.50	37 500	21	0.57	180 328	5.02
1997	–5 530	–3 078	–577	–9 186	93 109	49	7.73	60 151	31	5.36	38 000	20	0.85	191 260	5.55
1998	111	–1 012	–557	–1 459	105 278	51	12.96	63 197	31	4.96	38 600	19	1.48	207 075	8.16

Notes:
%   = the share of each level of government in total debt (annual = horizontal)
Δ real = the annual rate of growth of the debt compared to the previous year, in real terms
        (nominal rate deflated through the index of price inflation.

Source: *Finances publiques en Suisse 1998*, AFF, Berne, pp. 2–3 + own computation.

Table 10.2, columns 7, 10 and 13 give the respective share of total indebtedness for the three layers of government. The federal proportion has considerably increased for the last 18 years, from 34 to 51 per cent of the total debt. The cantons' share is almost stable, at around 31 per cent. The communes have been in a position to successfully control their debt, with a relative share falling from 36 to 19 per cent in the relevant period. Columns 8, 11, 14 and 16 give the annual real rate of growth of the public debt (that is, gross rate deflated by the consumer price index). For 1981 to 1990, the relative weight of total communal indebtedness diminished; from 1992 on, it was modest, with results lower than 1 point for 5 out of 8 years. The (self?) control of borrowing and debt at the local level has been tight, with the result that the present fiscal position of the communes is certainly better than that of both the federal and cantonal layers. This clearly appears in Figure 10.1, which shows the relative growth of indebtedness of the three layers in real terms, based on indices of 100 in 1982, compared with the rate of growth of GDP in real terms. For the period 1991–98, the federal and cantonal governments were unable to properly control their deficits and the negative evolution of their own fiscal situation. In fact, from the beginning of the 90s and today, the Confederation and several cantons are debating the introduction of constitutional amendments with the aim of curbing deficits and controlling the debt. For this purpose, past communal experiences and best practices will be useful.

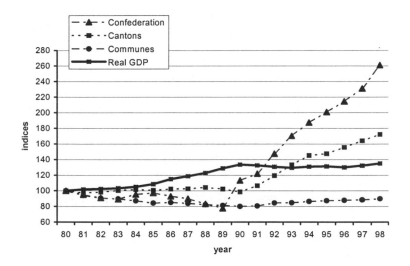

Figure 10.1   Comparative growth of debt, Confederation, cantons and communes, 1980–1998, in real terms based on GDP

214   *Local public finance in Europe*

10.2.3   The Maastricht Criteria

So far, the Maastricht criteria on deficit and debt have not been a major issue in the debate on budget accountability and sound governance in the field of public finances. The reason is simple: despite the importance of the deficits and a growing debt in the late 1990s, the limits of [deficit < 3 per cent of GDP] and [debt < 60 per cent of GDP] have been respected since 1996. Table 10.3 shows these proportions.

Table 10.3   Respect of the Maastricht criteria

Year	GNP mio SFr.	Deficit %	Debt %
1994	357 463	3.2	45.0
1995	363 329	2.1	46.9
1996	365 833	2.4	49.3
1997	371 372	2.5	51.5
1998	380 940	0.4	54.4

However, this was not the case for the period 1991–1994. The bad results of these years brought about drastic ad hoc measures for restoring balanced accounts and curbing the debt. The federal government introduced in 1997 a package of measures called "frein à l'endettement" ("slowing down indebtedness") and discussed their consolidation at the constitutional level. Most cantons have already introduced such regulation for their own finances or for the communes (Novaresi, 2001). Recently, the cantons have expressed their worries that the limits set by the Maastricht criteria could be reached again, with particular concern for the increasing level of indebtedness. They commissioned a first study on this question to examine (and defend?) their "right" to deficit and debt quotas (Jeanrenaud, 2001).

10.3   BUDGET ORTHODOXY AT THE LOCAL LEVEL

The fairly extensive autonomy of local governments for their finance is not unlimited. There are usually two sets of limitations in cantonal constitutions or laws: (i) internal limitations which pertain to public finance rules and budgetary processes and (ii) democratic institutions which are susceptible to considerable modification of budget outcomes in conveying the household preferences of citizens into public budgeting (Dafflon, 1999).[3]

10.3.1 Accountability

In the Swiss tradition, the two requirements of (1) a balanced budget and (2) debt limitation express the principle of accountability, which aims at coincidence between the three circles of "deciders", "beneficiaries" and "payers". They must be viewed in the perspective of the communal autonomy for public expenditures and access to own revenue sources as described above. If, on the one hand, local governments have direct access to taxation and a fairly large (though diminishing) amount of autonomy to decide the provision of local public services, then it is expected, on the other hand, that they will act in a responsible way and finance without excess borrowing what they are asked to provide, either in response to their electorate's own demands (the "choice" model) or by law (the "principal-agent" model). This is definitely a classical approach to fiscal federalism (Tollison and Wagner, 1986).

The first rule is concerned with the requirement of a more or less *balanced budget* for providing goods and services. Due to the financial legislation for the communes in many cantons, it is quite difficult to run or to accumulate deficits in their (current) budgets. If a large budget deficit occurs, expenditures would have to be cut and/or taxation would have to be increased. If a local authority does not follow this rule, the cantonal government might decide to raise the annual coefficient of taxation in place of the commune.[4]

In general, the "golden rule" applies in the following form:

- Short-term borrowing may be used to finance capital expenditures or to cover an unexpected deficit in the current account. In this last case, budgeting for sufficient revenue in the ensuing year must eliminate the deficit.
- Long-term borrowing is restricted to the financing of capital expenditures only. It is theoretically justified on a pay-as-you-use finance basis with the benefits from the project expected to fall on future users and taxpayers.

This of course requires a distinction between the current budget, which must be balanced, and the capital budget, which can be financed by borrowing. Referring to Chapter 1, figure 1.1, the result of the current account includes items 32 and 33, for the latter with the rates of amortisation normally set on a pay-as-you-use basis for each capital asset financed by borrowing. The result must be a surplus or a zero (current) deficit.

As a second rule, local current revenues net of current expenditures must be sufficient to pay for debt interest and the running costs of past and new investment. Whether this rule includes the effective annual reimbursement of the debt concomitant with amortisation in the accounts remains a much debated and controversial issue (Dafflon, 1998, p. 180). This rule also necessitates a clear distinction between current and capital expenditures and, of course, separation of the current from the capital budget. Again, the definition of the latter is not identical across cantons in particular with regard to the possibility (i) to transform capital expenditures into current outlays through leasing contracts to shortcut limitation, or (ii) through outsourcing of some expenditures to external budgets not accounted for by the public sector.

The third rule concerns borrowing and *debt limitation*. Public debt is allowed in many cantons only for financing capital expenditures and on condition that the local and/or cantonal government has the financial capacity to pay interest and debt amortisation out of its current budget. The rates of amortisation should be fixed according to the kind of investment and its possible duration. In some cantons, the law on the communes goes even further, requiring that, in addition to the financial costs of the debt, future operating and maintenance costs should be evaluated and included in the calculation of the debt limit. Thus the first debt limitation is given by the resources of the current budget and the willingness of local politicians and residents to affect a more or less substantial share of local taxes, or to cut other current expenditures, for servicing a new loan and the future costs resulting from the investment.

Other rules for debt limitation are possible either directly or as a benchmark for debt management. One of the most popular rules is the ratio of interest paid to current own revenues, or – in a more restrictive comparison – to tax revenues. In the case of Swiss municipalities, the average is 7 per cent for the first ratio and 12 per cent for the second. It is considered "low" and acceptable (Dafflon, 1998, p. 208).

10.3.2   Democratic Institutions

The Swiss political system also has some special characteristics which reinforce accountability at the local level.

- Direct democracy. Direct democracy participation is provided for in most cantonal constitutions for small and medium-size communes so that the citizens themselves may take part in the decision-making process on all important political and economic issues (current budget, tax coefficients, user charges regulations, investment projects and financing, sale or purchase of local public property, association to special purpose district for the joint production of public facilities, amalgamation of communes).

- *Initiative and referendum.* When democracy is representative, which is the case in large municipalities, cities and urban areas, voters express their preference on political and economic issues mainly via referenda, which may be brought up for vote several times during a year. Together with popular initiatives, these institutions form a real opposition (or at least an excellent decision filter) for local governments, as usually all important public decisions are subject to voters' approval. At the local level, the most common items which might be included in the initiative or in the referendum process are: investment projects and their financing, tax coefficients, user charges regulations, property sales or purchases, association with other communes or constitution of special purpose districts, amalgamation of communes.
- *Audit competencies.* The communal assembly of citizens, or the communal "parliament" where it exists, elects an internal finance committee for the political term. The committee has not only audit powers, but must also be consulted for reporting to the assembly on the budget, fiscal matters, taxation and investment projects. It has the power to investigate any budget item, current or capital, or financial matters without warning. If necessary, it might lodge a complaint against individual members of the local authorities for mismanagement of public funds.

Obviously these institutions of the federal system do not have the unique purpose of (economic) efficiency in the performance of expenditures and taxation. The more direct and democratic the institutions are, the better is their general capacity to strengthen the system of checks and balances, by both dividing and sharing political decision-making power. They give citizens/voters/taxpayers multiple access to government, increase their capacity to control the budgets and reduce political and bureaucratic leeway in rent-seeking forms of behaviour. In Hirschman's terminology, they not only have the "exit" solution (Tiebout-style mobility), but also the "voice" solution. The outcomes are that the growth of government activity has been significantly lower than in representative democracy, the size of government is limited and public expenditures are demand driven (Feld and Savioz, 1997; Feld and Kirchgässner, 1999). In Switzerland, per capita local public expenditures are, on average, 10 per cent lower in the cities where referenda, facultative or compulsory, exist and nearly the same result obtains in communes with direct democracy.

10.4   THE "GOLDEN RULE" REVISITED

Since each of the 26 cantons has its own set of rules for local public budgeting and debt control, it is only possible within this chapter to give a flavour of the existing cantonal laws. The chosen example comes from the canton of Fribourg and is interesting for two reasons. First, in this canton there is a long tradition of a balanced budget rule at the local level, which goes back to the previous law of 1894 on the communes. The 1894 law already contained the basic concept of the "golden rule". It was replaced in 1981 with the current law, which has only modernised the rule, introducing more clarity in its application. A second reason is that statistical data are available for the more recent period 1985–1998. This allows henceforth to evaluate the incidence of the changes introduced in the new law.

10.4.1   The capital expenditure decision

Let us first turn to the procedure for deciding capital expenditure in a commune. The following sequence applies: (i) the decision is made on the basis of a fully descriptive investment programme; (ii) if not decided in direct democracy by the local assembly, but in representative democracy by the local parliament, the project is submitted to facultative referendum; (iii) the actual capital expenditure is possible only when some budget requirements are satisfied; (iv) when the capital investment is financed by borrowing, there is a control from the cantonal authority. The main objective of this four-step process is to avoid the usual difficulties that capital budgeting elicits at the local level (Kitchen, 1984, pp. 134–7).

Investment programme
First, each investment to be decided by the assembly (or the local parliament) shall be explained in a message that gives the following information (art. 48 of the Application Act of 28 December 1981, of the Law on the communes – AALCo):

a)   the nature and the purpose of the investment;
b)   the gross and net capital outlays; the total financial funding, including grants and contributions of non-governmental parties; the annual credit if the installation works last more than one year;
c)   the types and terms of the borrowing to be undertaken, its length of time and the rate and the annual amount of amortisation;
d)   an estimation of annual maintenance and operating costs in addition to debt service.

These four pieces of information are cumulative. The decision is not valid and cannot be implemented if one of them is lacking. Clearly, the primary concern is that of ensuring solvency insofar as the legislative body of the commune cannot take a capital expenditure decision without knowing exactly the amount of the financial costs (interest and amortisation) as well as the future maintenance and operating costs. To be sure, some municipalities do not have sufficient management expertise to assess fully and carefully the impact of these expenditure programmes on their local budgets. Casual estimation is thus possible. But these shortcomings can be avoided by appealing to professional external bureaux or with the help of the cantonal administration in charge of communal affairs. In addition, two further steps, referendum and budget requirements, place the local authorities in such a position that they cannot escape the obligation to give explicit information.

Referendum
Five categories of decision are submitted to referendum when one tenth of the citizens in the commune lodge a written demand (art. 52 of the law of 25 September 1980, on the commune – LCo):
a) a capital expenditure that cannot be paid in cash within one annual budget, or a guarantee or a lease that could lead to such an expenditure;
b) the communal tax coefficients and user charges;
c) the creation of an association of communes or a special purpose district, or membership of such an association;
d) the amalgamation of the commune with another;
e) a local application act of general concern.

There is no referendum possible on a negative decision of the local parliament.

Budget requirements
Budget requirements are based on two rules. First, in addition to the future operating costs of investment and debt service if it is loan financed, the law requires that the asset be amortised and that the annual debt instalment corresponds to amortisation. Second, these new current costs (operating costs + interest payments + amortisation) added to the existing ones must not jeopardise balancing future current budgets.

First, local public debt must be amortised (reimbursed) within a period of time equal to the number of years in which the capital asset thus financed yields consumption services (art. 52 AALCo). Annual amortisation is calculated on the initial amount of the loan, or on the net outlay of the commune after deduction of grants and private contributions, whichever is the lowest. The annual rates of amortisation are flat rates, fixed by law (art.

53 AALCo) at 1 per cent for real-estate immovable; 2 per cent for river embankments and water reservoirs; 3 per cent for administrative buildings, schools, sport centres, theatres, garages; 4 per cent for water systems, sewerage systems, installations for the treatment of wastewater, or for the treatment and deposal of solid waste, for roads, pavements, pedestrian zones; 7 per cent for road surfaces; and 15 per cent for technical equipments, furnitures and vehicles.

Second, the current budget, including interest and amortisation (reimbursement) of the public debt plus future operating costs of the investment, must be balanced. If current expenditures are in excess of current revenues by 5 per cent or more, the tax coefficient must be increased to restore balance (art. 87 LCo).[5]

1894–1980: what is new?

The 1980 law on the communes is in keeping with the general pattern of budget accountability already called for at the turn of the twentieth century. Since the 1894 law already contained the "golden rule", what changed with the 1980 law? Three points may be singled out.

- The new law prescribes that the decision on capital expenditures is made on the basis of a comprehensive investment programme: letters (c) and (d) above have been added. Owing to information on the financial costs (interest and amortisation) and on future maintenance and operating costs, the decision cannot ignore future costs, which have to be properly discounted.
- The prescription of amortisation rates conforming to the length of use of the investment is also new. Whereas the pay-as-you-use rule (length of use → amortisation = annual instalment of the debt) already existed in the 1894 law and is maintained, the old law did not give any precision about the rates of amortisation, and the habit developed around a 3 per cent rate, which proved insufficient.[6]
- The principal innovation is the automatic sanction when a deficit of the current budget/account (including the prescribed amortisation) occurs; that is, the obligation to raise the local tax coefficients if current expenditures exceed by 3 per cent or more current revenues.

10.4.2 Control over Local Capital Budget and Borrowing

The most obvious constraint on local capital spending is the requirement that a governing body superior to local councils and their related boards and commissions must approve loan-financed capital expenditures. The extent to which these governing bodies oversee local capital spending and their financing varies across cantons. In the canton of Fribourg, the department of communes is in charge of this control.

- A first control (art. 95 LCo) refers to solvency. It is a general control reviewing the commune's total borrowing. It confronts total borrowing at the end of the fiscal year with the residual value of the capital assets if the amortisation has been properly recorded over the past years. Excess indebtedness exists when net debt is greater than the residual value of the capital assets.

- A second control (art. 149 LCo) is in respect of the decision-making process at local level: investment programmes have to be comprehensive and include the evaluation of future costs. It is a control on the legality of the decision, not of its opportunity or the technical accuracy of its content. This control intervenes only when capital expenditure is loan financed. If the commune has no excess indebtedness and the decision was correctly taken, then the authorisation to spend is given.

A number of issues must be addressed in exercising control over local capital budgets (Kitchen, 1984, p. 135).

- Whereas it is generally considered that cantonal authorisation and review of total borrowing are advantageous, what is the reasonable extent of this control? Should it include detailed drawings and descriptions of the capital project to be undertaken? If the rationale for a body approving local capital projects is the maintenance of solvency, then this body ought to be concerned with controlling total borrowing and not specific projects. This is exactly what happens in the Canton of Fribourg with the first control. Total indebtedness is the issue. Authorisation of an individual capital project does not concern its technical details[7], but whether its funding through borrowing is acceptable with respect to the existing debt and the fiscal capacity of the commune.

- The second control is clearly intended to protect local governments from costly burdens in the future. But the ways and means for achieving this are indirect. The basic idea is that democracy will prevent local authorities from ignoring or underestimating the future costs of the project when this information is explicitly given in the investment programme. So it is sufficient for the canton to verify the respect of the decision. This is true for the financial costs of the investment, because the rates of interest and amortisation can be easily checked, but there is no presumption that accuracy in estimating future operating costs automatically comes out of this procedure. Those familiar with local finance know that seriousness and accuracy depend more on the ability and the common sense of the actors in the decision-making process than on the process itself.

What this form of cantonal control does not do is as follows:

- It does not verify if individual capital projects or annual capital budgets are comprehensively and carefully integrated into a growth management programme. Five-year financial planning is not compulsory, and only a few communes prepare and use such a policy. Thus political ad hoc decisions are not excluded and priority is not always respected. Time consistency is not required. Ad hoc changes in priority can be damaging because capital expansion tends to be uneven in nature: a large expenditure in one year may preclude investment in subsequent years with little consistent pattern emerging.
- It does not distinguish replacement from new investment projects. Priority given to the latter projects may lead the communes to a dead end, with dramatic financial consequences when the renewal of old capital assets is not carefully planned and funded.
- It does not avoid the fact that local governments frequently undertake projects for which grants contribute a large proportion of total construction costs. In some cases federal and cantonal grant programmes induce municipalities to spend in ways that may not accurately reflect local priorities, a practice leading to inefficiencies in the allocation of local resources.
- It is not a *bailout* clause. A bailout clause would assume that, because of the cantonal control, the canton would be a payer of last resort in case of irresponsible financial behaviour of the communes or in case of local bankruptcy. This is foreign to any tradition of budget accountability. First, since the communes have their own taxation powers, the question of a cantonal guarantee of the debt would arise only when the local tax coefficients reach the maximum limits set in the tax law. Second, the usual answer is the freezing of the public finances of a commune that runs into this situation (art. 151 LCo). In a few cases the cantonal government repaid the debt, forcing the amalgamation of the commune with a neighbouring larger one.

In sum, control by the cantonal body is budget-oriented and addresses the question of solvency and excess indebtedness. It is also a control of sound amortisation of capital assets (past investment). It is neither concerned with efficiency in resource allocation, nor with priority between capital projects, two issues that are exclusively a local concern.

10.5 RESULTS

10.5.1 Current and Capital Accounts

From 1985 to 1997 local government finance in the Canton of Fribourg was characterised by 13 consecutive years of net positive results for the current budget. Only in 1998 and 1999 were the outcomes negative (Table 10.4, column 4). Capital expenditures represented about 36 per cent of current expenditures for the period 1985–89 and 1990–94, but reduced to 28 per cent for the period 1995–99, a clear indication that there is a time lag in the adjustment of investment decisions to the economic performance. Because of the lag in political decisions on capital investment between when work effectively begins and when the first payments are made, most investment projects implemented in the first half of the 1990s were decided during the more optimistic late 1980s. With recession, the current revenue diminished (see years 1996 to 1999 in column 3), which created financial difficulties for some local governments leading them to postpone investment projects. Thus total capital expenditures did not vary much between 1995 and 1997, with a slight up-turn later on.

Total current expenditures include amortisation of the capital assets listed in the balance sheet, and this also coincides with annual instalments of the debt following a pay-as-you-use legal requirement. The annual amortisation, which does not appear directly in Table 10.4, can be inferred from the following formula:

Amortisation = [final debt – (initial debt + net investment) – result of the current account].

Two indicators are generally given to estimate the annual results: the *financial need* and *the rate of funding*.

- The amount of *financial need* represents the volume of external funding necessary for one single year for the (consolidated) administrative account: this is the sum of columns 4 and 7 in Table 10.4 or, in other words, the annual net expenditure of the capital account minus the revenue surplus of the current account (or minus the deficit of the current account).
- The *rate of funding* is the proportion of the annual net result of the capital account that is covered by own financial resources without borrowing. It corresponds to the ratio between the "gross result" of the current account (current surplus + amortisation) and net investment expenditures. The annual rates are given in Table 10.4 column 11.

For 1999, the calculations are the following:

A net result of the capital account	(col. 7)	161,507 million SFr
+B net result of the current account	(col. 4)	32,854 million SFr
C financial need	(col. 10)	194,361 million SFr
−D variation of net debt	(col. 9)	114,516 million SFr
E amortisation		79,845 million SFr

Without amortisation, the result of the current account would have been a surplus: 79,845 million SFr minus the current deficit of 32,854 million SFr, that is, a cash flow of 46,991 million SFr. Since net investment was 161,507 million SFr, the increase in net debt was (161,507–46,991) = 114,516 million SFr.

The rate of funding was (B+E)/A above, that is (−32,854+79,845)/161,507 =0.29. This result means that for 1999, only 29 per cent of net investment (the net result of the capital account) was financed with the communes' own resources. This is a low figure compared with previous years. It is interesting to note that, following the new (harmonised) system of accounts for the cantons and the communes, a 60 per cent rate of funding is recommended. From 1985 to 1999, this target was reached 10 times. Note also that the rate of funding is positive throughout the time series: this indicates that the communes are always able to finance a large proportion of their capital expenditures with current net surpluses or, alternatively, that annual debt variation is always lower than total net investment. The "golden rule" of a (current) balanced budget is thus respected.

10.5.2 Deficits and Excess Indebtedness

Since the general pattern of local public accounts correctly combines the golden rule and pay-as-you-use finance, the second part of this case study explores the question of the deficits and excess indebtedness of individual communes. Table 10.5 summarises the results of the analysis from 1978 to 1999.

Table 10.4 Communal accounts in the canton of Fribourg, 1979–1999: results and net debt, in SFr.

Years	Current account Expenditures	Current account Revenues	Current account Result	Capital account Expenditures	Capital account Revenues	Capital account Result	Net debt Total	Net debt Variation	Financial need 10 = 7 – 4	Rate of funding
1	2	3	4	5	6	7	8	9	10	11
1979	n.d.	n.d.	n.d.	n.d.	n.d.	n.d.	-295 130 777	n.d.	n.d.	n.d.
1980	n.d.	n.d.	n.d.	n.d.	n.d.	n.d.	-245 455 378	49 675 399	n.d.	n.d.
1981	n.d.	n.d.	n.d.	n.d.	n.d.	n.d.	-255 181 006	-9 725 628	n.d.	n.d.
1982	n.d.	n.d.	n.d.	n.d.	n.d.	n.d.	-274 883 269	-19 702 263	n.d.	n.d.
1983	n.d.	n.d.	n.d.	n.d.	n.d.	n.d.	-299 995 009	-25 111 740	n.d.	n.d.
1984	n.d.	n.d.	n.d.	n.d.	n.d.	n.d.	-277 521 574	22 473 435	n.d.	n.d.
1985	411 702 428	454 197 625	42 495 197	155 626 835	60 793 188	-94 833 647	-330 172 006	-52 650 432	-52 338 450	0.44
1986	436 917 588	484 919 775	48 002 187	161 894 366	53 907 757	-107 986 609	-351 139 283	-20 967 277	-59 984 422	0.81
1987	476 109 315	512 803 164	36 693 849	157 537 581	62 912 602	-94 624 979	-374 205 278	-23 065 995	-57 931 130	0.76
1988	508 736 059	536 214 232	27 478 173	203 511 138	83 432 366	-120 078 772	-395 108 479	-20 903 201	-92 600 599	0.83
1989	559 927 094	614 989 061	55 061 967	214 485 242	98 455 591	-116 029 651	-434 475 611	-39 367 132	-60 967 684	0.66
1990	610 301 364	628 535 189	18 233 825	257 451 902	89 997 823	-167 454 079	-493 274 066	-58 798 455	-149 220 254	0.65
1991	639 597 321	664 405 007	24 807 686	245 397 700	100 079 161	-145 318 539	-580 792 415	-87 518 349	-120 510 853	0.40
1992	690 278 145	695 687 869	5 409 724	224 632 854	88 269 687	-136 363 167	-633 090 845	-52 298 430	-130 953 443	0.62
1993	n.d.	n.d.	n.d.	n.d.	n.d.	n.d.	-689 193 712	-56 102 867	n.d.	n.d.
1994	766 168 879	794 635 020	28 466 141	255 920 366	112 968 980	-142 951 386	-695 832 309	-6 638 597	-114 485 245	0.95
1995	806 653 807	831 243 878	24 590 071	227 219 733	86 958 028	-140 261 705	-740 148 202	-44 315 893	-115 671 634	0.68
1996	863 312 243	917 734 731	54 422 488	241 324 448	80 873 143	-160 451 305	-744 887 149	-4 738 947	-106 028 817	0.97
1997	878 476 854	883 887 387	5 410 533	230 059 866	70 855 672	-159 204 194	-792 431 855	-47 544 706	-153 793 661	0.70
1998	897 636 540	888 900 788	-8 735 752	261 722 109	84 538 596	-177 183 513	-866 737 515	-74 305 660	-185 919 265	0.58
1999	904 879 067	872 024 815	-32 854 252	275 594 691	114 086 976	-161 507 715	-981 254 333	-114 516 818	-194 361 967	0.29

Note: According to the statistical sources, "expenditures" in the current account include basic amortisation ("basic" in the sense that it follows the rule that a capital asset must be amortised at an annual flat rate on a number of years corresponding to the effective use of that asset). Supplementary amortisation and pure accounting entries are not taken into account.

Source: Statistical yearbook of canton Fribourg, various years, tables T18-12, -13 and -14; columns 9, 10 and 11: own calculation.

Table 10.5   Number of communes with current budget deficit and excess indebtedness

Year	Number of communes	Current account deficit	N	SFr	Fribourg city	Col. 5 + 6 in % of the net debt	Col. 5 in % of the net debt (F)
				Excess indebtedness			
1	2	3	4	5	6	7	8
1978	266	55	76	13 493 297	0		
1979	266	51	72	13 269 567	0	0.0450	0.0475
1980	262	11	51	11 003 134	0	0.0448	0.0425
1981	261	15	42	12 693 394	0	0.0497	0.0475
1982	260	23	44	9 726 534	0	0.0354	0.0341
1983	260	36	52	11 271 383	0	0.0376	0.0371
1984	260	18	34	11 379 320	0	0.0410	0.0390
1985	260	53	44	12 329 858	0	0.0373	0.0368
1986	260	51	28	4 739 782	0	0.0135	0.0135
1987	260	41	27	4 202 028	0	0.0112	0.0116
1988	260	21	28	4 865 939	0	0.0123	0.0128
1989	259	36	35	6 011 798	0	0.0138	0.0149
1990	259	27	45	1 054 529	10 050 954	0.0480	0.0302
1991	256	53	59	1 954 099	23 942 216	0.0730	0.0350
1992	255	45	52	4 041 395	41 387 577	0.0927	0.0307
1993	254	n.d.	46	3 801 004	54 244 153	0.1069	0.0321
1994	253	19	25	1 851 308	78 237 758	0.1222	0.0115
1995	252	23	23	1 772 867	77 704 363	0.1121	0.0084
1996	252	14	21	1 421 518	5 054 181	0.0153	0.0102
1997	249	21	23	1 768 880	19 104 173	0.0351	0.0133
1998	246	31	36	5 641 846	45 954 278	0.0711	0.0221
1999	245	46	n.d.	n.d.			

Source: Table 4 and Department of communes of canton Fribourg

column 2   The number of communes in the canton of Fribourg. This number is decreasing owing to a cantonal incentive policy for the amalgamation of communes.
column 3   Number of communes with a deficit in the current accounts (definition below).
column 4   Number of communes with excess indebtedness (definition below).
column 5   Total annual sum of excess indebtedness without Fribourg City.
column 6   Annual excess indebtedness of Fribourg City.
column 7   Proportion of excess indebtedness to total net debt (Table 10.4, column 8).
column 8   Same result without Fribourg City.

A current deficit exists when current expenditures including basic amortisation exceed current revenues. Book entries that do not involve cash, such as cost accounting, are not taken into account.

- Excessive deficit of the current account is a legal concept: the deficit is excessive when current expenditures exceed current revenues by 5 per cent (see section 10.4.1). The result in this case is an increase of the communal tax coefficients to restore balance. How many communes have a current deficit higher than 5 per cent is not examined here.

- Excess indebtedness is a concept of political economy, and only indirectly a question of solvency. It compares the maximum value of the debt at the end of a fiscal year (assuming that debt instalments have been paid on a regular basis that coincides with amortisation of the loan-financed assets) and the residual value of these assets (submitted to amortisation at flat rates corresponding to the life cycle of the assets).

Fribourg City has encountered heavy financial management problems with the recession since the beginning of the 1990s. Its total net debt, which was 43.4 million SFr in 1990, rocketed to 158.7 million SFr in 1998 with continuous current deficits higher than the 5 per cent limit set by law, thus incurring excess indebtedness as shown in Table 10.5, column 6. An increase of the tax coefficients is almost impossible in the present circumstances because of tax competition within the urban area as well as with respect to other capital cities of the same importance in Switzerland: such a policy would price the town out of the market insofar as regional development is concerned. This situation is the Achilles' heel of the cantonal decentralisation policy; solutions are being sought in the form of horizontal financial transfers, tax equalisation and a new larger jurisdiction, such as an institutionalised agglomeration with exclusive powers for the delivery of specific local public services.[8]

If we disregard the particular case of the capital town, the consequence of the 1980 law requiring a balanced budget, inclusive amortisation, is clear. Table 10.5 shows that excess indebtedness has been continuously decreasing since the introduction of this law (column 5), and that the proportion of excess indebtedness to total net debt is also on the decline (column 8). Figure 10.2 depicts this situation. Although there are only three reference years (1979–1981) before the introduction of the 1980 law on the communes (the 1981 budget was set up following the old law), the average proportion of excess burden was around 4.5 per cent. During the period of implementation 1982 to 1985, this proportion fell to 3.6 per cent, then to less than 2 per cent in the following years. Even with recession, when excess indebtedness soared, this proportion remained around 3.3 per cent (which was lower than the result of any previous year between 1979 and 1985). And this proportion fell again from 1994 onwards, a trend that corresponds exactly to the adjustment lag. The general conclusion strengthens the argument that institutional rules have a positive effect on fiscal accountability. In the present case study, the starting point does not record a very high proportion of excess indebtedness because of the long tradition of balanced budgets resulting from the 1894 law on the communes. Nevertheless, the new (1980) law has reinforced fiscal accountability at the local government level.

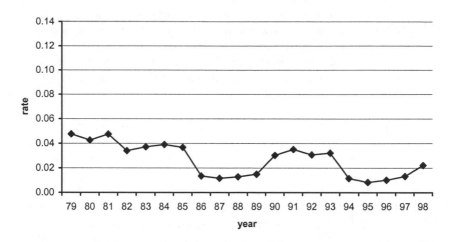

Figure 10.2   Excess indebtedness in % of net debt (without Fribourg City)

10.6   CONCLUSION

In the Swiss communes, budget orthodoxy is a tradition: the requirement of a balanced budget and rules of debt limitation are the expression of the accountability principle. When local governments have direct taxation powers and a fairly large autonomy to decide the provision of local collective goods and public services, it is then expected that they act in a responsible way and without excessive borrowing. Thus the "golden rule" applies *de facto* at the local level. In addition, direct democracy and the possibility of launching referenda against capital investment or changes in the tax rates force local governments to conduct their financial affairs in a household fashion, with caution and restraint. Yet, these are essentially internal processes.

Basic questions remain as to whether control by cantonal authorities is useful. First, in many cantonal laws, no sanction applies if the requirement of a current balanced budget is not respected. Second, whereas local borrowing is limited by law to capital expenditures, cantonal control generally covers the legality of the decisions to fund investment. It does not concern the merits of an investment as such, or that all future maintenance and operating costs have been accurately calculated or if new investment projects are decided instead of replacement projects. Third, whereas the rates of amortisation set by law tend to correspond to the life cycle of the assets, amortisation in the accounts does not always correspond to reimbursement. This disconnection may lead to excess indebtedness. Only a few cantonal laws on the communes have embedded satisfactory corrective processes in order to prevent these circumstances. But when a cantonal law addresses these questions seriously and coherently, an effective solution emerges, as the case study of the Canton of Fribourg shows.

Fourth, with general indebtedness at the three levels of government slowly approaching the Maastricht ceiling, no discussion has yet taken place on the distribution of this limit between government layers and between governments within one layer: cantonal rules decided in isolation could rapidly prove to be obsolete. This issue has yet to be debated in order to call for an acceptable solution.

NOTES

1. The administrative account combines current and capital accounts. Its presentation is designed to facilitate comparisons between governments and to allow consolidation of the financial statements of the different levels of government, for example in the perspective of controlling the respect of the Maastricht criteria regarding deficits and indebtedness.

2. Normally, the situation of total indebtedness of the public sector corresponds to the accumulated deficit of government. This is not the case in Table 10.2. Statistical differences are very important at the federal and cantonal level, but not as large at the communal level. At the cantonal level, for example, the total 1998 deficit was 1,012 million SFr, whereas the debt increased by 3,046 million SFr. This difference is partly explained by expenditures that are related to the patrimonial assets of the cantons, but this is far from satisfactory. Patrimonial assets are capital investments that a government decides as if it were a private entrepreneur (housing development and the tourist industry, for example). These projects are not directly needed for the delivery of public services: they fall outside the scope of "public administration" or public law. Though the investment decision is taken according to the same procedure for both "private" and public capital expenditures, "private" investments are sometimes recorded directly on the balance sheet, without entries in the annual capital account. But this is only *part* of the explanation. Important differences remain unexplained in official reports and no publication has yet tackled this question. For local governments, the harmonised accounting rules have been more rigorous since 1981, with the result that annual statistical differences are much lower: from 1990 to 1998, the total deficit accumulated to 9,338 million SFr, whereas total indebtedness increased by 9,600 million SFr (the unexplained cumulated statistical difference is 262 million SFr).

3. Of course, there are other economic limitations to local fiscal autonomy, such as interjurisdictional mobility and fiscal competition. These questions are not discussed here, for they are outside the domain of the present chapter.

4. For example, in September 1994, the Council of State (executive government) of Canton Berne imposed on the commune of Berne (the capital city of the canton and also the federal city) an increase of the tax coefficient from a multiple of 2.2 to 2.4 of the cantonal direct taxes levied in the commune. The reason was that the electorate of the commune had rejected for the third time the 1994 budget, which presented a deficit and required for balance an increase of taxation. In the Canton of Fribourg, the cantonal department of local affairs controls the books and the public debt of the communes on a yearly basis. It intervenes if the current account is not balanced or if the amortisation of capital assets financed by debt and the effective reimbursement of loans are not sufficient according to legal minimum rates. Cantonal intervention takes several forms, but it can go so far as to

impose a higher tax coefficient on the commune at fault in order to restore its financial situation.
5. This article contains other technical details on the budgeting process and the system of local public accounting.
6. In 1978, the local Association of Banks warned the cantonal authority that some communes were asking for new loans for the same investment items as those with pending debts. It was clear at that time that replacement projects were being funded with new loans while the existing debt was not fully repaid. The Association asked for stricter controls and higher rates of amortisation by law.
7. But each project, private or public, requires a permit of construction, which is delivered after a technical control of its compliance with urban planning rules in that area.
8. On this question, see Dafflon and Ruegg (2001).

REFERENCES

Dafflon, B. (1998), *La gestion des finances publiques locales*, Economica, Paris, 2nd edition.
Dafflon, B. (1999), "Fiscal Federalism in Switzerland: A Survey of Constitutional Issues, Budget Responsibility and Equalisation", in Fossati, A. and Panella, G. (eds), *Fiscal Federalism in the European Union*, Routledge Studies in the European Economy, London and New York, pp. 255–294. Revised edition (2001), Centre for Studies in Public Economics, University of Fribourg, Working paper No. 278.
Dafflon, B. and J. Ruegg (2001), "The case of Fribourg: A Model for Switzerland? Some Notes on a Recent Institutional Innovation", *Swiss Political Science Review*, 4, 134–141.
Feld, L. and G.Kirchgässner (1999), "Public Debt and Budgetary Procedures: Top Down or Bottom Up? Some Evidence from Swiss Municipalities", in Poterba, J. and von Hagen, J. (eds), *Budgeting Institutions and Fiscal Performance*, Chicago University Press and NBER, Chicago.
Feld, L. and M. Savioz, (1997), "Direct Democracy Matters for Economic Performance: an Empirical Investigation", *Kyklos*, 50 (4), pp. 507–538.
Jeanrenaud, C. (2001), "Conséquences d'une intégration à l'Union Européenne pour la politique financière des cantons", in Conférence des gouvernements cantonaux (ed.), *Les cantons face au défi de l'adhésion à l'Union Européenne*, Schulthess, Zürich, pp. 103–156.
Kitchen, H.M. (1984), "Local Government Finance in Canada", *Financing Canadian Federation: 5*, Canadian Tax Foundation, Toronto.
Novaresi, N. (2001), "Discipline budgétaire: étude de l'influence du référendum financier et des règles d'équilibre budgétaire sur les finances publiques des vingt-six cantons suisses", BENEFRI Centre for Studies in Public Sector Economics, University of Fribourg, Switzerland, Série: Thèse de doctorat.
Tollison, R.D. and R.E. Wagner (1987), "Balanced Budget and Beyond", in J.M. Buchanan, C.K. Rowley, and R.D. Tollison (eds), *Deficits*, Basil Blackwell, Oxford, pp. 374–390.

11. Local government financing and borrowing: Spain

Carlos Monasterio-Escudero and Javier Suárez-Pandiello

11.1 INTRODUCTION

3 April 1999 witnessed the 20th anniversary of a historic date for Spanish municipal governments. On that day democracy was restored in city councils after the long period of dictatorship. Nevertheless, this restoration took place within a particularly innovative institutional framework, characterised by a territorial public administration that, for the first time with the Constitution, used a new model that aspired to create a high degree of decentralisation. In fact, except in the terminology (we use the term "Estado Autonómico" – Autonomous state), Spain became in practice a federal country, since, as outstanding constitutionalists have pointed out, it displays all their essential features (Aja, 1999, pp. 31-39).

1. The division of competencies among central and autonomous governments is settled at constitutional level.
2. Legislative and executive powers of autonomous communities (regional parliament and president) are elected and are only responsible to their own electorate.
3. Conflicts between central and autonomous governments are resolved by the constitutional court.
4. There exists an objective and guaranteed system of financing for each level of government.

Regarding the dimension of the decentralisation process, from the very beginning this generated admittedly ambitious expectations, in such a way that it soon became a commonplace objective that at the end of the process the central government would only manage 50 per cent of public expenditures, 25 per cent remaining in the hands of the autonomous communities and the last 25 per cent having to be administered by the local authorities. Compared with neighbouring countries, the achievement of these quantitative objectives would have placed Spain at the level of the most decentralised federal countries, even when from the outset it became apparent that the 50–25–25 per cent target seemed more oriented by the magic of rounding off numbers than the result of a reasonable economic and administrative analysis.

In fact (Table 11.1), the evolution of the decentralisation process has increasingly strengthened the management capacities of the autonomous communities whose levels of expenditures will be well over 25 per cent at the time of completing the transfer of health responsibilities, which they have not yet assumed. In turn, the central expenditures are close to the forecast limits of 50 per cent. Local expenditures differ the most from the implicitly forecast amount. Thus it might appear that the important decentralisation process following the application of the 1978 constitution has been stopped at the level of the autonomous communities without pervading the area of local government, closest to the citizens. However, as we shall see, there is no sound reason for such a severe judgement; a more subtle interpretation is necessary regarding the structure of the local governments and the widening of the scope of their responsibilities.

Table 11.1   *Evolution of public expenditures decentralisation in Spain (% of total public expenditure)*

Year	Central government	Autonomous communities	Local governments
1978	89.00	—	11.00
1984	72.60	14.40	13.00
1987	63.31	20.58	16.11
1990	59.52	23.91	16.57
1991	57.10	26.20	16.70
1992	58.03	26.26	15.71
1993	58.10	26.63	15.27
1994	59.51	26.42	14.07
1995	57.49	28.09	14.42
1996	57.70	27.97	14.33
1997	57.49	28.22	14.29
1998	55.17	29.12	15.72

Notes: (*) Excluding social security pensions and public debt refunds.

Source: Ministerio de Administraciones Públicas.

Regarding revenues, several attempts have been made over the last 20 years to adjust the system of local finance[1] to the requirements of the new constitutional model, based on the principles of autonomy and sufficiency. The persistence of a financial system initially based on taxes, which were obsolete in their conception as well as in their collection capacity (frozen tax bases and, therefore, scarce income elasticity), aroused criticism from the local government authorities. They found themselves powerless to comply with citizen pressure demanding more and improved services in the light of the explosive quest for the return of civil liberties, and urged a radical reform of a system that was progressing dangerously down the path towards indebtedness.

Thus overspending became a matter of concern that although commonplace was none the less real. The search for permanent financial solutions to this situation of insufficiency has been ongoing up to the present time, with moments of greater or lesser tension in the institutional relations between the local authorities and the central administration. Successive attempts to reform the local finance system were accompanied by diverse local debt assumption operations by the state, according to which the debts of local authorities was bailed out by central government. Two were particularly noteworthy:

- The first took place in autumn 1980, when Act 42/1980 came into force on 1 October. It concerned extraordinary budgets at the local level financing debt repayments. This Act enabled the city councils to "approve extraordinary credits to repay debts undertaken or legally accrued before 31 December 1979". At the same time, the central government committed itself to assume 50 per cent of the debt burden (amortisation and interests) for the credits contracted with the Banco de Crédito Local (Public Bank) over the years 1976 to 1978. But this law was only a one-shot solution for a situation of sheer financial insufficiency, as it was not accompanied by new permanent resources.

- Act 24/1983, of 21 December on Urgent Measures for Restructuring the Local Finances was more ambitious. Its main aim was to make a first transitional step toward a more stable system. It contained two types of dispositions. On the one hand, it was an Act bailing out local debts that implicitly recognised the evident inability of the local authorities to assume their powers within the prevailing finance system. Consequently this Act aimed to place local governments at a more convenient starting point in order to demand henceforth greater responsibility from them. Central government committed itself to cover by grants (financed out of its general budget) the current deficits presented on 31 December 1982 by the local authorities and local enterprises with legal status that depended exclusively on them – for which the corresponding accounts audits would be made. Besides this, an attempt was made to eradicate the causes of deficit by the arbitration of a follow-up system for the management of the local governments receiving these grants and for sanctioning through the devolution of the grants cases of mismanagement. In addition, this Act tried to bestow on local governments new resources to improve future management and, more important perhaps, would give them greater autonomy in fiscal matters. In particular, for the first time municipal governments were allowed to set freely and without restrictions the tax rate of the Contribuciones Territoriales (forerunner of the Property Tax) and, as a novelty, to establish a surcharge (also with total freedom as to its amount) on the quota of the Individual Income Tax.

Nevertheless, these bailing out laws did not fulfil their objectives adequately. In the first case, as already pointed out, the law was not accompanied by measures reinforcing local government's own revenues. In the second place, the poor legal structure of the Act on Urgent Measures for Restructuring the Local Finances led the Spanish constitutional court to declare anti-constitutional the rule granting local governments an absolute freedom for setting tax rates without limits, just the very measure that was aimed at strengthening their capacity to generate independent resources. The consequence could not have been more unfortunate, in that it has generated an excessive load for those local governments that, protected by the prevailing acts, had assumed their responsibility, increasing the fiscal pressure on their citizens in order to improve the provision and finance of public services within their territories. Having to return the collected tax revenues to which they were not entitled, they found themselves immersed in a difficult political and economic situation for which they were not at all responsible, given their legal dependence on the central law in this matter.

A wide ranging reform of the local finances was therefore pending, but it was not fully undertaken until the enactment of the 1988 Law Regulating the Local Finances (Ley Reguladora de las Haciendas Locales, LRHL henceforth). When enacted, it was hailed by the local authorities for inspiring the hope that it would solve the chronic lack of sufficient financial resources.

Starting at this point, this chapter will review the recent evolution of local borrowing in Spain, beginning with a brief description of the institutional and financial framework in which local governments have been operating. The work is structured as follows. In the next section we will describe the main constitutional and administrative characteristics affecting the regulation of local governments, with special reference to the restrictions on expansion in relative terms of the local public sector beyond the current limits. Section

11.3 presents the main features of the resources forming the financial structure of local governments, excluding debt. In section 11.4 we shall analyse the regulation of local borrowing and in section 11.5 we present some particularly relevant figures concerning its evolution. The chapter will end with a short conclusion and present future expectations.

11.2 LOCAL AUTHORITIES: CONSTITUTIONAL RESTRICTIONS AND ADMINISTRATIVE CHARACTERISTICS

Figure 11.1 shows the current system of administrative decentralisation prevailing in Spain following the enactment of the 1978 constitution. There are two levels of sub-central government, the autonomous communities and the local governments. The former were created "ex novo" by the constitution. They assume important responsibilities especially in areas of education and health and can approve their own laws in their field of competencies. The functional management of those services is organised in a great variety of forms from one autonomous community to another, although most of them use types of internal decentralisation structures listed down the left-hand side of Figure 11.1. Their aims are to improve the administration and to assimilate the behavioural patterns of the private sector.

For local governments (Figure 11.1), two general institutionalised administration levels exist: (1) the provincial level, including the diputaciones provinciales, the consejos and cabildos insulares, and (2) the municipal level. Additional forms of local government are typical in certain parts of the territory, sometimes based on mechanisms of voluntary co-operation between municipalities (mancomunidades, áreas metropolitanas, agrupaciones de municipios), sometimes based on institutional designs found in some autonomous communities (comarcas), or elsewhere on the specific requirements of municipalities with a population particularly spread out throughout the territory (entidades locales menores).

This chapter focuses exclusively on the analysis of the two main levels of local government, provincial and municipal. Within the new Spanish constitutional framework, both levels are no longer mere executors of state policies, but they have also seen their autonomy recognised. This autonomy can certainly not be directly assimilated to that of the autonomous communities: it lacks the political component, in the sense that local governments do not have all the institutional organs of self-government that deplete the traditional division of powers. Local governments depend legally to a greater extent on other levels (state and autonomous communities). Nevertheless, the possibilities of designing and implementing their own budgets and adopting their own internal organisation schemes (centre of Figure 11.1), linked to the increasingly greater discretionary power in setting their tax revenues, especially at the municipal level, are particularly relevant aspects in the current functioning of local administrations.

The matters in which local governments may exercise their powers are listed in Act 7/1985, of 2 April regulating local competencies. For the municipalities, these competencies vary in terms of the population size. Table 11.2 summarises the main ones.

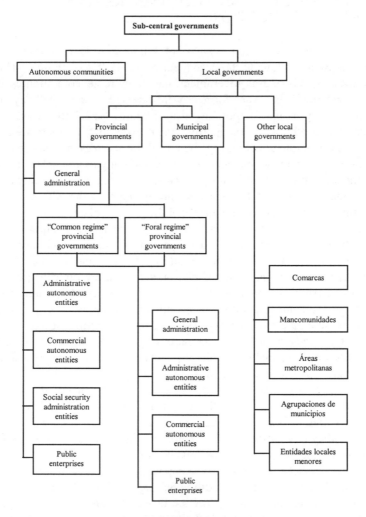

Figure 11.1   Administrative decentralisation in Spain

Table 11.2 Municipal responsibilities

- General services
  - Water supply
  - Urban refuse management
  - Lighting
  - Sewerage
  - ...

- Social services
  - Promotion and social rehabilitation
  - Primary health care
  - ...

- Education
  - Co-operation in creation, building and maintenance of schools

- Leisure
  - Culture
  - Sport
  - Tourism
  - ...

- Public works and urbanism
  - Parks and gardens
  - Urban management
  - Paving of urban public streets and roads
- ...

Municipalities with more than 50,000 inhabitants:

- Urban collective transport for people
- Protection of the environment

Provincial governments and the consejos and cabildos insulares should coordinate their respective municipal services, guaranteeing the principles of solidarity and equilibrium between the municipalities within their territory,

- providing them with legal, economic and technical assistance,
- securing collaboration (especially between municipalities with smaller economic capacity and management skill) and
- provide public services of a supra-municipal and, should it be necessary, supra-comarcal nature.

But, as shown in Figure 11.1, not all provincial governments are the same. Besides the common regime, the three so-called diputaciones forales, based in the autonomous community of the Basque Country, have specific characteristics. The fact that they have a much greater tax autonomy, based on the constitutional recognition of a special finance system for their territories, makes them in practice more similar to regional than local governments.[2]

All in all, the framework of competencies for the local governments sometimes clashes with responsibilities that are constitutionally attributed to the regional governments. Such are the cases, for example, of activities in culture, tourism and urbanism. It is often said that this clash of interests causes inefficiencies in service management, either because costs are unnecessarily duplicated or because such a clash inhibits both administrations, as a consequence of the lack of co-ordination between them. These problems would apparently be overcome should there exist a clearer delimitation of respective powers in such a way that the responsible administrations were explicitly identified. In this sense, the application of the principle of subsidiarity would help so that, as a basic guide line, what could be done by the administration closest to the residents should not be done by the further one.

Nevertheless, this type of reasoning runs the risk of being over-simplistic. In fact, there are many fields in which the clash of interests, far from taking away authority, does actually increase it. Consider, for example, the responsibilities of infrastructures linked to the objective of local development or to economies of scale that could be generated by the territorial co-ordination of public transport in metropolitan areas.

Recently the Spanish parliament has approved a new framework for the division of responsibilities between the regional and local levels of government termed pacto local (local agreement). This new regulation has influenced the reorganisation of powers of the local administrations and their expansion into certain sectors in such a way that the local governments have seen their powers strengthened in diverse matters, such as traffic and road safety, public transport (both urban collective transport and taxis), consumption, planning and management of sports facilities and activities, training and employment policies, youth areas, the environment, women, social services, tourism and urbanism, among others.[3]

However, even with this wider range of powers, it will prove difficult in practice to increase public expenditure up to the 25 per cent target worked out at the beginning of the decentralisation process. Neighbouring countries, where local governments reach a dimension of this calibre or even higher, have in common the fact that local authorities have full responsibility for primary education. Therefore it seems difficult in practice for Spanish local governments to cover 25 per cent of public expenditure unless their power also includes primary school. Indeed this is a very difficult objective if no ambitious process of reorganisation of the municipal powers is undertaken, setting a minimum population in order to make the most of the scale economies for the efficient management of a service of such importance. This seems an impossible task with the current local fragmentation: over 85 per cent of the approximately 8,000 municipalities existing in Spain have fewer than 5,000 inhabitants (Table 11.3).

Table 11.3   *Structure of municipalities in Spain by autonomous*
communities (according to the number of inhabitants)

Autonomous community	Total	Up to 100 inhabit.		From 101 to 1 000		From 1 001 to 5 000		From 5 001 to 50 000		More than 50 000	
		N	%	N	%	N	%	N	%	N	%
Andalucía	770	2	–	175	23	347	45	225	29	21	3
Aragón	729	129	18	486	67	94	13	19	2	1	–
Asturias	78	–	–	16	21	31	40	26	33	5	6
Baleares	67	–	–	10	15	28	42	28	42	1	1
Canarias	87	–	–	1	1	27	31	55	63	4	5
Cantabria	102	1	1	30	29	54	53	15	15	2	2
Castilla-La Mancha	915	177	19	457	50	220	24	55	6	6	1
Castilla y León	2 247	401	18	1 552	69	246	11	40	2	8	-
Cataluña	944	30	3	496	52	260	28	139	15	19	2
Valencia	540	18	3	214	40	174	32	123	23	11	2
Extremadura	382	1	–	178	47	160	42	40	10	3	1
Galicia	314	–	–	11	4	173	55	123	39	7	2
Madrid	179	11	6	56	31	66	37	33	19	13	7
Murcia	45	–	–	2	4	7	16	33	73	3	7
Navarra	272	34	13	157	58	65	24	15	6	1	–
País Vasco	250	3	1	108	43	76	31	56	22	7	3
La Rioja	174	44	25	103	59	20	12	6	3	1	1
TOTAL	8 095	851	11	4 052	50	2 048	25	1 031	13	113	1

Source: Dirección General de Coordinación con las Haciendas Territoriales.

The currently valid regulation attributes to the autonomous communities the authority to modify municipal borders and to create or suppress municipalities. But the normative procedure is rather complex.[4] In this sense, a task not undertaken to date but necessary if the decentralisation process is to be completed in terms of efficiency in the provision of goods and public services, is that of the reorganisation of the territory and the redefinition of the municipal map, even when this implies overcoming local passivity and resistance, mostly lacking in justification from an economic point of view.

11.3   THE LOCAL FINANCE SYSTEM

Table 11.4 and Figure 11.2 show the structure of the financial resources of
the Spanish local governments. This structure is notably different in the
municipalities and in the provincial governments, and within the latter, as
indicated in the previous section, neither the dimension nor the financial
structure of the diputaciones forales in the Basque Country are similar to that
of the rest of the provincial governments. In fact, any lay reader would be
surprised to find that the revenue of the three diputaciones forales are over
1,000,000 million pesetas, of which 92 per cent is from taxes, whereas the
total non-financial revenues of the remaining 47 provincial governments only
reach 700,000 million, with taxes amounting to only 11 per cent. The reason
behind these figures is that the three foral institutions collect practically all of
the taxes in their territory, including those that in the rest of the country are
the responsibility of central government such as the individual income tax,
the authority profit tax and the value added tax. Yet at the same time, the
diputaciones forales are responsible for granting the municipalities and the
Autonomous Community of the Basque Country.[5]

Table 11.4   *Revenue structure of Spanish local governments (1998)*
(millions of Pts)

	Municipalities*	"Common regime" provincial governments**	"Foral regime" provincial governments**	Internal transfers	Total consolidated local governments
Taxes	1 329 961.14	83 888.47	1 024 232.81	–	2 438 082.42
Fees, public prices and fines	648 330.76	87 628.22	19 505.16	–	755 464.14
Grants	1 576 723.24	547 962.51	39 948.87	255 919.27	1 908 715.35
Other revenue	232 022.69	16 413.31	4 107.98	–	252 543.98
Total non financial revenue	3 787 037.83	735 892.51	1 087 794.82	255 919.27	5 354 805.89

Notes: *   Only general administration.
        ** Consolidated data with their administrative autonomous entities.

Source: Dirección General para la Administración Local.

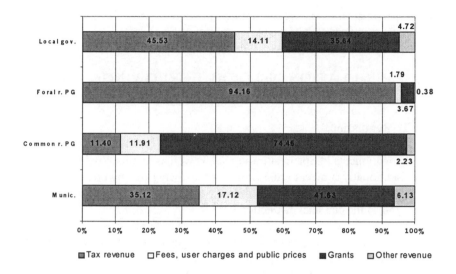

Figure 11.2   Structure of local government revenue (1998)

Figure 11.2 sufficiently illustrates up to what point the financial structure of Spanish local government is determined by that of the municipal level, that thus appears as the basic reason behind this. As can be seen, slightly more than half of the non-financial revenues of the municipalities comes from their own fiscal resources (35 per cent from taxes and 17 per cent from user charges). Spanish municipalities have five taxes of their own: (a) three (property tax, business tax and vehicle tax) should be obligatorily required by all the municipalities; (b) the other two (tax on land increase value and tax on building, plant and works) are optional. In all cases, the municipal governments freely choose a tax rate to be applied between a range (maximums-minimums) established by an act of central government.

A further 40 per cent of the municipalities' non-financial revenues have their origin in diverse types of grants from other levels of government. Of these, three-quarters are unconditional grants from central government[6] and the rest are grants for specific investment projects from the central government itself, the autonomous communities and the provincial governments. The other municipal revenues have their origin in market activities into which local governments engage.

The provincial governments in the "common regime" find three-quarters of their total revenues via grants, mainly unconditional and from central government (84 per cent of the total). They can levy user charges (12 per cent of the total). As own tax, they can only collect a surcharge on the municipal business tax, freely setting the rate of this surcharge up to a maximum of 40 per cent of the basic amount of business tax.

11.4   REGULATION OF LOCAL BORROWING: OBJECTIVES AND LIMITS

11.4.1   Regulation

Local governments in Spain, at provincial as well as at municipal levels, have been traditionally subject to rules limiting borrowing. At the present time, the 1998 law on local finance LRHL deals with this matter in articles 49 to 56, starting from the classical distinction between

- short-term debt (under 1 year), designed only to cover liquidity problems and not being permanent, and
- long-term debt (over 1 year), for which the "golden rule" holds, that forces debt resources to be allocated to financing investments.

This is the most widespread regulation regarding sub-central debt, since it was valid before the LRHL and is applied not only to local government, but also to autonomous governments. The LRHL debt limits are of a general nature and the same rules apply to small municipalities of under 100 inhabitants as to large cities with several million inhabitants, Madrid or Barcelona included.

In 1998, some aspects of the LRHL concerning borrowing were reformed, although the general scheme was maintained. It is noteworthy that despite the fact that Spain is a country with a federal structure since the democratic constitution of 1978, the powers to authorise and supervise local indebtedness continue to be in the hands of central government and are exercised by the Ministry of Finance.[7]

The model limiting local borrowing chosen in Spain does not act on the budgetary process, requiring the economic balance of the local annual budgets, but rather acts on the final result of the budget, directly setting limits to local indebtedness. With no access to issuing money, and since borrowing is the only instrument to finance the deficit within the scope of local governments, limiting indebtedness amounts to the same as limiting the size of the possible deficit.

There is no difference between the current budget and capital budget; the budgetary document is unique and although legally it must be presented in a balanced form, this balance is purely formal and for bookkeeping purpose only, in the sense that the total expenditure (current, capital and financial) is equal to total revenues. So the required balance is a tautology and does not mean a true balance in an economic sense.[8]

The limits valid for local borrowing are of diverse types. In most cases, these are objective rules that force the indebtedness to be stopped when certain ceilings have been reached, regarding the level of gross saving or amount of debt with respect to current revenues. Moreover, authorisation must be obtained from the Ministry of Finance when indebtedness is going to take the form of certain types of liabilities, such as issuing public debt or indebtedness in foreign currency. The limits are permanent, and should be individually respected by each local government at all times.

From 1992, limits of another type have been added to the LRHL limits, as the consequence of the European Monetary Union (EMU) process and the need to reduce deficits and total debt of the Spanish public sector. Based on this, agreements on budget consolidation plans (BCP) have specified the commitment of each level of public administration and their contribution to restructuring public finances. Unlike the LRHL limits, the BCP agreed upon by the local governments are temporary and are based on the overall control of deficit and the total local debt, without specifying the liabilities of individual local government units. But each local government must inform the Ministry of Finance about local borrowing operations, even about those not subject to authorisation and even when the local government respects the established limits.

The process of settling BCP is as follows. Central government and autonomous communities decide in a co-ordination forum – the Council of Fiscal and Financial Policy (CFFP) – the distribution by levels of government of the maximum amounts of deficit and debt, according to the stability and growth pact of Spain. These amounts are individualised for each autonomous community and for central government and globalised for the local authorities. The results of the BCP application can be qualified globally as positive because the deficit and debt levels have fallen since 1993. Moreover some problems have been detected in the individual behaviour of certain autonomous communities, who have gone above the agreed ceilings. With reference to local authorities, there are no individual limits for each municipality. In this sense the Spanish organisation grouping local authorities – Federación Española de Municipios y Provincias (FEMP) – is now claiming its inclusion in the CFFP to negotiate the various borrowing limits limits. Nevertheless the high concentration of local debt in the biggest cities is currently opening a debate about the need to set individual targets of debt and deficit for this type of local government.

Within the diverse limits setting a maximum amount for local debt, there do not exist additional requirements as to the structure and forms of local borrowing. Both can be freely decided by local governments, according to the conditions of the financial markets. The appropriate financial management of local indebtedness thus becomes an important factor for local governments: they can choose the period and form of the loan, the type of lending institution (public or private bank) and the currency.

11.4.2 Objectives

Considering the regulation of local borrowing as a whole, the objectives pursued by the diverse restrictions are the following

- Reach intergenerational equity. The main aim of linking the permanent (long-term) debt with the financing of investment expenditures is for future generations to receive a greater stock of public capital, together with the burden of the debt.
- Attain a balanced budget and solvency for local governments. Fixing the maximum limits for the debt attempts to ensure that excessive borrowing does not burden future budgets, in such a way that the repayment of loans in the local public sector is assured and the financial system considers the local governments as solvent. There is no rule of amortisation linked to the length of the physical life of the investment. Acording to the definition of debt amortisation by LRHL, the rules of annual repayment of loans are simply those agreed between the contractors.
- Collaborate in the country's stabilisation policy. Although central government is responsible to the authorities of the European Union (EU) for the fulfilment of the Maastricht convergence criteria regarding the limits of the deficit and the debt, the decentralisation process carried out in Spain has caused the relative weight of the central government budget to decrease notably. But central government is responsible for controlling the total deficit and debt of the Spanish public sector in spite of only deciding on a decreasing share of total public expenditure. So effective mechanisms to co-ordinate budget and borrowing are necessary to put into practice the guidelines of the general economic policy in order to ensure the collaboration of the other levels of government in the pursuit of EMU goals. The commitment of the local public sector set down in the BCP is necessary to put into practice these guidelines, which in turn serve to achieve this objective.

11.4.3 General Limits

Short-term debt
Short-term borrowing concerns the type of debt that lasts for less one year. It is designed to cover temporary liquidity problems. The local governments have set down a maximum amount for short-term debt: cannot be over 30 per cent of the current revenues of the last closed financial period. Therefore, both capital and financial revenues are excluded to calculate the maximum amount of short-term debt. In addition, the reference to the last closed financial period avoids an overestimation of the budgeted revenues being used as a means of getting round this limitation.

In order to reinforce the effectiveness of the limit, the 1998 reform of the LRHL has added the list of operations considered as short-term. It includes:

- Advances from financial entities, in anticipation of the collection of certain local taxes (in particular the property tax and business tax).
- Local public debt, under one year.
- Borrowing from financial entities to cover liquidity problems, also under one year.

In any case, even below this one-year limit, local governments need the prior authorisation of the Ministry of Finance to issue public debt or apply for loans in foreign currency. In an attempt to speed up this type of financial operation, the local authority empowered to decide short-term borrowing is the mayor if the amount of the short-term debt (including the new operation to be arranged) is not over 15 per cent of the current revenue, and the plenary session for higher amounts.

Long-term debt
The recourse of local government to long-term borrowing must fulfil two conditions:

- The debt must be assigned to finance investment expenditures (real investments or capital transfers).
- Long-term borrowing operations cannot be arranged without previously obtaining authorisation from the Ministry of Finance, should the local government have negative saving or when its total debt (short- and long-term) is over 110 per cent of the current revenue in the last year whose real data (not forecasted) are known.

The second requirement does not entail an absolute limit to long-term borrowing. What it really amounts to is the annulment of local autonomy regarding indebtedness and shifting decision-taking to central government. If the local government presents a financial restructuring plan, proposing appropriate measures to re-establish the required balance regarding the positive current saving or maximum amount of debt, the Ministry of Finance can authorise a new borrowing transaction.

The current definition of this limit, made in 1998 by a modification of the LRHL, replaces the pre-existing limit, set at 25 per cent of current revenues, valid for a longer period compared with local borrowing that fixed a maximum for the debt service (amortisation plus interest).

If we give a value R_t to the current revenue of a local government in the year t, D_{t-1} to the real debt at the end of the previous period t–1, r to the market interest rate and m to the fraction of the debt amortised annually, the previous limit of the debt burden, applied to year t can be expressed as

$$D_{t-1} (r + m)_t \leq 0{,}25 \, R_t \qquad (11.1)$$

Fixing a limit of the debt burden on current revenue has the effect that the correct debt management allows a local government to maintain a higher volume of debt than that of another local government with similar current revenue, but with bad (worse) conditions regarding repayment periods or interest rates.

With the change introduced in 1998, the above expression (11.1) is replaced by

$$D_{t-1} \leq 1{,}1 \, R_{t-2} \qquad (11.2)$$

Assuming constant current revenue over the time

$$R_{t-1} = R_t = \ldots = R \qquad (11.3)$$

We would know which will be the maximum amount of debt according to the two different debt limits in expressions (11.1) and (11.2). Given that the two expressions will be equivalent if

$$0.25 / (r + m)_t = 1.1 \qquad (11.4)$$

It is interesting to ascertain how the values $(r + m)_t$ have evolved during this period:

- Observing the evolution of the interest rates of the long-term public debt, an important decrease can be noted from the mid-1990s and as the restructuring of Spain public finances brought its economy closer to meeting the convergence conditions established in Maastricht. The nominal interest rate of the long-term debt dropped from 11.7 per cent in 1992 to 8.7 per cent in 1996 and 6.4 per cent in 1997.

- The average life of the debt has not changed significantly throughout the 1990s and it can be generally considered to be constant.

Since the average period of contracting local debt in this period is six or seven years, starting from a value of b = 0,1538, according to expression (11.1), reaching the limit to the debt burden would be equivalent to having a volume of debt equal to 103.82 per cent of the current revenue in 1996 and would have increased to 114.78 per cent in 1997 as a consequence of the fall in interest rates. The process of decreasing interest rates that has continued from that year, would have widened the possibilities of local indebtedness. Therefore, rather than as a change in the rules of borrowing, the 1998 modification can be regarded as an implicit toughening-up of the limits on long-term indebtedness.

The requirement of positive current saving is also an addition from 1998. This limit is legally defined as the difference between total current revenues, less current expenditures including interests and amortisation.

Another important new feature of the borrowing regulations was introduced in 1998. Municipalities with over 200,000 inhabitants are henceforth also obliged to obtain the authorisation of the Ministry of Finance when either one of the two limits is exceeded. But such an authorisation will not be necessary for those municipalities which have applied for and obtained the approval of an individual BCP over three years, on condition that it respects the maximum limits of debt and deficit fixed in its BCP.[9]

Beyond the obligation to allocate the long-term debt to financing investment expenditure, there is no relationship between the average life span of the local investments financed and the amortisation period of the debt used to finance them. The life span of most local infrastructures (roads, housing, sports facilities, hydraulic works) is clearly longer than the period of validity of the long-term debt, over 50 per cent of which is arranged for a period of less than five years.

Authorisation to accord long-term borrowing operations is a matter for the mayor if the annual amount of these transactions is not over 10 per cent of the current revenue, and the competence of the plenary session should this amount be higher (unless the previously mentioned state authorisation is necessary).

Authorisation of certain liabilities
In addition, even if local governments meet the above-mentioned

requirements and limits, they still need prior authorisation to contract debts in foreign currency or issue public debt bonds. This requirement may be linked to the objective of guaranteeing the coherence of local borrowing with the needs of the general economic policy, since foreign currency borrowing may not be advisable in certain situations, depending on the country's forecasted balance of payments. In the case of issuing local public debt bonds, the authorisation procedure gives priority to state borrowing in the financial market.

Since the recourse to these types of liabilities is almost exclusive to large municipalities (section 11.5), which run the higher levels of deficit and debt, the procedure of prior authorisation constitutes a powerful instrument of control for central government. Overall however, this requirement, taken in isolation, will not avoid an indefinite borrowing process for local governments, as it only affects these types of liabilities.

11.5 THE EVOLUTION OF LOCAL BORROWING AND BCP COMPLIANCE

Since 1992, deficit and debt ceilings have been established for local government in connection with the convergence programme. As such limits are general (because of the difficulty of setting individual limits for each of the 52 provinces and over 8,000 municipalities), budget consolidation plan results in the period 1992–97 should be seen more as guidelines for judging the compatibility of the general budgetary policy of the local public sector with the fulfilment of the convergence criteria than as an effective brake for each of the local governments. As a whole, BCP outcomes can be valued satisfactorily in the period since the local deficit was below the established national limits and the weight of the local debt with respect to GDP has been reduced (Table 11.5).

Table 11.5   Local deficit and borrowing and economic convergence in the EU (% of GDP)

	1991	1992	1993	1994	1995	1996	1997
Forecast deficit of convergence programme	–	–0.15	–0.15	–0.25	–0.22	–0.23	–0.10
Real deficit		–0.10	–0.10	–0.10	0.00	0.00	0.00
Real borrowing	4.1	3.90	4.30	4.20	4.20	4.10	3.70

Source: Ministerio de Economía y Hacienda and Banco de España.

However, the apparent compliance of the total local public sector conceals different behavioural patterns. On the one hand, small and medium municipalities and provincial governments have generally oscillated between budgetary balance and surplus. The capital cities and large municipalities are the local governments which have generated the deficit. Hence, the 1998 change in the conditions of local borrowing involves an incentive for municipalities with over 200,000 inhabitants to present an individual BCP and respect their limits since, in the case of approval, they can contract debt without having to obtain an authorisation from central government as mentioned in section 11.4. The 1998 modification of the rules limiting local indebtedness should also be clearly interpreted as an attempt to make a more technical definition of its limitations and to apply the experience gained in the application of the BCPs for the period 1992–97.

In order to further reinforce its capacity to control local debt, central government considers the possibility that the Budget Act sets an overall limit to local borrowing as part of its general economic policy. This may lead us to think that the BCPs have been the instrument through which central government has exercised this power. In the future, the BCPs should be a pathway to promote budgetary balance for local governments (Table 11.6).

Table 11.6   Targets for local public sector (% of GDP)

	1998	1999	2000	2001
Deficit	–0.08	–0.08	–0.08	0.00

Source: Ministerio de Economía y Hacienda.

Table 11.7 shows that in the period 1990–97, approximately a third of the real investments of all the public administrations were made by local governments, with a clear predominance of municipalities (as the main agents of the local public sector) over provincial governments. It can also be observed that the evolution of local investments is pro-cyclical, in such a way that when the effects of the economic crisis cause a fall in local revenue (period 1993–95), the local governments also curb the investment process.

Turning now to the sources for financing local investments, and taking the total local investments as a reference (real investments, plus capital transfers and financial investments in shares and other financial assets), one can observe that, on average in the period 1990–97 (Table 11.8), borrowing reached slightly less than 50 per cent, received capital transfers were used to finance a further 25 per cent and current saving (growing since 1995) and the sale of municipal properties provided the remaining 25 per cent. In the evolution of total local investments, we can appreciate the previously mentioned fact of pro-cyclical behaviour, with a marked decrease in 1993 and the subsequent recovery of the investment rhythm in 1995.

Table 11.7   *Evolution of real public investment by public sector agents (data from budgets); in percentages by agents*

	Municipalities	Provincial governments	Local governments	Autonomous communities	Central government*	Total
	1	2	3 = 1 + 2	4	5	6 = 3 + 4 + 5
1990	24.4	6.9	31.3	31.3	37.4	100.0
1991	21.1	6.8	27.9	32.6	39.5	100.0
1992	23.5	7.0	30.5	36.7	32.8	100.0
1993	23.4	6.2	29.6	36.8	33.6	100.0
1994	23.3	6.2	29.5	36.0	34.5	100.0
1995	21.9	6.5	28.4	36.8	34.8	100.0
1996	25.8	7.2	33.0	36.5	30.5	100.0
1997	31.0	7.1	38.1	35.3	26.6	100.0
Mean	24.3	6.7	31.0	35.3	33.7	100.0

Note: * Excluding defence expenditure as this is the unique responsibility of central government.

Source: Informe Económico-Financiero de las Haciendas Territoriales, MAP.

Regarding the division of debt between the different types of local government and the evolution of total local borrowing during the last 15 years (1984–98), one can observe a fall in the local debt-GDP ratio since the application in 1989 of the LRHL promoting the fiscal autonomy of local governments. The decrease is even more marked from 1993, when the BCP began to be applied to the local public sector. As for distribution between local governments, the six largest municipalities with populations over 500,000 inhabitants account for about a third of the total debt. If the debt of the municipalities with over 200,000 inhabitants is added, most of the municipal debt would be accounted for. Thus the target of the 1998 reform becomes obvious: municipalities with more than 200,000 inhabitants should present individual BCPs.

The three "foral regime" provincial governments absorb a third of total provincial debt due to their previously mentioned special characteristics. They can be considered more similar to the autonomous communities than the rest of the provincial governments.

Table 11.8 *Budgetary investments by local governments*
(preliminary budgets of municipalities with over 20,000 inhabitants and provincial governments)

	(Million ptas)			Total to be financed =Total financing (Million ptas)	Financing sources for the investment							
	Real investment	Financial investment	Capital transfers		Selling of estate		Borrowing		Capital transfers		Saving or self-financing	
					Million ptas	%	Million ptas	%	Million ptas	%	Million ptas	%
	1	2	3	4=1+2+3=5+7+9+11	5	6=(5/4)*100	7	8=(7/4)*100	9	10=(9/4)*100	11	12=(11/4)*100
1990	463 407.1	33 163.4	85 503.8	582 074.3	67 355.7	11.57	311 095.5	53.45	141 755.3	24.35	61 867.8	10.63
1991	414 738.6	32 685.2	95 979.3	543 403.1	70 315.1	12.94	289 545.1	53.28	155 285.3	28.58	28 257.6	5.20
1992	436 964.6	35 456.7	94 031.5	566 452.8	93 321.4	16.47	314 155.8	55.46	149 055.9	26.31	9 919.7	1.75
1993	399 341.7	33 526.2	11 870.7	549 738.6	88 129.3	16.03	289 926.6	52.74	145 624.0	26.49	26 058.7	4.74
1994	426 938.1	27 223.3	12 532.5	581 693.9	86 069.8	14.80	288 092.0	49.53	160 165.1	27.53	47 367.0	8.14
1995	408 947.4	21 983.3	152 423.0	583 353.6	76 174.5	13.06	264 837.1	45.40	164 089.6	28.13	78 252.4	13.41
1996	469 034.3	27 705.9	159 783.5	656 523.8	102 795.4	15.66	271 468.5	41.35	175 041.4	26.66	107 218.6	16.33
1997	568 798.6	19 887.2	170 722.7	759 408.5	106 368.0	14.01	316 120.9	41.63	184 614.1	24.31	152 305.5	20.06

Table 11.9 Local public borrowing (billions of pesetas)

	TOTAL	Total *	Total municipalities	Municipalities with over 500,000 inhabitants	Rest of municipalities	Total provincial and insular governments	"Common regime" provincial governments	"Foral regime" provincial governments	Off-budget debt	Off-budget debt/TOTAL (%)	Total (% of GDP) **
	$1=2+9$	$2=3+6$	$3=4+5$	4	5	$6=7+8$	7	8	9	$10=9/1$	$11=2/PIB$
1984	598	571	412	156	256	159	137	22	27	4.5	2.2
1985	719	698	523	227	296	175	155	20	21	2.9	2.5
1986	989	962	694	336	358	268	189	79	27	2.7	3.0
1987	1 126	1 064	752	337	415	312	218	94	62	5.5	2.9
1988	1 381	1 287	833	359	474	454	244	210	94	6.8	3.2
1989	2 359	2 224	874	312	562	1 350	278	1 072	135	5.7	4.9
1990	2 300	2 129	1 108	398	710	1 021	333	688	171	7.4	4.2
1991	2 515	2 287	1 488	496	992	799	398	401	228	9.1	4.2
1992	2 624	2 354	1 646	552	1 094	708	447	261	270	10.3	4.0
1993	2 936	2 646	1 860	601	1 259	786	487	299	290	9.9	4.3
1994	3 095	2 811	2 002	611	1 391	809	489	320	284	9.2	4.3
1995	3 298	3 002	2 136	640	1 496	866	492	374	296	9.0	4.2
1996p	3 383	3 110	2 243	669	1 574	867	495	372	273	8.1	4.1
1997p	3 336	3 010	2 303	702	1 601	707	476	231	326	9.8	3.8
1998p	3 465	3 139	2 405	682	1 723	734	508	226	326	9.4	3.7

Notes:
p   Provisional data.
*   Debt according to the excessive deficit protocol.
** Calculated according to GNP directive.

Source: Banco de España, Boletín Estadístico.

252

The "off-budget" debt of local public enterprise has increased in importance compared with the total since the early 1990s. This phenomenon should be observed with caution, in order to avoid opening the floodgates to a trend of overrunning the limits of local borrowing by satellisation of local functions, shifting the debt towards local public enterprise or even outside the local public sector through "privatisation", a concern that extends throughout Europe (see Table 11.9).

Finally, Table 11.10 shows the structure of local debt in its percentage distribution according to types and periods. In the vast majority of cases, Spanish local debt takes the form of loans and credits from commercial and savings banks. Only the large cities with over 500,000 inhabitants and the foral provincial governments have made a significant use of other instruments such as the direct issue of public debt bonds or arranging credit in foreign currencies. Local debt is basically medium- and long-term. More than 85 per cent is debt over one year. Once again the foral provincial governments break slightly with this criterion: it is more than likely that their peculiarity of being governments financing other administrations forces them to carry out temporary treasury operations more frequently.

Table 11.10   Structure of Spanish local debt (1997)

	Debt instrument (%)			Debt period (%)			
	Financial system loans	Issue of debt	Foreign banking and foreign currency loans	Less than 1 year	From 1 to 6 years	More than 6 years	Unknown
Municipalities	83.61	6.51	9.87	12.61	43.10	42.85	1.44
Less than 50,000	*99.95*	*0.00*	*0.05*	*12.91*	*44.33*	*41.00*	*1.76*
From 50,000 to 500,000	*98.07*	*0.18*	*1.75*	*11.79*	*42.43*	*44.17*	*1.61*
More than 500,000	*50.47*	*20.37*	*29.16*	*13.79*	*42.12*	*43.71*	*0.38*
Provincial governments	42.87	33.56	23.57	34.67	21.89	43.44	0.00
"Common Regime"	*99.84*	*0.16*	*0..00*	*7.15*	*14.28*	*28.57*	*50.00*
"Foral Regime"	*42.87*	*33.56*	*23.57*	*34.67*	*21.89*	*43.44*	*0.00*
Other local governments	100.00	0.00	0.00	22.79	53.39	23.49	0.33
Total local governments	80.27	8.81	10.92	13.90	42.33	42.43	1.34

Source: CIRLOCAL.

11.6   CONCLUSION AND FUTURE PERSPECTIVES

The local public sector in Spain comprises two types of local government: municipalities and provinces. The municipalities have a greater weight.

Following the democratic 1978 constitution, the decentralisation process was much more intense toward the regional level (autonomous communities) than for local government. But the latter have an important economic weight in providing public services which are essential for the welfare of their residents.

Prior to the 1988 LRHL change, the system of local finance was based on taxes of low revenue capacity and low income elasticity. Local government lacked autonomy in taxation. As a result, the two operations of bailing out that emerged in 1980 and 1983 were indicative of the dangers of an unsuitable tax system and of the lack of operative control mechanisms for local debt.

The LRHL changed this panorama. The rules limiting local borrowing embodied in the LRHL and applied from 1989 are based on the classical distinction between short-term debt, addressing liquidity problems only, and true long-term debt, arranged to finance investments. The new legislation was an attempt to obtain the solvency of local governments and henceforth to maintain a budgetary margin without the debt burden becoming excessive. These rules have been strongly influenced by the EMU process and the obligation to fulfil the commitments of budgetary discipline established in the Maastricht Treaty. On the one hand, a medium-term budgetary commitment by local governments was added to the previous rules. This operation was linked to the Spanish convergence programme, specifying the evolution of the maximum local deficit and debt during the prevailing period of 1992–97. On the other hand, the experience gained in applying the borrowing limits led to the reform of the local borrowing regulation in 1998, defining the limits more accurately. Furthermore, attempts were made to encourage large municipalities with over 200,000 inhabitants to present individual BCPs, since it is this type of local government that issues most debt.

The local public debt has financed a little less than half of total local investments. The rest has been covered by capital transfers from the centre and current saving. The weight of local debt in relation to GDP decreased in the 1990s, particularly from 1994 onwards. The control mechanisms have worked satisfactorily in general. For the future, the new role designed for the municipalities and provincial governments in the "local agreement" may require the local tax and grants system to be reconsidered. Similarly, the control mechanisms should not attempt to produce a shift of the local debt towards off-budget firms and entities if the effectiveness of the rules limiting indebtedness is to be maintained. This objective is reinforced by the rules of the new European System of Accounts, ESA 95, because local enterprises ought to be consolidated within the general account in those cases where more than 50 per cent of their revenues are grants from the municipality. In the same way, in the new decentralised framework of the Spanish public sector, one can ask whether the control of local finance could correspond to that of the autonomous communities, although this matter has recently aroused political apprehension in the Spanish Local Government Federation (FEMP) and could make it difficult for central government to exercise its powers in economic policies.

NOTES

1. For a more detailed view of the most relevant issues concerning local finance in the democratic stage see Monasterio and Suárez-Pandiello (1998), chapter 4.
2. On the content of the *foral system*, see Suárez-Pandiello (1999) for a schematic presentation and Zubiri and Vallejo (1995) for a more detailed analysis.
3. For further analysis see MAP-FEMP (1999).
4. For a complete legal analysis see Sosa Wagner (1999).
5. See note 1.
6. Except in the case of municipalities in *foral* territories, in which grants basically come from *foral* provincial governments.
7. In some regions, this responsibility is exercised by the autonomous communities and not the central government.
8. At this time (April 2001) the Spanish parliament is debating a new Law of Budgetary Stability which will change the budget balance definition. So the new requirement will be a zero deficit in accordance with the European System of Accounts (ESA 95) delimitation of net borrowing.
9. The authorisations for borrowing could be enlarged in the future to all the municipalities that do not accomplish the requirement of budgetary balance in accordance with the ESA rules, if the Law of Budgetary Stability comes into force.

REFERENCES

Aja, E. (1999), *El Estado Autonómico. Federalismo y Hechos Diferenciales.* Alianza Editorial. Madrid.
MAP-FEMP (1999), *El Pacto Local. Medidas para el Desarrollo del Gobierno Local.* Ministerio de Administraciones Públicas, Federación Española de Municipios y Provincias, Instituto Nacional de Administración Pública,. Madrid.
Monasterio, C. and J. Suárez-Pandiello (1998), *Manual de Hacienda Autonómica y Local.* Ed. Ariel. Barcelona.
Sosa Wagner, F. (1999), "Creación y supresión de municipios y alteración de sus términos", in Jeménez-Blanco, A. and Parada, J.R. (eds), *La Administración Pública: Reforma y Contrarreforma*, Fundación para el Análisis y los Estudios Sociales, Papeles de la Fundación, no 46, Madrid.
Suárez-Pandiello, J. (1999), "Fiscal Federalism in Spain: An unfinished task", in A. Fossati and G. Pannella (eds), *Fiscal Federalism in Europe*, Routledge, London.
Zubiri, I. and M. Vallejo (1995), *Un análisis metodológico y empírico del sistema de cupo*, Ed. Fundación BBV, Bilbao.

12. Local government capital expenditure in England

Peter A. Watt

12.1 INTRODUCTION

In the ongoing struggle over spending between central and local government that has continued for at least 20 years in Britain, it is current spending rather than capital spending that has sometimes hit the headlines, especially during the infamous poll tax experiment, widely credited with Mrs Thatcher's downfall (Gibson, 1990). Academic interest has also mainly focused on the revenue side of local government expenditure, with, for example Foster et al.'s (1980) 634-page volume devoting only two or three pages to the subject of capital expenditure but two or three chapters at least to current expenditure. Yet, as this chapter shows, it is capital expenditure that has been more severely constrained and the subject of more central direction.

In theory, capital expenditure is expenditure that yields a stream of future benefits, although in practice the definition may focus on expenditure on physical assets. Hence, although education generates a stream of future returns, in practice teachers' salaries are usually defined as revenue rather than capital (Musgrave, 1959, pp. 558–562; Jones and Pendlebury, 1996, p. 64).

Capital expenditure is largely financed by loans in England. The practice of funding capital projects by borrowing can be seen as stemming from the pay-as-you-use principle of attempting to make the payment pattern match the pattern of benefits from the asset (Musgrave, 1959, p. 558). This pay-as-you-use principle is also evident in the current UK government's Code for Fiscal Stability discussed below (HM Treasury, 1998a).

Traditionally the way for local government to generate a stream of benefits from an asset has been for it to become the *owner* of the asset. Thus, for example, the local authority typically owns the town hall. However, in recent years the unthinking acceptance of the "in-house" solution for provision has given way to the "enabling" approach of considering purchase from the private sector either voluntarily or under compulsory competitive tendering (Musgrave, 1959, p. 42; Ostrom et al., 1961; Ridley, 1988; Clarke and Stewart, 1988). The Private Finance Initiative (PFI) broadly aims to extend this approach to public investment projects, with the objective being to encourage consideration of the option of keeping ownership of proposed public sector investments in the private sector. The benefits the investments provide are then bought by the public sector through a stream of payments geared to the actual receipt of these benefits.

This chapter considers the recent history of government control of capital expenditure by local authorities, describes the current system and outlines current proposals for change. The chapter also examines the recently developing avenues for capital investment now opening up under the PFI.

12.2   THE RECENT HISTORICAL PATTERN OF LOCAL AUTHORITY CAPITAL EXPENDITURE

The details of the UK local authority capital expenditure system differ between England, Northern Ireland, Scotland, and Wales, although there is a broad general similarity. This chapter provides details of the system for England only, although we start by looking at the historical pattern of expenditure for the whole of the UK.

Local government capital expenditure in the UK currently comprises about 0.7 per cent of total domestic expenditure and has been close to this level since the 1980s. The pattern since 1958 is shown in Figure 12.1.

In the past, local government capital expenditure generally formed a higher proportion of domestic spending than it has recently, rising from around 2.5 per cent in the late 1950s to a peak of 3.8 per cent in 1974, just before the major reorganisation of local government in England and Wales that year. The following year saw the cuts imposed on the government as a condition of the IMF loan and Anthony Crosland's declaration to local government that "the party's over" (Butler and Butler, 1994, p. 274).

Figure 2 shows that, as well as declining in relation to all domestic expenditure, capital expenditure has also declined dramatically as a proportion of total local government expenditure. Figure 2 shows capital expenditure as a share of all local government expenditure falling from a fairly stable 30–35 per cent in the 1960s and early 1970s to a fairly stable 10 per cent in the 1980s and 1990s. The overall picture is that as local government expenditure has been cut as a percentage of all domestic expenditure from the mid 1970s onwards, it is capital expenditure that has absorbed most of the cuts.

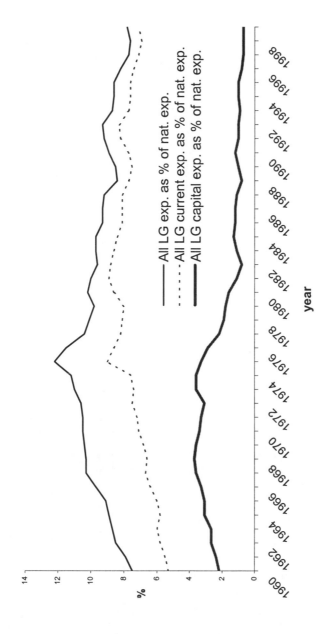

Figure 12.1 Local government expenditure as a percentage of all domestic expenditure in the UK

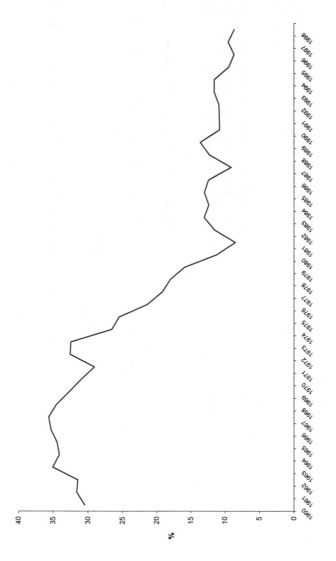

Figure 12.2 Local government capital as a percentage of all local government expenditure, UK

Table 12.1 shows the distribution of proposed local government capital expenditure by programme area. Housing is still the largest area of spending, although education is an important priority for the government and it can be seen that it is planned to make rapid spending increases in this area in the next few years.

Table 12.1   *Local authority investment 2001/2 – 2003/4 - major spending areas*

	2001/02 (£m)	2002/03 (£m)	2003/04 (£m)
Housing	2,392	2,553	2,634
Transport	1,378	1,651	1,856
Education	1,673	1,929	2,555
Health	65	87	87
Regeneration	360	337	362
Home Office (Fire, Police)	214	240	242
Electronic service delivery	25	135	190
Total	6,107	6,932	7,926

Note: Education figures exclude PFI credits and ICT expenditure

Source: DETR (2000a)

12.3   A BRIEF HISTORY OF CAPITAL EXPENDITURE CONTROL

Great Britain is a *unitary* state with central government having the authority to reorganise, create or destroy units of local government and control their actions as it sees fit. British local government is controlled in law by Acts of Parliament and by secondary legislation in the form of regulations laid before Parliament.

There is a long history of central government control of local government capital expenditure in the UK. Page (1985, p. 6) argues that the constitutional basis of such control lies in the right to levy taxes being the fiscal prerogative of the crown. Borrowing involves a commitment to local taxes for repayment and this is the source of the requirement for approval. Page (1985, p. 53) traces the first statutory borrowing provisions to a local Act of Parliament of 1663 "An Act for the repairing the Highways within the Counties of Hertford, Cambridge and Huntington", which allowed a sum to be borrowed at interest for a maximum of nine years against the security of road toll payments.

The Local Government Act of 1933 consolidated practices that had evolved in the control of borrowing. The act did not define capital expenditure, but provided a systemisation whereby local authorities could borrow "for any purpose the Minister considered proper" (Page, 1985, pp. 169–70). The Act listed "acquisition of land and erection of buildings, execution of permanent works, provision of plant, and the doing of any other thing the cost of which the sanctioning authority agreed ought to be spread over a term of years", but added that "borrowing might be undertaken for any other purpose for which borrowing was authorised by statute or statutory order". *Loan sanction* from central government was effectively necessary for all borrowing and the purpose of all loans was subject to ministerial scrutiny and approval.

In 1970 the Department of the Environment circular 2/70 (DoE, 1970) gave the objectives of the system it introduced as "regulating the total level of capital expenditure, ensuring that individual projects meet the standards set by departments and monitoring the overall level of local authority borrowing on the market" (DoE, 1970, cited in Page, 1985, p. 195). Services were divided into "key sector", where projects were individually "loan sanctioned", intermediate, which did not count against overall totals for loan sanction, and minor locally determined schemes, which were controlled by a block allocation set at a low level. Local authorities had been pressing for all services to be dealt with under a block allocation, but only achieved this for the locally determined schemes element, which together with the intermediate sector accounted for less than 10 per cent of capital expenditure.

Key sector services included education, social services, housing, highways, police and urban programmes and constituted about 90 per cent of capital expenditure. The intermediate group related to land purchase, as distinct from other capital expenditure, for education, highways and housing. Seen from a centralist viewpoint the system failed to provide control in two ways. First, control was not exerted over schemes financed through revenue, and second the granting of a loan sanction did not necessarily mean that the money would be spent in the year it was given (Watt, 1982, p. 91).

The system of control introduced in 1981 under the provisions of the Local Government, Planning and Land Act, 1980 was designed to *extend* control to these two aspects of the former system which had allowed a degree of local autonomy. A major change introduced with this system therefore was that control was exercised not over *loans* but capital *payments* whether financed by loans or from revenue. Capital payments were defined in Schedule 12 to the Act to include most items of capital expenditure. The total for a local authority's payments was allocated for a year at a time, rather than extending open-endedly into the future as had loan sanctions, and this imposed a new requirement for a local authority to manage its scheduling of capital projects more closely.

Local authorities were required to submit capital expenditure plans to the relevant central government department for housing, education, transport and social services and would be notified of their allocation near the end of the calendar year. The new capital payments system integrated administratively with the cash limits system of public expenditure control introduced by the Treasury in 1976.

In practice the system failed to deliver the control it promised in the way that central government wanted. The interest focused on controlling the local authority borrowing requirement (LABR) as part of the public sector borrowing requirement (PSBR).

Part of the difficulty of control stemmed from local authority capital receipts. Since 1980, local authorities had received considerable *capital receipts* from the sale of their housing stock as a result of the 1980 Housing Act, which gave their tenants the right to buy at discounted prices. Central government restricted the proportion of these receipts that could be spent but did not have full control over when the remaining *usable receipts* might be spent. The government therefore had to estimate likely spending of capital receipts. Its estimates often turned out to be very inaccurate, with the outcome level of capital spending being considerably above or below the level the government had been seeking to obtain. (Watt, 1988, p. 162).

The government was also concerned by the growth of "creative accounting" methods for circumventing controls by leasing and barter arrangements that had the effect of capital expenditure, but escaped being defined as such. At times such arrangements could also be poor value for money.

Consideration of these weaknesses led to the introduction of the current system through the Local Government and Housing Act, 1989, which moved control away from capital payments back to sources of finance, and provides an explicit definition of capital expenditure in order to restrict opportunities for creative accounting in this area. We now describe the current system.

12.4   THE CURRENT SYSTEM OF CONTROL

12.4.1   Central Government Structures and Objectives

In the UK HM Treasury has responsibility for UK fiscal policy, macroeconomic policy and public expenditure allocation across the UK (HM Treasury, 1999). Under the Scotland Act (1998), Government of Wales Act (1998) and Northern Ireland Act (1998) the devolved administrations "have freedom to make their own spending decisions on devolved programmes within the overall totals" (HM Treasury, 1999). Funding for the devolved administrations' budgets is determined in the spending review round at the same time as it is determined for departments of the UK government.

This chapter will focus on the system that applies to England. In England, the Department for Transport, Local Government and the Region (DTLR) administers central government control over local authorities capital spending. The department with responsibility for local government in England was called the Department of the Environment (DoE) until 1997, and the Department of Environment, Transport and the Regions (DETR) until June 2001.

In 1997 the Conservative government, which had been in power since 1979, was replaced by a Labour government. The new government has introduced a system of spending reviews, carried out every two years, to control overall government spending, including local government spending, and setting plans for three years ahead (Twigger, 2000). This replaced the previous system of annual public expenditure surveys.

The new government has set out its approach to public spending in its "Comprehensive Spending Review" (HM Treasury, 1998b) and in its "Economic and Fiscal Strategy Report" (HM Treasury, 1998a). The government set out two overall fiscal rules:

- the golden rule: over the economic cycle the government will borrow only to invest and not to fund current spending; and
- the sustainable investment rule: net public debt as a proportion of GDP will be held over the economic cycle at a stable and prudent level (HM Treasury, 1998a, p. 5)

The new public expenditure planning process involves a new aggregate quantity called total managed expenditure (TME). TME is composed of departmental expenditure limits (DELs) set for three years, and annually managed expenditure (AME), which is determined annually.

Local government capital expenditure is included within DELs, except that part which is self-financed out of capital receipts, which is classified as annually managed expenditure. Central government therefore aims to control local authority capital expenditure, categorised under DELs and also self-financed capital expenditure, categorised under AME, although it recognises that the latter category is less easy to control. The government's interest in controlling local government capital expenditure stems from its effects on public sector net borrowing (HM Treasury, 1998a, p. 39) and the public sector net cash requirement.

Other new features of the public expenditure planning process include a move to resource accounting and budgeting (HM Treasury, 2001). This moves the public accounts from a cash basis to an accruals basis and also involves the publication of a public sector balance sheet. The 2000 spending review has been carried out on a resource accounting and budgeting basis (HM Treasury, 2000a, b).

12.4.2 Mechanisms for the Control of Local Authority Capital Spending

The major recent legislation on local authority capital expenditure is the Local Government and Housing Act 1989, which establishes the current framework of control.

Although the broad aim of control of local authority capital expenditure is to contribute to an overall objective of keeping government expenditure in line with fiscal rules, the objectives can be broadened to include seeking *prudence* in local authority capital finance, as well as controlling the level of capital expenditure and in addition steering it towards specific central government policies (DoE, 1997a, p. 3).

Central government has a number of prudential objectives for local authority finance imposed through legislation.

- First, it does not in general allow local authorities to pay for current expenditure out of capital resources.
- Second, it seeks to ensure that local authorities make adequate provision to meet their debt and credit liabilities.
- Third, regulations prevent local authorities choosing financing options which represent poor value for money but would otherwise be attractive as a way of evading controls (e.g. sale and leaseback arrangements).
- Fourth, the ways in which local authorities can borrow money are controlled, they are encouraged to become debt free, and they are discouraged from engaging in speculative forms of investment (DoE, 1997a, p. 3).

12.4.3 Legislation and Control Mechanisms

The objective of controlling the level of capital expenditure and steering it towards central government priorities is achieved by controlling its finance. There are four sources of finance for local authority capital expenditure and all are regulated either directly or indirectly by central government. These sources are, in order of importance, (1) borrowing and other forms of credit,

(2) capital grants, (3) the use of capital receipts and (4) the use of revenue funds. The first two of these sources of finance, borrowing and grants, are directly controlled by central government. Borrowing is subject to credit approval issued by central government and it also controls grants.

Hence, all capital expenditure must be paid for out of revenue funds unless (a) it is met from usable capital receipts, or (b) it is borrowing or credit that has central government *credit approval*, or (c) it is met from a *grant*. These three categories of expenditure are all controlled by central government and if the expenditure does not fall into these categories it is met from revenue expenditure, which is also controlled by central government's powers to "cap" local authority revenue expenditure (although these powers have not been used since 1998).

Table 12.2 shows the relative importance of these different sources of finance over recent years in relative and absolute terms. The controls exerted by central government on these various routes for capital expenditure other than revenue finance, will now be discussed in turn.

Table 12.2   *The finance of capital expenditure: 1995/96 to 1999/00, England*

	1995/96		1996/97		1997/98		1998/99		1999/00	
	£m	%	£m	%	£m	%	£m	%	£m	%
Borrowing:										
Basic credit approvals	1,493	21	1,291	20	968	15	1,048	16	1,052	15
Supplementary credit approvals	771	11	829	13	1,131	17	1,286	19	1,254	18
Government grants	1,484	21	1,388	21	1,262	19	1,160	17	1,154	17
Other grants and contributions	230	3	281	4	389	6	485	7	599	9
Use of capital receipts	1,216	17	1,192	18	1,184	18	1,223	18	1,517	22
Revenue finance	1,591	23	1,425	22	1,382	21	1,255	19	1,043	15
Other	236	3	172	3	196	3	253	4	234	3
Total capital expenditure as defined in s. 40(6) of 1989 Act	7,021	100	6,578	100	6,512	100	6,710	100	6,853	100

Source: *Local Government Financial Statistics 2000*, DETR (2000b).

Capital receipts

Capital receipts arise when a local authority sells an asset such as a piece of land or a council house. Since 1980 local authorities have been required by law to sell houses to tenants who have wanted to buy them and this has been their main source of capital receipts.

The use of capital receipts to finance new capital spending is controlled in two ways. First, not all capital receipts are *"usable"*, because the government requires that a high percentage of these receipts are used to repay debt or pay off liabilities under credit arrangements. This is called provision for credit liabilities (DoE, 1997a, p. 23). Only 25 per cent of receipts from the sale of housing are usable on capital expenditure and only 50 per cent of the receipts from the sale of other land or buildings (DoE, 1997c, p. 140; CIPFA, 2000, p. 49). These proportions can be varied by regulation and have been varied a number of times in attempts to fine-tune the system or encourage particular short-term policy objectives (DETR, 1998).

Second, central government makes assumptions about how much of its capital receipts a local authority will use to finance capital expenditure, and makes a corresponding reduction in the amount of borrowing it approves for the authority, as discussed below under credit approvals.

Credit approvals
The government controls local authority borrowing by issuing *credit approvals*. Borrowing is defined as either taking out a loan or entering into arrangements that have the effect of offering credit (such as leasing). This inclusive definition was introduced under the 1989 Act as part of the restrictions it places on creative accounting and is used to prevent local authorities from entering into leasing arrangements purely to avoid central government control. As credit arrangements are subject to *credit approval* in the same way as loans, there is no incentive to construct artificial leasing arrangements in order to escape these controls.

Credit approvals are of two kinds: *basic credit approvals* (BCAs) and *supplementary credit approvals* (SCAs). BCAs can be used for any kind of capital expenditure whereas SCAs can only be used for specifically approved projects, such as coast protection schemes or major transport schemes (CIPFA, 2000, p. 47) and hence the degree of control that is exerted by central government with SCAs is greater than the degree of control exerted with BCAs. Table 12.2 shows that the level of supplementary credit approvals has been rising relative to basic credit approvals over time, leading to reduced local discretion.

BCAs are calculated as the sum of a number of elements – *education*, *social services*, *housing* and *other* although local authorities are allowed to vire spending between categories. Virement therefore allows local authorities to use basic credit approvals for any capital spending (CIPFA, 2000, p. 47).

Basic credit approvals are regulated as part of a process whereby the government sets out an *annual capital guideline* (ACG) for each authority which broadly indicates how much it believes the authority should spend on capital projects. Decisions on ACGs are arrived at by a combination of methods including consideration of bids and the use of formulae (Henley et al., 1992, p. 67; DETR, 1998). The government makes an estimate of how much of each local authority's capital spending it could finance itself out of capital receipts. This is called receipts taken into account (RTIA – usually pronounced "Rita"). These receipts taken into account are subtracted from the annual capital guideline to give for each authority a BCA issued by the Department of Transport, Local Government and the Regions. Hence

$$BCA = ACG - RTIA$$

Some authorities have few capital receipts. The effect of the formula is that for a given total of credit approvals relatively more is allocated to authorities that have low capital receipts. The RTIA system is sometimes criticised as being effectively a tax on authorities' usable capital receipts, which redistributes towards authorities with low holdings (DETR, 1998).

To summarise, the government only allows a certain proportion of capital receipts to be used on capital expenditure: usable capital receipts. It then estimates how much of these will be used to finance capital spending (RTIA) and subtracts this amount from the amount it believes the authority should be spending on capital (ACG) to determine how much it will allow the authority to borrow (BCA) via credit approvals controls.

Grants

Apart from revenue finance the other main source of capital finance is government grants. Grants are given by government departments mainly for housing, transport or urban regeneration purposes, or by non-departmental public bodies, such as the National Lottery distributors (DETR, 1998). There can also be inputs from the private sector associated with "planning gain". In order to receive capital grants, detailed plans have to be submitted and the grants are tied to these plans. The importance of grants has also been slowly rising as a proportion of total capital finance, and this has entailed a further reduction in local discretion.

12.4.4   How Capital Resources are Allocated to Local Authorities

Central government decides annually how much in the way of ACGs, SCAs and grants to allocate to local authorities. The amounts provided are composed of allocations made by the relevant central government departments, and the methods used are "complex and vary significantly amongst departments" (DETR, 1998). The most important areas are housing, transport and education which together account for nearly two-thirds of the overall sums involved. The allocation methods used are briefly discussed under these headings.

Housing

Each local authority receives a *housing investment programme* (HIP) allocation. The national total for housing ACGs is divided among the ten *regions* of England (each with their associated government office) on the basis of the *generalised needs index* (GNI) – a statistical indicator designed to relate to local authorities' need for housing capital expenditure. The GNI is calculated from indicators of the types of housing stock in an area and measures of overcrowding and is subject to discussion with local authority associations. The government office for each region then allocates an ACG to each of its local authorities. Each authority receives an amount based on its GNI, increased or decreased according to how relatively efficient and effective it is judged to be by its regional government office. This judgement is made on the basis of DETR criteria determined by ministers and takes into account each local authority's strategy for housing and its "performance" in previous years (DETR, 1998). Such criteria include the extent of a local authority's liaison with other organisations such as housing associations and the effectiveness of its use of information such as housing condition indicators. The HIP process also allocates resources for renovation grants for privately owned homes and for disabled facilities grants.

Transport

Capital resources for transport are allocated through the transport policies and programme (TPP) mechanism. Each year local authorities submit a bid to the DTLR in the form of a comprehensive plan for highways, public transport and traffic management, with an outline programme over five years. Resources are allocated for major schemes (over £2 million), structural road maintenance, bridge strengthening and minor works, and grants are given for projects of over £5 million.

Education

ACGs for education are allocated on the basis of a per capita formula and an assessment of the need for extra places called basic need (BN) calculated by comparing demand for places at schools with total capacity. Adjustments are made to reflect the requirement for places for pupils with special educational needs, and projects for cost-effective rationalisation of surplus places.

Other services

ACGs are distributed between the various classes of local authority on the basis of previous years' allocations. Different types of authority have their ACG allocated on the basis of different formulae. In counties and districts the allocation is on the basis of population, in metropolitan authorities on the basis of unemployment and in London boroughs on the basis of the previous year's allocation.

12.4.5   Borrowing and Repayment of Debt

Although the level of local authority capital expenditure is controlled by central government, the *financing* of capital expenditure is not particularly an issue for local authorities. Rather the question is one of securing central government approval for expenditure and the particular issue of finance is not in general an important constraint. The most significant source of loans to local government is the government Public Works Loan Board (PWLB) which financed 78 per cent of UK local authority debt in 1991 (Cook, 1993). The next most significant source is local authorities' internal borrowing from either reserves or capital receipts. The financing costs of borrowing are largely met by two government grants, the revenue support grant, which contains a capital finance element, and the housing revenue account subsidy for borrowing related to housing provision (DETR, 1998, p. 45).

Total debt (and liabilities equivalent to debt such as PFI agreements) must not exceed an authority's aggregate credit limit (ACL). The ACL for an authority is worked out each year by a complicated calculation largely based on the authority's total outstanding debt in March 1990, adjusted by adding new credit approvals and subtracting amounts required to be set aside from capital receipts (the unusable portion) and its revenue provision for repayment of debt (CIPFA, 2000; Challis, 2000).

A local authority must set aside a minimum level of revenue each year for repayment of debt. This is 2 per cent of the ACL credit ceiling due to housing items and 4 per cent of the credit ceiling due to non-housing items.

The present system for repayment of debt is recognised to have serious shortcomings. According to recent research commissioned by the government:

> Under the present system, councils are required to charge at least a minimum amount in their accounts each year for the redemption of debt. This sum, the minimum revenue provision (MRP), is calculated primarily by reference to the credit ceiling, a concept going back to 1989 with no relevance to current levels of borrowing. (DETR, 1999a, p. 5)

The government is currently seeking to develop a new approach to debt repayment through the Prudential Code Steering Group of the Chartered Institute of Public Finance and Accountancy.

12.5   THE PRIVATE FINANCE INITIATIVE

Local authorities have found that the regime of capital expenditure control has severely limited their ability to spend on capital projects, and any new avenues are likely to be of great interest. A currently developing route for capital spending is the private finance initiative (PFI). Local authorities' abilities to secure the use of capital assets for their residents has recently been supplemented by the options opened up by the private finance initiative (PFI) (HM Treasury, 1995). The PFI initiative seeks to move the public sector away from the traditional approach of *ownership* of capital assets.

The PFI was launched in 1992 in the autumn statement by the Chancellor. The basic idea is to encourage public bodies to use privately provided capital services. Private financing of government expenditure had hitherto been largely ruled out by the "Ryrie rules" which were based on the premise that the government can borrow more cheaply than the private sector, hence public investments should be publicly funded. This approach takes the public investment project as a "given". The PFI approach considers that the nature of the investment is not fixed but is likely to change with private involvement. Savings could therefore ensue not from finance but from a more appropriately defined investment.

PFI projects have to satisfy two fundamental requirements specified by the government. These are that "value for money must be demonstrated" and "the private sector must genuinely assume risk" (HM Treasury, 1996). Until 1992, private finance was very rarely used for public sector investment projects. Most projects were ruled out by the above mentioned "Ryrie rules" set out in the early 1980s. Sir William Ryrie was Second Permanent Secretary in charge of public finance at the Treasury. The Ryrie rules directed that privately financed projects still counted against the public sector borrowing requirement and that they must be evaluated against a theoretical public sector alternative. In addition government had access to the cheapest finance through its own borrowing through the National Loans Fund. Hence it was difficult to demonstrate value for money in privately financed projects (Thain and Wright, 1995; Terry, 1996).

In Autumn 1992 Norman Lamont announced that self-financed projects undertaken by the private sector would no longer need to be compared with theoretical public sector alternatives, and the public sector would have more opportunity to use leasing where it secured good value for money and a transfer of risk to the private sector.

The extension of PFI to local authority projects was not at first a very practical proposition. Such projects could bear resemblance to 1980s schemes to get round capital spending restrictions which had been barred by legislation. As was pointed out above, one of the purposes of the 1989 Act, which is the main legislative instrument for control of local authority capital finance, was a desire to prevent local authorities entering into leasing arrangements to evade capital expenditure controls. PFI arrangements are rather similar to such arrangements and for PFI schemes to be able to proceed a number of regulations under the 1989 Act have had to be changed (DoE, 1997b, Appendix 2). Legislation was changed to allow more scope for leases of non-housing property to be treated as revenue, making it easier for local authorities to participate in companies led by the private sector.

Some commentators have likened the PFI to hire purchase for consumers and have suggested that there may be dangers of local authorities constraining their future actions too heavily by over use of such arrangements.

The government route for the extension of the PFI in local authorities is through "design build finance operate" (DBFO) schemes.

The incentive for a local authority to enter into PFI schemes is that if the private sector takes on a sufficient level of risk in the projects, the capital investment does not score against the local authority's capital spending limits. The DBFO scheme is important here. In such a scheme, a private company might provide school buildings for a local authority and be paid by the local authority for "school building services" received. Certain risks would be borne by the private provider – for example if the buildings were unavailable due to, say, a heating breakdown, the payment would not be made. DBFO projects for local authorities must satisfy the following four main principles (DOE, 1996). First, there must be some transfer of risk to the private sector. Such risks could be in any or all of the financing, design construction and operation of the building. Risk in operation could be in the level of occupancy or usage of the asset. Second, specification of DBFO projects should be in terms of the *outputs* required, allowing the possibility of innovation in how the service is delivered. Third, the contractor should bear risks and take responsibility for the performance of the asset over a long-term period. Fourth, payment should be for services received and subject to performance.

It is envisaged that, as well as schools, DBFO schemes could provide buildings such as police stations, leisure centres and libraries. Local authorities have also been given new freedoms to participate in private sector-led joint venture companies (DoE, 1997b). The government announced that in 1998/99 the value of PFI projects that could be supported was £500m.

The relevance of PFI schemes to the system of capital expenditure control is that they effectively give the local authority the ability to expand capital beyond limits that would otherwise apply. The mechanism for doing this is that PFI schemes lead to the issue of either *notional credit approvals* or *non-*

scoring credit approvals. Such credit approvals in turn lead to revenue support through the revenue support grant.

12.6 PROPOSALS FOR CHANGE

A recent consultation paper has stated that is "not clear that the current system offers sufficient incentives for good corporate working and planning or enough encouragement for cross cutting initiatives. Councils that try to adopt a corporate approach and deliver cross-service programmes may face a bewildering array of independent allocation specific timetables, rules and mechanisms that can be difficult to manage in a coherent way" (DETR, 1998).

The government is therefore considering moving towards a "single pot" allocation to each local authority covering most capital resources and made on the basis of a system similar to the housing allocation system. The government recently commissioned research work in this area (DETR, 1999b). A White Paper due in autumn 2001 will contain proposals for a "simplified formula" for capital allocations "with targeted grants for councils with high levels of deprivation" (LGC, 2001).

REFERENCES

Butler, D. and G. Butler (1994), *British Political Facts 1900–1994*, 7th edn, Basingstoke: Macmillan.

Challis, P. (2000), *Local Government Finance,* London: Local Government Information Unit.

CIPFA (2000), *Councillors' Guide to Local Government Finance*, London: Chartered Institute of Public Finance and Accountancy.

Clarke, M. and J.D. Stewart (1988), *The Enabling Council*, Luton: Local Government Training Board.

Cook, P. (1993), *Local Authority Financial Management and Accounting*, Harlow: Longman.

DETR (1998), *Modernising Local Government: Capital Finance Consultation Paper*, London: Department of the Environment, Transport and the Regions.

DETR (1999a), *A Prudential Framework for Repaying Debt and Providing for the Replacement of Assets*, Lodon: PricewaterhouseCoopers, Department of the Environment, Transport and the Regions.

DETR (1999b), *Measurement of Relative Need for Capital Expenditure*, London: PricewaterhouseCoopers, Department of the Environment, Transport and the Regions.

DETR (2000a), *Local Authority Investment Overview*, London: DETR.

DETR (2000b), *Local Government Financial Statistics, England*, London: DETR.

DoE (1970), Circular 2/70, Department of the Environment.

DoE (1996), *The Private Finance Initiative and Local Authorities*, London: Department of the Environment, Welsh Office.

DoE (1997a), *A Guide to the Local Government Capital Finance System*, London: Department of the Environment.

DoE (1997b), *The Private Finance Initiative and Local Authorities* (Revised), London: Department of the Environment.

DoE (1997c), Annual Report, 1997, Department of the Environment, Cm 3607.

Foster, C.D., R.A. Jackman and M. Perlman (1980), *Local Government Finance in a Unitary State*, London: Allen & Unwin.

Gibson, J.G. (1990), *The Politics and Economics of Poll Tax: Mrs Thatcher's Downfall*, Cradely Heath: Emas.

Henley, D., A. Likierman, J. Perrin, M. Evans, I. Lapsley and J. Whiteoak (1992), *Public Sector Accounting and Financial Control*, London: Chapman and Hall.

HM Treasury (1995), *Private Opportunity, Public Benefit, Progressing the Private Finance Initiative*, London.

HM Treasury (1996), House of Lords Select Committee on Relations between Central and Local Government, Vol II Oral Evidence and Associated Memoranda, *Memorandum by H.M. Treasury*, HL Paper 97-I, pp. 280–283, London.

HM Treasury (1998a), *Stability and Investment for the Long Term: Economic and Fiscal Strategy Report*, Cm 3978, London.

HM Treasury (1998b), *Modern Public Services for Britain: Investing in Reform. Comprehensive Spending Review: New Public Spending Plans 1999-2002*, Cm 4011, London.

HM Treasury (1999), *Funding the Scottish Parliament, National Assembly for Wales and Northern Ireland Assembly*, London.

HM Treasury (2000a), *Prudent for a Purpose: Building Opportunity and Security for All 2000 Spending Review: New Public Spending Plans 2001–2004*, Cm 4807, London.

HM Treasury (2000b), *Resource Budgeting and the 2000 Spending Review, Explanatory note by HM Treasury*, London.

HM Treasury (2001), *Managing Resources: Full Implementation of Resource Accounting and Budgeting*, London.

Jones, R.H. and Pendlebury, M. (1996), *Public Sector Accounting*, (4th edn), London: Pitman.

LGC (2001), "Byers to Liberate Spending", *Local Government Chronicle*, 24 August.

Musgrave, R.A. (1959), *The Theory of Public Finance*, New York: McGraw Hill.

Ostrom, V., C.M. Tiebout and R. Warren (1961), "The Organisation of Government in Metropolitan Areas: A Theoretical Inquiry", *American Political Science Review*, 55, pp. 831–842.

Page H. (1985), *Local Authority Borrowing, Past, Present and Future*, London: George Allen and Unwin.

Ridley, N. (1988), *The Local Right: Enabling not Providing*, London: Centre for Policy Studies.

Terry, F. (1996), "The Private Finance Initiative – Overdue Reform or Policy Breakthrough?", *Public Money and Management*, January–March.

Thain, C. and M. Wright (1995), *The Treasury and Whitehall. The Planning and Control of Expenditure, 1976–1993*, Oxford: Clarendon Press.

Twigger, R. (2000), "Background to the 2000 Spending Review", House of Commons Library, Research paper 00/59, London.

Watt, P.A. (1982), "The Control of Local Authority Capital Expenditure", *Local Government Studies*, 8, (3), May/June, pp. 91–97.

Watt, P.A. (1988), "Topics in the Analysis of Government Expenditure and Intervention: A Public Choice Approach", DPhil, University of York.

13. Fiscal controls in Europe: a summary

Jørn Rattsø

13.1   INTRODUCTION

This volume has introduced the reader to the institutional complexities of fiscal controls in European local public finance. All countries apply restrictions to local government budgeting and borrowing, but in various forms and degrees. The restrictions are broadly understood as necessary components of a fiscal federalism, which has strong central government involvement in local government affairs. This design can be named administrative federalism, and is characterised by local governments integrated into a larger "public sector". Extensive fiscal controls look like natural ingredients of this administrative federalism, and the public sector hierarchy model works quite differently from the co-operative federalism and competitive federalism discussed in the US (Kenyon and Kincaid, 1991). Only Switzerland stands out as a decentralised model of public finance.

Local governments in Europe operate in a system of centralised financing with decentralised spending, that is vertical fiscal imbalance, and with great national political interest in the redistributive services provided by the local governments. The setting can be described as a double common pool problem (Rattsø, 2001). First, individuals claim excessive local government redistributive services when they are not financed by benefit taxation. Second, local governments demand central government funds financed by general taxation. This system will apply strong pressure for increased spending and has an associated threat of fiscal indiscipline. The broad arguments for control were discussed in Chapter 2. Using the formulations of Inman (2001), we have given up the first line of defence when local governments are not limited to resident-based taxation and low spillover services, and then the second line of defence when grants are not made costly. The third and last line of defence for hard budget constraint is to establish fiscal controls.

This book offers information and understanding about how European countries have designed their restrictions to balanced budgets and borrowing. It adds to the recent empirical literature on the working of systems with vertical fiscal imbalance, notably Rodden et al. (2001). In this short summary we will discuss some common aspects of fiscal federalism in Europe and some general characteristics of the fiscal controls observed. The concluding section discusses possibilities for future research in this area.

13.2   EUROPEAN VERSUS US LOCAL PUBLIC FINANCE

The dominant thinking in local public finance is the Musgrave-Oates-Tiebout model of fiscal federalism (Musgrave, 1959; Oates, 1972; Tiebout, 1956). The model offers a sharp understanding of the key mechanisms of local public finance in the US system. The theory is based on four key assumptions: local public goods, benefit taxation, mobility, and no spillovers. The strength of the local public sector in this setting is competition (Tiebout) and balancing of local benefits and costs (Oates' decentralisation theorem). Local governments in this design are like clubs established by the local population to solve common problems. Benefit taxation assures local accountability, and there is no case for central government financial controls.

To give room for central government intervention and control, we must go beyond this model. Concern about equity is the obvious candidate for central government involvement. In this respect, the US looks like a special case. The US federal government has been less involved in equalisation grants than most countries, and the emphasis on equity varies among the US states. When the central (federal) government is not much engaged in what is going on at the local level, the local governments can be allowed to work like a club. Interestingly, McKinnon and Nechbya (1997, p. 55) see more emphasis on equity as a major threat, even "the beginning of a slow collapse of the relatively successful US federal system into a unitary state".

There is another challenge to local fiscal discipline in the US that may be stimulated by the mobility, since mobility generates spillovers. It will be tempting to shift the financing of current spending on to future taxpayers if you can leave the place when the bill is due to be paid. Private credit markets may or may not prevent such deficit financing, which may appear in complicated ways (like pension underfunding). Inman (2001) clarifies the conditions for such "deficit-shifting" and studies more closely the exceptions to the US success, notably the recession in the 1930s and more recent big city crises (like New York City, Washington DC, Philadelphia and Miami). He identifies institutions promoting fiscal discipline, in particular powerful presidents, constitutional balanced budget rules, and fiscal oversight boards.

His major conclusion is that "this tradition of refusing to provide significant national fiscal relief to governments in distress continues to this day". Epple and Spatt (1986) report that the debt of local jurisdictions has been restricted by their state governments for more than 100 years. They emphasise externalities of default at the financial markets.

The European design presented in this book is quite different from the US federal system and the Musgrave-Oates-Tiebout model. Compared with that model, all four key assumptions are false. Local governments deal with redistributive services as well as local public goods. The financing is centralised rather than of local benefit character. Mobility is limited, and the redistributive services involve spillovers (like schooling). Rather than the result of the local population organising a club to solve common problems, local governments are established as part of a national "public sector".

Many European economists have expressed frustration with the limited relevance of the dominant US thinking in fiscal federalism. In my neighbourhood, Jørgen Lotz of the Ministry of Finance in Denmark has been the leader of the "anti-US" movement. In his historical account of Denmark, he states that "economic theory played no role in the design of the municipal reforms" (Lotz, 1998, p. 22). The background is an increasing central government concern about service provision at local level, primarily in relation to equity. Musgrave (1959) discusses this in relation to "merit goods", and concludes that the choice of institutional arrangement depends on political evaluation of the role of the state. The guidelines for design are less clear when local governments produce welfare services in heterogeneous communities, and issues of redistribution and preference aggregation are high on the agenda. Oates (1999) acknowledges the complexities of the vertical structure of the public sector in a recent essay.

Why have the Europeans chosen to break with the normative message of the Musgrave-Oates-Tiebout model? If local governments were allowed to concentrate on local public goods based on local financing, much of the basis for central government intervention into their affairs would disappear. But the public sector in general is larger in Europe, and the sector has higher expectation to influence the lives of the people. As formulated by Assar Lindbeck in Sweden, socialism ended up socialising the family and not the production. Whatever the explanation for the larger size of the public sector, with great redistributive ambitions, central government's direct handling of all redistributive activities would lead to administrative overburden. Decentralisation of redistributive spending, combined with mandated and centralised financing, is an administrative convenience. European fiscal federalism consequently can be called administrative federalism. At the local level, the local politicians have gladly accepted the increased responsibilities.

The local public sector across Europe is not a static entity. There is frustration both at national and local level. While central governments often express worry about control of spending and cost efficiency and productivity growth of service provision, local governments are unhappy about limited discretion and local democracy with little content. These frustrations do not point to one clear strategy of reform, but it seems that reforms generally should aim at clearer lines of responsibility between the centre and the locals and consolidation of grants to reduce earmarking. The recent wave of introducing competition and privatisation even in basic social services may change the conditions for local governments. If Europeans end up with a smaller public sector and less emphasis on equity, deconstruction of the fiscal controls and more emphasis on market controls may happen in the future.

13.3   VARYING FISCAL CONTROLS IN EUROPE

This volume has entered into the details of local government budgeting and borrowing across Europe, based on the definitions described by editor Bernard Dafflon in Chapter 1. The ambition has been to facilitate international comparison of fiscal design. The country studies presented show how complex and different fiscal arrangements for local governments are in the details. Although a general basis for comparison across countries has not been established, there is much to learn from the country studies.

13.3.1   Comparing Complex Designs

The first problem of international comparison is the diversity among definitions of the basic economic variables involved. The countries have different definitions of key elements of public expenditure, notably the definition of public investment. In addition, many different definitions of expenditure are in use in relation to fiscal controls. Needless to say, it is hard to interpret and compare budget balance requirements and borrowing limitations when the basic definitions vary in this way. Austria (in Chapter 3) may serve as an example, where local borrowing is said to be permitted only for "extraordinary and absolutely necessary expenditures", where extraordinary means "unusual in nature and size". While the meaning of this certainly is open for discussion, also the economic conditions for approval of loan financing vary between the Länder (regions) within the country.

The second problem of international comparison is the institutional design. Also here the devil is in the details. As discussed by Sergio Rossi and Bernard Dafflon in Chapter 2, the IMF made an earlier attempt at broad international comparison of fiscal federalism (Ter-Minassian 1997, in particular chapter 7 by Ter-Minassian and Craig), with country approaches to borrowing controls divided into four categories: market discipline, cooperative control, administrative control, and rule-based control. The concepts are clearly helpful in understanding how mechanisms of fiscal discipline are established and function. However, given the country descriptions of this book, the "cooperative control" of Ter-Minassian and Craig (1997) in Belgium and Denmark is hard to separate from their "administrative control" in Austria, Norway, Spain and the United Kingdom. They all have administrative control systems from the top with sufficient contact and negotiation with local units to call them cooperative. The loan restrictions reached "in co-operation" in Denmark certainly leave less room to manoeuvre than the combined rules and administrative controls in Norway. Since rules set by law must be interpreted, they always imply administrative discretion. The IMF classification of Italy and Germany as "rule-based" as opposed to "administrative" is challenged even by the country authors of the book (chapters 10 and 11 in Ter-Miniassian, 1997). Their "administrative control" in Norway and Spain has rules by law that seems to be even more clarifying than "rule-based" Italy.

13.3.2 Budget Balance versus Borrowing Restrictions

The extreme cases of fiscal control in our sample are Denmark and France. The designs of the two appear to be quite different on paper, but less so in practice. In Denmark (Chapter 5), the "main rule" says that all spending, including investment, is financed by current revenues. There are automatic and discretionary exceptions from the main rule, and the discretionary part is related to macroeconomic policy. Recently 40–50 per cent of investment has been financed by loans. This is more than in most countries. At the other extreme, in France (Chapter 6) fiscal control is delegated to the private market, and the communes can finance their investments by private loans without limits. But then central government controls the current budget balance, so that the debt burden can be financed by current surpluses. Loans finance about 40 per cent of local investment. Restrictions on the current balance substitute restrictions on borrowing.

While Denmark concentrates on borrowing control and France on current budget balance control, the other countries rely on both in different degrees. Belgium, Italy and Norway are oriented towards current budget balance control, while Austria, United Kingdom, Germany and Spain put more emphasis on borrowing restrictions. The fiscal requirements of the Maastricht Treaty have encouraged more emphasis on budget balance controls to satisfy the deficit criteria. This is certainly true in Austria, where the 3 per cent deficit allowed is shared out among the three levels of government and among the regions in great detail.

The emergence of fiscal controls is a separate area of research, and Von Hagen and Eichengreen (1996) share the view that the conditions of administrative federalism motivate restrictions on borrowing. In a broad dataset of 45 countries they test the relationship between vertical fiscal imbalance and borrowing restrictions. Vertical fiscal imbalance, a high degree of central government financing of local government, is a common characteristic of administrative federalism. They find econometric evidence that centralised financing is associated with borrowing controls. They also find that countries with borrowing restrictions have higher government debt. The understanding is that the fiscal pressure against the centre is higher when the centre controls the funds. Their result fits well with the situation in Austria, described here, where debt is understood as a result of limited local revenue sources. Spending pressure without local revenue instruments may lead to growth of debt and motivate restrictions. On the other hand, this is the opposite of the understanding in Denmark. The strict Danish controls are motivated by their freedom in local income taxation. Borrowing restrictions are seen necessary because the tax decisions of the large local public sector have notable macroeconomic consequences.

13.3.3   Performance under Controls

The restrictions imposed regarding balanced budgets and borrowing allow for administrative discretion at central government level. They typically involve some rules related to budgets and accounts, but the rules are always supplemented with supervision and discretion. Many countries report local activities to get around the rules and regulations, either in the form of innovative accounting or in organising enterprises outside the accounts under control. The chapters for Austria, Germany and Spain discuss experiences with "hidden debts", while France has similar problems in the control of budget balance. Presumably the importance of administrative evaluation is a way of compensating for the limited effects of formal limitations. Restrictions seem to work although they are imperfect.

All the countries are successful in that none of them are heading towards fiscal crisis in local public finance. This overall rosy picture does not mean, however, that the countries have avoided fiscal imbalances altogether. The episodes of local fiscal crisis experienced, notably in Italy and Spain in the late 1970s, motivated an overhaul of fiscal controls. Central government interventions and bail-outs were followed by institutional reforms to avoid future repetitions. The optimistic view is that the countries have learned their lesson. At present, Germany certainly has a challenge in the handling of the new eastern Länder, with weak fiscal capacities and high fiscal demands. Many authors report that the EMU process has been helpful in arranging sustainable balances. This is contrary to the negative assertion that EU governments attempted to shift the burdens of the fiscal criteria down to local level. The most recent observations certainly indicate that new fiscal imbalances have not resulted at the local level.

Control of budget balances and borrowing reduce local government flexibility and may induce fiscal bias. When current revenues are assumed to finance a large part of the investment, the investment pattern easily becomes pro-cyclical. Pro-cyclical local public investment is reported for Austria, Germany, Norway and Spain. In this case, the attempts at controlling local governments create new challenges at the national level, to counterbalance the pro-cyclical elements following controls. In Belgium, the investment variation over time is related more to a political cycle. In Denmark, strict borrowing controls are used as an active instrument of macroeconomic policy, but the cyclical pattern of local government investment is not reported. Another type of potential fiscal bias is reduced investment over time. Given strong national controls on overall local spending and rising pressure for services locally, the room for investment may be squeezed. Declining local public investment over time is reported in United Kingdom, Germany and Norway. A similar mechanism has led to the discussion of the "infrastructure problem" in the US (Hulten and Peterson, 1984). The bias towards current spending may lead to a deterioration of public infrastructure and construction over time.

In terms of design, the regional level seems to be the main challenge of the countries concerned. Sharpe (1988) introduced a bold and interesting classification in this respect, between "Napoleonic states" and "non-Napoleonic states". In our sample the Napoleonic states include Belgium, France, Italy and Spain, and their defining characteristic is the central government representatives at regional level overseeing local governments ("the prefects"). This kind of representation now seems to be the case in all the countries studied in this book, except for the federal states, Austria, Germany and Switzerland, where the regions (Länder and cantons) have a stronger independent position in relation to the local governments. The role of the "middle level" looks like an interesting area of further investigation.

The lesson from this book is that all the countries involved carry out their budget balance and borrowing controls within a complicated mixture of rules by law, administrative routines and supervision, and cooperative arrangements. Market discipline plays a limited role and mainly in France. This reflects the common European approach to fiscal federalism, where local governments are an integrated part of a national "public sector". Controls within this public sector appear in many forms and always allow some discretion at the centre. The controls are successful in that fiscal imbalances in the local public sector generally are avoided.

13.4   FUTURE RESEARCH

A set of country studies like in this book offer a broad understanding of institutional variation and economic performance. A long political and economic history explains the emergence of the administrative system, of rules and regulations based on law, and of decision making in each particular country. The stories told for each country are of interest in themselves, but do not allow for much generalisation about how different designs have different consequences for economic performance. The next step is to move to more explicit and quantitative comparative analysis of fiscal federalism. Europe presents a rich variation in federalist structures, and allows for comparative analysis of many aspects such as local tax systems, grant systems, degrees of monopoly or competition in service provision, and so on. Not many comparative analyses of this sort are seen, maybe there is too much variation in too many dimensions for them to be productive. Still I suggest that some attempts should be made.

13.4.1   Comparative Analysis 1: Fiscal Restrictions

The EU-oriented analysis of fiscal discipline by Von Hagen and Harden (1994) represents a fruitful approach that could be developed to include decentralised government. Their emphasis is on broader characteristics of the budget process, and the main conclusion is that budget stringency is associated with lower budget deficits and lower levels of government borrowing. Similar comparative analysis at the country level has been made for Latin–America (Alesina et al., 1999) and with the same conclusion that budget institutions matter.

More extensive econometric studies of the consequences of budget balance requirements and borrowing limitations are made for the US States, which, with their relative homogeneity and institutional variation, offer an attractive database for the investigation of fiscal restrictions. The states generally have balanced budget requirements and limitations on debt, but in different forms. Von Hagen (1991) did an innovative study of how these rules affect state indebtedness. The motivation for his study was the discussion about European monetary integration and the use of fiscal restraint. The US case represents an opportunity to investigate how fiscal restraints in a monetary union are functioning. His main conclusion is that fiscal restraints "do little to reduce the likelihood of extreme outcomes in fiscal performance" and thus that they cannot be expected to be effective in a European monetary union. The conclusion has since been challenged, and an overview is offered by Poterba (1997).

Most US States apply some kind of balanced budget rules for operating budgets, and their variation opens up for comparative analysis. Poterba (1997) classifies three main types: required submission of a balanced budget; required legislative decision of a balanced budget allowing for actual deficits; and combining a balanced budget from the legislature with a prohibition to carry forward the deficit. The empirical analyses apply an index of the stringency of the state's balanced budget requirements. The econometric analyses following up Von Hagen's study have generated broader models of economic and political variables affecting spending and revenue behaviour. There has been some discussion about what deficit concepts are most appropriate given that the balance restrictions apply to specific components of revenue, spending and funds. However, the analysts today seem to agree that the most restrictive fiscal limits do reduce the state indebtedness and also reduce the borrowing costs for a given deficit.

Since fiscal restrictions are stable over time, the econometric evidence primarily is based on cross-section evidence, with the associated problems of linking the performance to the restrictions in question. This problem will be even larger across countries (as compared to across US states), which may motivate other approaches.

13.4.2   Comparative Analysis 2: Shocks

If quantitative analyses of fiscal restrictions cannot be done, we have to look for simpler alternatives. A realistic approach is to do separate analyses of local government behaviour in each country, and in a design that can be compared. Analysis of economic responses to fiscal shocks and the handling of budget deficits are well suited for international comparison. Fiscal shocks can be understood as "natural experiments" that provide information about government behaviour.

Country studies of fiscal shocks in the local public sector already exist for Denmark, Norway and Sweden (Rattsø and Tovmo, 2000; Rattsø, 1998; Lundberg, 1998 respectively). Although the broad model of fiscal federalism is similar among the Scandinavian countries, there are distinct differences in control systems. As we have seen in Chapters 9 and 5 respectively, Norway has the most centralised control of financing with close to no local tax discretion, while the Danish system is particular in its strict control of loans and investments, where central government regulates the loan totals for each local unit and the design assumes that investment activity is financed within the current budget. Sweden has more centralised control of the welfare services through mandating and standardisation, but leaves more discretion in borrowing.

The different types of centralised control lead to distinctly different patterns of response to shocks. The strict borrowing restrictions in Denmark force local governments into immediate adjustments. Rattsø and Tovmo (2000) estimate that both current revenues and expenditures are adjusted in response to shocks, and that current revenues take most of the adjustment. The results are comparable to the most restrictive fiscal institutions analysed for the US States by Poterba (1994), where strong anti-deficit rules increase spending responses.

The controls in Norway are directed towards the current budget balance, and the amount of discretion within the current budget is limited by tax regulations and mandated spending. Rattsø (1998) finds no short run adjustments to shock in Norway, and all the adjustment is channelled through investment. The system clearly is based on central government handling of short-run stabilization issues by way of adjusting tax revenue sharing, grants and mandating. The result confirms the pro-cyclical investment observed in the text. Lundberg (1998) identifies no revenue adjustment to shock for Sweden, and surprisingly concludes that the expenditure side absorbs the shock. All three countries have adjustment mechanisms to avoid serious fiscal imbalances, but the adjustments are channelled in different directions, dependent on the fiscal arrangement. It is of interest to compare shock adjustments of this kind for several countries.

13.4.3 Comparative Analysis 3: Local Public Investment Behaviour

Fiscal constraints of budget balance and borrowing have consequences for investment behaviour, as discussed above. There are tendencies for pro-cyclical investment and long-run investment squeeze in the data. Public investment stagnation in the US has been analysed by Hulten and Peterson (1984). They show that state and local capital spending as a share of their total spending declined from 30 per cent in the mid-1960s to 15 per cent in the early 1980s. Some observers refer to deterioration of roads, mass transit systems, water and sewerage systems, and so on, as evidence of problems related to bad decision making. In Norway, the deterioration of local public sector capital stock is basically manifested in the declining quality of buildings, particularly schools and hospitals. Maintenance of buildings seems to suffer most. It is not self evident that this deterioration is suboptimal. But it cannot be concluded from direct observation that bad decision making explains the stagnating investment level. The slowdown may be the sensible response to reduced future revenue growth or demographic shift. Local and county governments have based their investment plans on expectations about future economic and social conditions, and investments are typically predicted to develop pari passu to revenue growth. Slowdown and stagnation may follow news about changes in permanent revenue growth and demographics. Changes in the age composition of the population may motivate a reorientation of the service production towards more labour intensive services; for example, care for the elderly is less capital intensive than education for children.

Econometric analyses of investment may supplement observations of country studies. Holtz-Eakin and Rosen (1993) innovated this field by estimating an intertemporal model of investment determination. Their conclusion is optimistic, that US States operate in accordance with the forward looking model. Rattsø (1999) analysed the investment decline in Norway using a similar approach and found it to be a consequence of a negative shift in the local government revenue growth. Consistent with Chapter 9, local public investment is pro-cyclical with respect to unexpected components of the cycle. Expected changes in gross domestic product and unemployment have no influence on the investment level, consistent with the forward-looking model. It follows that the fiscal restrictions in Norway have not limited the long-run behaviour of local governments "on average". Since most of them generate current surplus financing of investment, they have not been restricted by the balanced budget rule. The dynamics of local public investment is an interesting research area in other countries.

Poterba (1995) has made an econometric analysis of borrowing restrictions across the US States in order to test whether investment behaviour is affected. The main distinction is between states with unified budgets and states with separate budgets for capital and current spending. The background understanding is that investment spending is squeezed within unified budgets. Also the states vary with respect to restrictions regarding current revenue financing (pay as you go) of investment projects. Poterba concludes that separate capital budgets are associated with higher investments. Interestingly, differences in fiscal restrictions (possibly resulting in investment decline) can be compensated by local budgetary practices (like separating out a capital budget). European counterparts to these econometric regularities would certainly be of interest.

13.4.4   Comparative Analysis 4: Broader Issues

The fiscal constraints discussed primarily address short run imbalances. But as we discussed in Section 13.2, the European design implies vertical fiscal imbalance with potential effects also for the growth and size of the local public sector. The common pool problem associated with centralised financing leads to spending pressure on the central government. The fiscal restraints consequently can be seen as ways of handling this spending pressure. The broad question is how the national political system handles the spending pressure resulting from limited internalisation of the costs of decentralised government. Analyses of the spending growth of the total local public sector over time may reveal how changing conditions of central government influence the outcome. This is the approach for the study of US grants by Inman (1988) and local public spending growth by Borge and Rattsø (1997, 2001). The US study emphasises strong presidents as disciplining factors, while the Norwegian study points to the fragmentation of parliament as an important factor. This type of public sector growth study in principle can be made at regional and local government level to investigate the effects of variation in political and institutional design.

13.5   CONCLUDING REMARKS

The country analyses of this book show that fiscal stability of decentralised government can be achieved in different ways. The variation in administrative and institutional arrangements across countries reflects broad historical differences including cultural, social and political backgrounds. All the countries included in this volume have been successful in avoiding serious fiscal imbalances in the last 20 years. But the effects of these fiscal arrangements for the broader goals of the government sector are an open question. In this final chapter we have indicated alternative approaches for more explicit comparative studies of fiscal performance in the future.

REFERENCES

Alesina, A., R. Hausmann, R. Hommes and E. Stein (1999), "Budget institutions and fiscal performance in Latin-America", *Journal of Development Economics*, 59, 253–273.
Borge, L.-E. and J. Rattsø (1997), "Local government grants and income tax revenue: Redistributive politics in Norway 1900-1990", *Public Choice*, 92, 191–197.
Borge, L.-E. and J. Rattsø (2001), "Spending growth with vertical fiscal imbalance: Decentralized government spending in Norway 1880–1990", mimeo, Department of Economics, Norwegian University of Science and Technology.
Epple, D. and C. Spatt (1986), "State restrictions on local debt: Their role in preventing default", *Journal of Public Economics*, 29, 199–221.
Holtz-Eakin, D. and H. Rosen (1993), "Municipal construction spending: An empirical examination", *Economics and Politics*, 5, 1, 61–84.
Hulten, C. and G. Peterson (1984), "The public capital stock: Needs, trends, and performance", *American Economic Review*, 74, 166–173.
Inman, R. (1988), "Federal assistance and local services in the United States: The evolution of a new federalist fiscal order", in H. Rosen (ed.), *Fiscal Federalism: Quantitative Studies*, Chicago: The University of Chicago Press.

Inman, R. (2001), "Hard and soft budget constraints in the United States", in J. Rodden, G. Eskeland and J. Litvack (eds), *Fiscal Decentralization and the Challenge of Hard Budget Constraints*, Washington, DC: The World Bank.

Kenyon, D. and J. Kincaid (eds) (1991), *Competition Among States and Local Governments*, Washington DC: The Urban Institute Press.

Lotz, J. (1998), "Local government reforms in the Nordic countries, theory and practice", in J. Rattsø (ed.), *Fiscal Federalism and State-Local Finance: The Scandinavian Perspective*, Cheltenham: Edward Elgar.

Lundberg, J. (1998), "Local government responses to unexpected fiscal shocks and budget deficits: Evidence from Swedish municipalities", mimeo, Department of Economics, Umeå University, Umeå, Sweden.

McKinnon, R. and T. Nechbya (1997), "Competition in federal systems: The role of political and financial constraints", in J. Ferejohn and B. Weingast (eds), *The New Federalism: Can the States be Trusted?*, Stanford: Hoover Institution Press.

Musgrave, R. (1959), *The Theory of Public Finance*, New York: McGraw-Hill.

Oates, W. (1972), *Fiscal Federalism*, New York: Harcourt, Brace and Jovanovic.

Oates, W. (1999), "An essay on fiscal federalism", *Journal of Economic Literatur*, XXXVII, 1120–1149.

Poterba, J. (1994), "State responses to fiscal crisis: The effects of budgetary institutions and politics", *Journal of Political Economy*, 102, 4, 799–821.

Poterba, J. (1995), "Capital budgets, borrowing rules, and state capital spending", *Journal of Public Economics*, 56, 165–187.

Poterba, J. (1997), "Do Budget Rules Work?", in Auerbach, A. (ed.), *Fiscal Policy: Lessons from Economic Research*, Cambridge, MA: The MIT Press.

Rattsø, J. (1998), "Fiscal adjustment with vertical fiscal imbalance: Empirical evaluation of administrative fiscal federalism in Norway", mimeo, Department of Economics, Norwegian University of Science and Technology.

Rattsø, J. (1999), "Aggregate local public sector investment and shocks: Norway 1946–1990", *Applied Economics*, 31, 577–584.

Rattsø, J. (2001), "Vertical fiscal imbalance in a welfare state: Norway", in J. Rodden, G. Eskeland and J. Litvack (eds), *Fiscal Decentralization and the Challenge of Hard Budget Constraints*, Washington, DC: The World Bank.

Rattsø, J. and P. Tovmo (2000), "Fiscal discipline and asymmetric adjustment of revenues and expenditures: Local government responses to shocks in Denmark", mimeo, Department of Economics, Norwegian University of Science and Technology, Trondheim, Norvay.

Rodden, J., G. Eskeland and J. Litvack (eds) (2001), *Fiscal Decentralization and the Challenge of Hard Budget Constraints*, Washington, DC: The World Bank.

Sharpe, L. (1988), "Local government reorganisation: General theory and United Kingdom practice", in B. Dente and F. Kjellberg (eds), *The Dynamics of Institutional change*, London: Sage.

Ter-Minassian, T. (ed.) (1997), *Fiscal Federalism in Theory and Practice*, Washington, DC: International Monetary Fund.

Ter-Minassian, T. and J. Craig (1997), "Control of subnational government borrowing", in T. Ter-Minassian (ed.), *Fiscal Federalism in Theory and Practice*, Washington DC: International Monetary Fund.

Tiebout, C. (1956), "A pure theory of local government expenditures", *Journal of Political Economy*, 64, 416–424.

Von Hagen, J. (1991), "A note on the empirical effectiveness of formal fiscal restraints", *Journal of Public Economics*, 44, 199–210.

Von Hagen, J. and B. Eichengreen (1996), "Federalism, fiscal restraints, and European Monetary Union", *American Economic Review*, 2, 86, 134–138.
Von Hagen, J. and I. Harden (1994), "National budget processes and fiscal performance", *European Economy*, 3, 311–418.

Name Index

Subject Index

3 5282 00529 7620